BREAKING
THE SOUND BARRIER

AMY GOODMAN
EDITED BY DENIS MOYNIHAN

Haymarket Books
Chicago, Illinois

First published by Haymarket Books in 2009
© 2009 Amy Goodman

Haymarket Books
P.O. Box 180165, Chicago, IL 60618
773-583-7884
info@haymarketbooks.org
www.haymarketbooks.org

ISBN: 978-1931859-99-8

Trade distribution:
In the U.S. through Consortium Book Sales and Distribution, www.cbsd.com
In the UK, Turnaround Publisher Services, www.turnaround-psl.com
In Australia, Palgrave Macmillan, www.palgravemacmillan.com.au
All other countries, Publishers Group Worldwide, www.pgw.com

Special discounts are available for bulk purchases by organizations and institutions.
Please contact Haymarket Books for more information at 773-583-7884 or
info@haymarketbooks.org.

This book was published with the generous support of the Wallace Global Fund.

Cover design by Eric Ruder. Author photograph courtesy of *Democracy Now!*

Printed in Canada by union labor on recycled paper containing 100 percent post-consumer
waste in accordance with the guidelines of the Green Press Initiative,
www.greenpressinitiative.org

Library of Congress CIP Data is available.

10 9 8 7 6 5 4 3 2 1

PRAISE FOR AMY GOODMAN ·

"Amy Goodman has taken investigative journalism to new heights."

—Noam Chomsky

"You want public broadcasting to be balanced against all these elite establishment voices that get heard? Get Amy Goodman on public television."

—Bill Moyers

"What journalism should be: beholden to the interests of people, not power and profit."

—Arundhati Roy

"At times when people are told to 'watch what they say,' Amy Goodman is not afraid to speak truth to power. She does it every day."

—Susan Sarandon

"[Amy Goodman carries] the great muckraking tradition of Upton Sinclair, George Seldes, and I. F. Stone into the electronic age."

—Howard Zinn

"Amy Goodman continues the quest for global justice and awareness by bringing us stories and a perspective that we don't normally get from the mainstream media."

—Danny Glover

THE RULERS TAKE EXCEPTION
TO AMY GOODMAN

"Hostile, combative, and even disrespectful."

—President Bill Clinton

"A threat to national security."

—The Indonesian military

"I have advised my mother to talk to no reporters because of … people like you."

—Former Speaker of the House Newt Gingrich

CONTENTS

NEWS FROM THE UNREPORTED WORLD

GRASSROOTS ACTIVISM

ELECTIONS

OBAMA

LUMINARIES

FOREWORD

You can learn more of the truth about Washington and the world from one week of Amy Goodman's *Democracy Now!* than from a month of Sunday morning talk shows.

Make that a year of Sunday morning talk shows.

That's because Amy, as you will discover on every page of this book, knows the critical question for journalists is how close they are to the truth, not how close they are to power. Like I. F. Stone, she values the facts on the ground; unlike the Sunday beltway anchors, she refuses to take the official version of reality as the definition of news, or to engage in Washington's "wink-wink" game by which both parties to an interview tacitly understand that the questions and answers will be framed to appear adversarial when in fact their purpose is to avoid revealing how power really works. Quick: recall the last time you heard a celebrity journalist on any of the Sunday talk shows grill a politician on what campaign contributors get for their generosity. Try again: name any of those elite interrogators who skewered any politician for saying that "single-payer" wasn't on the table in the debate over health care reform because "there's no support for it." OK, one last chance: recall how often you have heard any of the network stars insist that Newt Gingrich reveal just who is funding his base as the omnipresent expert on everything.

See?

Now read this book for a reality check. And tune in to *Democracy Now!* to hear and see the difference an independent journalist can make in providing citizens what they need to know to make democracy work.

It takes the nerves, stamina, and willpower of an Olympic triathlete to do what Amy Goodman does. That's just who she is, this quiet-spoken tornado of muckraking journalism: Edward R. Murrow with a twist of Emma Goldman, a *Washington Post* reporter once noted—willing to take on the powers that be to get at truth and justice, then spreading the word of those two indispensable gospels to the republic and the world beyond.

Amy Goodman goes where angels fear to tread. Beaten by Indonesian troops while she and a colleague—also beaten—were covering East Timor's fight for independence. Hiking dangerous African deltas to get to the bottom of Chevron Oil's collusion with the Nigerian military. Or closer to home, in New Orleans or Appalachia or facing down the police when her colleagues were arrested in Minneapolis during the 2008 Republican National Convention (they threw her in the slammer, too).

Through her reporting, we hear from people who scarcely exist in news covered by the corporate-owned press. We learn about issues of war and peace and social wrong. She is impervious to government subterfuge or spin. "Goodman is the journalist as uninvited guest," that *Washington Post* reporter wrote. "You might think of the impolitic question; she asks it."

And once it's been asked, she refuses to take "no comment" for an answer. She returns to a story time and again, continually digging, refusing to let her audience or investigative target forget how important it is to nail down just who's responsible and what needs to be done.

On top of everything else she finds time to take her message out to a broad public with speeches and books and a weekly newspaper column, from which this collection of essays, *Breaking the Sound Barrier*, has been selected. I'd be envious if it didn't appear unseemly. Let's just say I'm in awe.

Read this collection and revel in the truth-telling. Be outraged by what you learn from it and renew your oath as a citizen. "We stand with journalists around the world who deeply believe that the mission of a journalist is to go where the silence is," Amy Goodman said in December 2008 when she accepted the Right Livelihood Award for personal courage and transformation. "The responsibility of a journalist is to give a voice to those who have been forgotten, forsaken, beaten down by the powerful."

And, at a time when the future of journalism is in question, this ringing rationale for our embattled but essential craft: "It's the best reason I know for us to carry our pens, our microphones, and our cameras, both into our own communities and out to the wider world."

Right on.

Bill Moyers

Dedicated to my mother, Dorrie Goodman—
The most remarkable woman I have ever known

INTRODUCTION:
BEYOND THE NINE-SECOND SOUND BITE

My goal as a journalist is to break the sound barrier, to expand the debate, to cut through the static and bring forth voices that are shut out. It is the responsibility of journalists to go where the silence is, to seek out news and people who are ignored, to accurately and clearly report on the issues—issues that the corporate, for-profit media often distort, if they cover them at all.

What is typically presented as news analysis is, for the most part, a small circle of pundits who know so little about so much, explaining the world to us and getting it so wrong. While they may appear to differ, they are quibbling over how quickly the bombs should be dropped, not asking whether they should be dropped at all.

Unfortunately, as a result, people are increasingly turning away from the news at a time when news media should be providing a forum for discussion—a forum that is honest and open, that weighs all the options, and that includes those deeply affected by U.S. policy around the globe. I am not talking about a fringe minority or the silent majority, but a silenced majority, silenced by the corporate media. The media's job is to be the exception to the rulers, to hold those in power accountable, to

1

challenge, and to ask the hard questions—to be the public watchdog. The media also need to find stories of hope, to tell stories that resonate with people's lives in the real world (not the reel world).

The media are going through profound changes. The Internet undermines traditional business models that have enriched for-profit media companies. Newspapers are folding at an alarming rate, like Denver's *Rocky Mountain News*, shuttered after almost 150 years. Others have stopped printing paper editions, moving online, like the *Seattle Post-Intelligencer* and the *Christian Science Monitor*. In fact, most papers are still profitable— just not profitable enough for Wall Street. Shareholders demand a return on investments, attaching no value to the crucial role that journalism plays in society.

Increasingly restless, people are looking for alternative sources of information in this complex world. They are getting savvier at pursuing the news sources they want, when and how they want it—on websites, through audio and video podcasting, on mobile platforms. They critique, share, excerpt, and repost the content they appreciate, adding their insights, running circles around the old networks while building their own trusted online communities. Many contribute reporting, joining the global ranks of the increasingly important citizen (and non-citizen) journalists.

All this was enabled because the Internet has been free and unfettered, driven by "net neutrality," the rules of the Internet that have kept its content and uses equal—that have made web sources like democracynow.org as readily available as the sites of the major media corporations. These large corporations, however, are trying to control the Internet, to restrict the free flow of information, to restore their historical role of for-profit arbiter of what we can and cannot read, watch, or hear. Preserving net neutrality will prevent their digital oligopoly, keeping the Internet a level playing field.

Despite the opportunities this new media environment provides, there is still no replacing the historically crucial role played by the seasoned muckraker in our society. How can journalism be supported sustainably? There has been much discussion of "nonprofit" journalism. *Democracy Now!* has been practicing nonprofit journalism for 14 years, following the lead of Pacifica Radio, which has been at it for more than 60 years, brought to you by the audience—not by corporations that profit from war.

Democracy Now! is a national, daily, independent, award-winning news program, pioneering the largest public media collaboration in the United States. We broadcast on Pacifica, NPR, community, and college radio stations; on public access, PBS, and satellite television; and on the Internet at democracynow.org. *Democracy Now!*'s podcast is one of the most popular on the web. We shepherd our resources carefully, invest in people, develop and use open source technology, and don't answer to advertisers.

I remember as the bombs were falling on Baghdad in 2003, when we got an e-mail from Radio Skid Row, a Sydney, Australia, community radio station that carries *Democracy Now!* They received a comment from a listener asking, "How is it that the best coverage of the war is coming from the poorest station in Sydney?" This is what independent media is all about: unembedded, investigative, international journalism.

The columns collected here are stories from both the streets and the suites, bringing out voices from all over this increasingly globalized world. Unprecedented changes are affecting everyone, everywhere. I have tried to go beyond the nine-second sound bite to bring you a taste of the whole meal. I see the media as a huge kitchen table that stretches across this globe, one we all sit around to debate and discuss the most critical issues of the day: war and peace, life and death. Anything less than that is a disservice to a democratic society.

WAR

THE ART OF WAR AND DECEPTION

"Every great work of art goes through messy phases while it is in transition. A lump of clay can become a sculpture; blobs of paint become paintings which inspire."

No, this is not Pablo Picasso speaking, but Major General William B. Caldwell IV, spokesman for the Multinational Force–Iraq, comparing the carnage in Iraq to a work of art in another audacious attempt to paint Iraq as anything other than a catastrophe.

The general's remarks do bring the great artist to mind. Picasso's epic painting *Guernica*, named after the city in Spain, captured the brutality of the bombing of that city during another civil war, the Spanish Civil War.

The painting, almost 30 feet wide, is a globally recognized depiction and artistic condemnation of war. Picasso shows the terror on the faces of people, the frightened animals. He shows the dead, the dying, the dismembered. A tapestry reproduction of it adorns the lobby outside of the United Nations Security Council.

In February 2003, before then–U.S. Secretary of State Colin Powell gave his major push for war at the United Nations—a speech he would later call

7

a "blot" on his record—a blue curtain was drawn across the tapestry so that the image would not be the backdrop for press statements on the coming war. Immediately, posters and banners of Picasso's *Guernica* began appearing at the antiwar demonstrations sweeping the globe.

The attempted control of imagery and propaganda, language and spin has been a high priority of the Bush administration. Yes, the Pentagon forbade photographing the flag-draped coffins of fallen soldiers. But the manipulation goes beyond the war.

President Dwight D. Eisenhower once said, "Every gun that is made, every warship launched, every rocket fired, signifies, in the final sense, a theft from those who hunger and are not fed." If Eisenhower worked for the government today, he would have to revise his statement. Recently, the Bush administration stopped using the words "hunger" or "hungry" when describing the millions of Americans who can't afford to eat. Instead of suffering from hunger, the Agriculture Department now says these people are experiencing "very low food security."

While the Bush administration has had some success in covering up the truth, it seems like reality is finally beginning to outpace its efforts.

Take, for example, Hurricane Katrina. A side effect of the Bush administration not responding to that disaster in a timely fashion is that when the network reporters went to New Orleans, there were no troops to embed with. What we saw for one of the first times was the network correspondents reporting from the victims' perspective. Day after day, unspun, unfiltered. Bodies floated across our TV screens. I remember a young woman reporter interviewing a man whose wife's hand had just slipped out of his, as she told him to take care of their children. After telling his story, the man waded into the water in shock with his boy. The reporter started to cry. The reports galvanized the country. Could you imagine if for one week we saw those images in Iraq: babies dead on the ground, women with their legs blown off by cluster bombs, soldiers dead and dying. Americans are a compassionate people. They would say no—war is not an answer to conflict in the twenty-first century.

The debate now in vogue is whether Iraq is in a civil war. Sectarian violence on a mass scale is acknowledged all around: Gone are the harangues that the media are not covering the "positive stories" or the "good news"— there simply is no good news in Iraq.

The Iraqi Ministry of Health estimated that 150,000 Iraqis have died since the invasion. An October medical journal article estimated the civilian death toll as somewhere near 655,000.

The U.S. invasion and occupation of Iraq has now lasted longer than the U.S. involvement in World War II. Iraqis suffered the most violent day in the entire war while Americans were celebrating Thanksgiving.

Iraq, like Spain in the 1930s, is in a civil war. A civil war started by the U.S. invasion and fueled by the U.S. occupation. The shroud over the UN's *Guernica* tapestry is gone. Now the only shrouds worth noting are those that wrap the victims of the daily slaughter in Iraq.

RESISTANCE TO WAR CANNOT BE JAILED

You can jail the resisters, but you can't jail the resistance. George W. Bush, take notice as U.S. Army Lieutenant Ehren Watada is court-martialed next week. Congress, take heed. Young people in harm's way are leading the way out of Iraq. It is time you followed.

Watada was the first commissioned officer to refuse deployment to Iraq. He joined the military in March 2003. He believed President Bush's claims that Saddam Hussein had weapons of mass destruction, connections to 9/11 and al-Qaeda, and that Iraq was an imminent threat to the United States.

After signing on, he studied intensively to be well prepared to lead troops in Iraq. His studies, and the daily news coming out of Iraq of civilian deaths and no WMDs, led him to the conclusion that the war was not only immoral, but also illegal.

On June 6, 2006, Watada said, "My moral and legal obligation is to the Constitution and not to those who would issue unlawful orders ... As the order to take part in an illegal act is ultimately unlawful as well, I must, as an officer of honor and integrity, refuse that order."

He refused to deploy. The army charged Watada with missing the troop movement, contempt toward officials, and conduct unbecoming an officer. Watada hoped that his court-martial would be a hearing on the legality of the war. He was not claiming conscientious objection; rather, he says, he simply refused an illegal order. He offered to resign his commission. He offered to serve in Afghanistan. The army refused his offers. A military judge ruled Watada cannot present evidence challenging the war's legality or explain what motivated him to resist his deployment order.

On our *Democracy Now!* news hour, Watada said of his upcoming February 5 court-martial, "it will be a non-trial. It will not be a fair trial or a show of justice. I think that they will simply say: 'Was he ordered to go? Yes. Did he go? No. Well, he's guilty.'"

Several journalists to whom Watada spoke were subpoenaed in order to testify, first at his pretrial hearing, then at the court-martial. The journalists fought back, and in each case, the army backed down. Sarah Olson, one of the independent journalists involved, said, "I am glad the growing number of dissenting voices within the military will retain their rights to speak with reporters."

Dissent within the military against the war in Iraq is growing. Iraq Veterans Against the War has quadrupled in size in the past year. More than 1,200 soldiers have signed on to an Appeal for Redress, with which active-duty soldiers can appeal to Congress for an end to the war with legal protections against retaliation from the military. The appeal simply reads: "As a patriotic American proud to serve the nation in uniform, I respectfully urge my political leaders in Congress to support the prompt withdrawal of all American military forces and bases from Iraq. Staying in Iraq will not work and is not worth the price. It is time for U.S. troops to come home."

Sergeant Ronn Cantu signed the Appeal for Redress, which soldiers can do confidentially online at appealforredress.org. In a *Democracy Now!* exclusive, Cantu spoke to us over a crackly cell-phone connection from the front lines in Iraq: "I'm scared out of my mind right now ... It's a belief of the soldiers I've talked to that any troop increase over here, it's just going to be more sitting ducks, more targets."

Since Watada and other active-duty resisters are facing years in military prison, I recently asked two of the most progressive members of the new Senate, Senators Bernie Sanders, I-VT, and Sherrod Brown, D-OH, what Congress could do for the soldiers facing court-martial. Both replied, "I don't know." As Congress wrangles over nonbinding resolutions condemning Bush's war-making—or as he calls it, his "surge"— these brave young patriots are making binding decisions.

Without Congress taking decisive action, these soldiers are left to fend for themselves. How many must die, how many must be sent to prison or flee to Canada, before Congress ends this war?

CLINTON TO ANTIWAR VOTERS: BRING 'EM ON

Hillary Clinton is a once and future warrior. Campaign events in New Hampshire suggest the majority antiwar electorate has problems with her vote for the Iraq war and with her position on Iran.

On February 10, New Hampshire resident Roger Tilton asked Senator Clinton at a town hall meeting, "I want to know if right here, right now, once and for all and without nuance, you can say that war authorization was a mistake."

Clinton responded, "Well, I have said, and I will repeat it, that knowing what I know now, I never would have voted for it ... The mistakes were made by this president who misled this country and this Congress into a war that should not have been waged."

A week later, in Dover, New Hampshire, she dug in: "If the most important thing to any of you is choosing someone who did not cast that vote or said his vote was a mistake, then there are others to choose from. But for me, the most important thing now is trying to end this war."

Her tough talk to antiwar voters is reminiscent of President Bush's taunt to the Iraqi insurgents: "Bring 'em on."

People's concerns about Clinton's Iraq war vote are of more than historical interest. History has a frightening way of repeating itself. Drop the "q," add an "n." Iran.

New Hampshire Peace Action Director Anne Miller asked Clinton about her recent comments to AIPAC, the American Israel Public Affairs Committee. Clinton had told AIPAC, "We cannot, we should not, we must not permit Iran to build or acquire nuclear weapons. And in dealing with this threat ... no option can be taken off the table."

Miller, who has visited Iran, expressed "deep concern ... that we have a Democratic presidential candidate who is a militarist of this nature and that she isn't coming out and saying we need strong diplomatic action with Iran, which is really the only answer."

Clinton continues to invoke the now largely discredited Bush administration claim that the government of Iran is supplying high-tech weaponry to Iraqi insurgents. Even General Peter Pace, chairman of the Joint Chiefs of Staff, says there is no evidence of Iranian government involvement.

Senator Robert Byrd, D-WV, fought the resolution authorizing the use of force in Iraq. He said the president wants "to have the power to launch this nation into war without provocation and without clear evidence of an imminent attack on the United States, and we're going to be foolish enough to give it to him." Byrd seems to have known then what Clinton says she knows now. He called the resolution "dangerous" and a "blank check," and now, with more than 3,145 U.S. soldiers killed, and with Iraq war costs through 2008 projected at more than $1 trillion, it appears he was right.

Representatives Barbara Lee and Lynn Woolsey also seemed to know then what Clinton says she knows now. They were lauded by the 50 activists who, on January 30, 2007, occupied Clinton's Senate office, weaving a web with pink yarn "to symbolize the senator's web of deception and the innocent people—Americans and Iraqis—caught in it." Protesters have promised to "bird-dog" Clinton at all of her public appearances. These actions recall the student sit-in at Clinton's New York office on October 10, 2002, while Clinton stood on the Senate floor and made her case for war.

Fully a year before she died, columnist and arch Bush critic Molly Ivins wrote, "Enough. Enough triangulation, calculation and equivocation. Enough clever straddling, enough not offending anyone ... Sen. Clinton is apparently incapable of taking a clear stand on the war in Iraq, and that alone is enough to disqualify her."

And then there's Ralph Nader. He admits that there are good antiwar candidates but says that if Clinton wins the Democratic nomination, he will be more likely to run.

Senator Clinton has drawn the line in the sand over Iraq. She will not admit that her vote to authorize Bush to use military force in a unilateral, unprovoked war based on lies was a mistake. She is open to a military strike on Iran. Her latest message to voters: "There are others to choose from." Antiwar voters already know that, and are lining up behind candidates Barack Obama, John Edwards, Dennis Kucinich, and, perhaps before long, Ralph Nader.

CARLOS ARREDONDO
EXPLODING INTO ACTION

The United States is entering the fifth year of its violent, failed occupation of Iraq, a war that has lasted longer than the United States was involved in World War II. Through the grimly deepening quagmire, a strengthening, pervasive U.S. antiwar movement is emerging. An increasingly powerful voice comes from soldiers and their families, turning grief into action. Take the Arredondo family.

On August 25, 2004—Carlos Arredondo's 44th birthday—a U.S. Marine van arrived outside his house. He thought that his son Alex had managed to come home from his second deployment to Iraq to surprise him. Instead, the marines informed him that Alex had been killed in action in Najaf.

Carlos lost his mind. He asked, he begged, the marines to leave. He pleaded. They didn't leave, so he ran to his garage and grabbed a hammer, gasoline, and a blowtorch. He began pummeling the van. He climbed in, pouring the gasoline. His mother, distraught and wailing, tried to pull him from the van. The blowtorch accidentally sparked, and Carlos was blown from the van into the yard, in flames.

Then his wife, Melida, arrived. She saw her husband burning. Carlos' younger son, Brian, 16 years old, in Bangor, Maine, later saw the incident on television. This was the day he learned that the brother he loved and emulated was dead.

Carlos suffered burns on more than one-quarter of his body. The physical healing was the easy part. It is the emotional healing that he pursues in his tireless and remarkable odyssey to end the war. To honor Alex's memory, he has been crisscrossing the country, from Capitol Hill to Crawford, Texas, pulling a flag-draped coffin. He calls it his public mourning: "I want the caskets coming home to be very public. The government doesn't want you to see them."

Carlos stopped for a few days this week in New York. He parked outside the military recruiting station in Times Square, where activists have established what they call the Endless War Memorial. For six days ending Friday, March 16, sunrise to sunset, hundreds of people are taking turns reading the names of the Iraq war dead—all the dead whose names could be discovered. The roughly 3,200 U.S. military fatalities, the other "coalition" casualties, the journalists, and the 7,733 Iraqi names they were able to find. The organizers point out that there are 200 unnamed dead Iraqis for each of the thousands they have gathered (based on a study by the British medical journal *The Lancet* that estimated more than 650,000 Iraqi dead).

The scene is surreal and unforgettable. Passersby stop by the flag-draped coffin Carlos has rolled out of the back of his pickup truck. There are army boots of loved ones lost, and large photos of grieving Iraqi women and one of Alex in an open casket. This is all set against the massive video display atop the recruiting station. Among its slogans: "There is nothing on this green earth stronger than the U.S. Army." Above that, an even larger display promotes Fox News and Bill O'Reilly and flashes phrases like "Gitmo justice." The famous Dow Jones news zipper runs its endless recitation of stock quotes and the daily count of dead and injured. A video ad for sunglasses flashes the words "Never Hide."

Carlos is heading next to Washington, D.C., to lead this weekend's march on the Pentagon.

As we part, Carlos shows me the latest recruiting letter sent to his son Brian. It contains a fake red, white, and blue credit card with Brian's name on it. It says, "This is not a credit card. It is money in the bank." An earlier letter promises him a bonus of up to $20,000. "What can you do with $20,000? A new car? Pay off credit cards? Help your family? … Remember the decisions you are making right now will have a huge impact on how the rest of your life turns out." Which is exactly why Carlos prays his surviving son will not join up.

Meanwhile, around the corner, each name read represents a once living, breathing, complex human being whose life was snuffed out as a result of this four-year-old war. Alongside the named dead are living people, like Carlos, following their consciences, making connections, building a movement, each day bringing the end of the war one day closer.

HANG UP ON WAR:
CLAIM YOUR TELEPHONE TAX REBATE

If you are upset that Congress won't defund the war in Iraq, there's something you can do: Stop paying taxes. Legally.

The Internal Revenue Service is giving a rebate this year on a telephone war tax. This is one of those line items at the bottom of your phone bill. The tax was instituted in 1898 to help the United States pay for the Spanish-American War. Individuals and businesses have one chance to obtain a refund on this telephone war tax, by asking for it in their 2006 income tax returns.

Remarkably, the IRS has made it easy to request the refund, yet IRS Commissioner Mark Everson says that many taxpayers are overlooking it. Obtaining the refund is easy. But first, a little history.

The Spanish-American War lasted from April to August of 1898 and was predicated on a U.S. government demand that Spain abandon its colony in Cuba, which the United States subsequently occupied. By the end of 1898, the United States had also taken over the Philippines, Guam, and Puerto Rico.

The war was also used as an official pretext to take over Hawaii. The Senate debated over the annexation in secret, some arguing for total an-

19

nexation, others for just Pearl Harbor. Senator Richard Pettigrew of South Dakota derided the annexation plan as money "thrown away in the interest of a few sugar planters and adventurers in Hawaii." Military bases and raw materials—sound familiar?

The telephone tax was instituted as part of a War Revenue Bill, which expanded the government's ability to collect taxes, ostensibly to pay for the war. As with the myriad controversial "pork" items added to the recent Iraq war funding authorization, the 1898 bill was the subject of scores of amendments that benefited big business. These included tax breaks for powerful industries like the insurance companies and tobacco dealers.

The telephone tax of one cent per call targeted the wealthy, who were generally the only ones who had telephone access in 1898. After the war, the tax was eventually raised to 3 percent. Since the Vietnam War, it has been the target of war tax resisters, people who refuse to pay taxes because they do not want to fund war.

Tax resistance has a long history. Henry David Thoreau promoted it in his essay "Civil Disobedience" to fight slavery: "If a thousand men were not to pay their tax bills this year, that would not be a violent and bloody measure, as it would be to pay them, and enable the State to commit violence and shed innocent blood." The IRS has vigorously targeted full-fledged tax resisters—ranging from those refusing to pay the Pentagon's percentage of their taxes to those who outright refuse to pay anything to the government—making an example of them by garnishing wages, sending them to prison for tax evasion, and confiscating their homes.

Tax resisters figured out that they could protest the telephone tax simply by writing their checks to the phone company, withholding the amount of the tax. The IRS deemed the collection of the tax too expensive, relative to the small amount of the tax itself. According to the National War Tax Resistance Coordinating Committee, early collection efforts by the IRS included the auctioning of Jim Glock's bicycle for $22 in 1973 and of George and Lillian Willoughby's VW Bug in 1971 for $123 (in 2004, Lillian, at 89, with the support of her husband, George, 94, was jailed for protesting the Iraq war).

Court losses convinced the IRS to dump the telephone war tax in 2006 and to offer the retroactive rebate for phone taxes paid between March 1,

2003, and July 31, 2006. Typical refunds will be between $30 and $60. Ironically, while the IRS has dropped the tax on long-distance and "bundled" services, like high-speed Internet, the tax remains for older, standard local phone services and on rental of equipment that enables the disabled to use phones. Thus, this tax on the rich is now a tax on the poor. Congressman John Lewis, D-GA, has submitted a bill to permanently wipe this remnant clean. Two-thirds of the bill's cosponsors are antitax Republicans, so Democrats might be leery about passing it.

The website www.refundsforgood.org lists step-by-step instructions on how to recoup the telephone tax rebate, and recommends donating it to charity. While Congress and President Bush trade barbs over war funding, with a simple check mark on your tax return you can help to defund the war. Claim your telephone tax rebate. Let the Pentagon hold a bake sale.

WAR AND CENSORSHIP
AT WILTON HIGH

Last Sunday night, as millions of Americans tuned in to the two Tonys—the final episode of *The Sopranos*, to see whether Tony Soprano lived or died, and the Tony Awards, celebrating the best in American theater—actor Stanley Tucci (who played Nigel in *The Devil Wears Prada*) was in an off-Broadway theater, the Culture Project, watching high school students perform a play about war.

The production, *Voices in Conflict*, moved the audience to tears, ending with a standing ovation for the teenage actors, still reeling from a controversy that had propelled them onto the New York stage. Their high school principal had banned the play.

Bonnie Dickinson has been teaching theater at Wilton High School in Connecticut for 13 years. She and her students developed the idea of a play about Iraq, initially inspired by the September 3, 2006, death of Wilton High graduate Nicholas Madaras from an IED (improvised explosive device) blast in Baqubah, Iraq. The play uses real testimonials from soldiers, from their letters, blogs, and taped interviews, and Yvonne Latty's book *In Conflict*, with the students acting the roles. The voices of Iraqis are also included.

In mid-March, after students spent months preparing the play, the school administration canceled it. Superintendent Gary Richards wrote, "The student performers directly acting the part of the soldiers ... turns powerful material into a dramatic format that borders on being sensational and inappropriate. We would like to work with the students to complete a script that fully addresses our concerns." (The students have modified the script; they perform Richards' letter, its cold, condescending bureaucratese in stark relief against the play's passionate eyewitness testimonials.)

The story struck a chord with Tucci. He was already producing a video piece about his high school alma mater, John Jay High School in Cross River, New York, where high school girls were suspended for performing an excerpt of Eve Ensler's play *The Vagina Monologues*. Their crime: uttering the word "vagina" after being warned not to.

Following the performance of *Voices in Conflict*, Tucci participated in a public conversation with the student actors, noting that "Cross River and Wilton are only 15 miles apart. There's obviously something in the water."

After the *New York Times* published an article on the Wilton High censorship scandal, Ira Levin, the author of *The Stepford Wives*, wrote the paper a letter:

> Wilton, Conn., where I lived in the 1960s, was the inspiration for *Stepford*, the fictional town I later wrote about in *The Stepford Wives*. I'm not surprised ... that Wilton High School has a Stepford principal. Not all the Wilton High students have been Stepfordized. The ones who created and rehearsed the banished play *Voices in Conflict* are obviously thoughtful young people with minds of their own.

Wilton High School principal Timothy Canty was quoted in the *New York Times* article saying that the play might "hurt Wilton families 'who had lost loved ones or who had individuals serving as we speak,' and that there was not enough classroom and rehearsal time to ensure it would provide 'a legitimate instructional experience for our students.'"

I asked the student actors about their opportunities to discuss the war at school. Jimmy Presson, 16 years old, said his U.S. history class has a weekly assignment to bring in a current-event news item, with one caveat: "We are not allowed to talk about the war while discussing current events." The students said that they can discuss the war in a Middle Eastern studies class, but, they said, it is not being taught this year. "Theater Arts II was the only class in the school where students were discussing the war," Dickinson said. Jimmy added, "We also get to speak about it with the military recruiters who are always at school."

Following Sunday's production, Allan Buchman, the Culture Project's artistic director, summed up, "What we saw tonight was the reason to have a theater."

With the evening winding down, the kids were already talking about their next performance, this one at the famed Joseph Papp Public Theater, another prominent New York institution, which will be attended by some of the soldiers the student actors play. Jimmy said, "It means a lot that we can share their stories. We got word from India, Japan … and even Iowa." The audience laughed. It was getting late. As the students packed up to head home to Connecticut, they wondered if they would ever be allowed to perform the play where it all began, at Wilton High.

THE TIME IS RIGHT FOR NEW PENTAGON PAPERS

Of the Democratic presidential candidates, Senator Mike Gravel is probably the least well recognized. His dark-horse candidacy may be the butt of jokes on the late-night comedy shows, but that doesn't faze former Pentagon analyst Daniel Ellsberg: "Here is a senator who was not afraid to look foolish. That is the fear that keeps people in line all their lives."

The famed whistle-blower joined Gravel this past weekend on a panel commemorating the 35th anniversary of the publication of *The Pentagon Papers* by the Beacon Press, a small, nonprofit publisher affiliated with the Unitarian Universalist Association. It was this publisher that Gravel turned to in 1971, after dozens of others had turned him down, to publish the 7,000 pages that Ellsberg had delivered to Gravel to put into the public record.

The story of the leak of the Pentagon Papers to the *New York Times* is famous, but how they got published as a book, with Gravel's face on the jacket, reads like a John Grisham novel.

Ellsberg was a military analyst working for the RAND Corporation in the 1960s when he was asked to join an internal Pentagon group tasked

25

with creating a comprehensive, secret history of U.S. involvement in Vietnam. Ellsberg photocopied thousands of documents and leaked them to the *New York Times*, which published excerpts in June 1971.

President Richard Nixon immediately got a restraining order, stopping the newspaper from printing more. It was the first time in U.S. history that presses were stopped by federal court order. The *Times* fought the injunction, and won in the Supreme Court case *New York Times Co. v. United States*. Following that decision, the *Washington Post* also began running excerpts. Ellsberg gave the Pentagon Papers to the *Post* on the condition that one of its editors, Ben Bagdikian, deliver a copy to Gravel.

Gravel recalled the exchange, which he set up at midnight outside the storied Mayflower Hotel in Washington, D.C.: "I used to work in intelligence; I know how to do these things." Gravel pulled his car up to Bagdikian's, the two opened their trunks, and Gravel heaved the boxes personally, worried that only he could claim senatorial immunity should they get caught with the leaked documents. His staff aides were posted as lookouts around the block.

Thwarted in his attempt to read the Pentagon Papers into the public record as a filibuster to block the renewal of the draft, Gravel called a late-night meeting of the obscure Subcommittee on Buildings and Grounds, which he chaired, and began reading the papers aloud there. He broke down crying while reading the details of Vietnamese civilian deaths. Because he had begun the reading, he was legally able to enter all 7,000 pages of the Pentagon Papers, once top-secret, into the public record.

Though ridiculed by the press for his emotional display, Gravel was undaunted. He wanted the Pentagon Papers published as a book so Americans could read what had been done in their name. Only Beacon Press accepted the challenge.

Robert West, the president of the Unitarian Universalist Association at the time, approved the publication. With that decision, he said, "We started down a path that led through two and a half years of government intimidation, harassment and threat of criminal punishment." As Beacon weathered subpoenas, FBI investigations of its bank accounts, and other chilling probes, Gravel attempted to extend his senatorial immunity to the publisher. The bid failed in the U.S Supreme Court (the first time that the U.S. Senate appeared before the court), but not without a strongly worded dissent from Justice William O. Douglas: "In light of the command of the First Amendment we have no choice but to rule that here government, not the press, is lawless."

Which brings us to today. Sitting next to West and Gravel, Ellsberg repeated the plea that he is making in speeches all over the United States:

> The equivalent of the Pentagon Papers exist in safes all over Washington, not only in the Pentagon, but in the CIA, the State Department and elsewhere. My message is to them: Take the risk, reveal the truth under the lies of your own bosses and your superiors, obey your oath to the Constitution, which every one of those officials took, not to the commander in chief, but to the Constitution of the United States.

THE UNCOUNTED CASUALTIES OF WAR

U.S. Marine Lance Corporal Jeffrey Lucey is not counted among the Iraq war dead. But he did die, when he came home. He committed suicide. His parents are suing the Department of Veterans Affairs and R. James Nicholson, the secretary of veterans affairs, for wrongful death, medical malpractice, and other damages.

Kevin and Joyce Lucey saw their son's rapid descent after he returned from combat in Iraq in June 2003. Kevin said, "Hallucinations started with the visual, the audio, tactile. He would talk about hearing camel spiders in his room at night, and he actually had a flashlight under his bed, which he could use to search for the camel spiders. His whole life was falling apart."

Jeffrey told his family that he was ordered to execute two Iraqi prisoners of war. After he killed the two men, Jeffrey took their dog tags and wore them until Christmas Eve 2003, when he threw them at his sister, calling himself a murderer. A military investigation concluded the story is without merit, but Kevin Lucey says, "An agency investigating itself, I have a lot of problems with that. We fully believe our son." Joyce Lucey added, "It really, to us, didn't make a difference what caused Jeffrey's PTSD [post-traumatic stress disorder]. We know that he came back different, so something happened to him over there."

Jeffrey got worse, secluding himself in his room, watching TV and drinking heavily. Jeffrey was reluctant to seek care, fearing the stigma that he felt accompanied mental-health treatment. Finally, on May 28, 2004, the Luceys had Jeffrey involuntarily committed. The Veterans Affairs hospital released him after three days.

On June 5, 2004, Jeffrey had deteriorated significantly. His sisters and grandfather brought him back to the VA. Joyce said the VA "decided that he wasn't saying what he needed to say to get involuntarily committed. Later we were to find out that they never called a psychiatrist or anybody that could have evaluated him. And they have this all on the record. It said that the grandfather was pleading for his grandson to be admitted."

The Luceys later learned from staff notes that Jeffrey talked about three ways to commit suicide. His father explained:

He told them that he would suffocate himself, he would overdose or he would hang himself. He also shared with the psychiatrist how he had bought a hose. And, of course, on June 5, when we tried to admit him the second time and the VA declined, Joyce and I went through the house, we took everything that he could hurt himself with, but we never thought of a hose.

Turned back by the Veterans Affairs Medical Center, Jeffrey spent his last two weeks alive at home. Kevin Lucey describes the night before his son killed himself: "It was about 11:30 at night, and I was exhausted, Jeff was exhausted. He asked me if he would be able to sit in my lap. And so for 45 minutes we rocked in silence, and the therapist told us after Jeff died that that was no doubt his last place of refuge, his last safe harbor that he felt that he could go to."

The next evening, after returning home from work, Kevin raced inside: "I went to his bedroom, and the one thing I noted was that his dog tags were laying on his bed." He made his way to the cellar, where he found his son Jeffrey dead, a hose double-looped around his neck.

Three years later, his parents have filed suit. They are not alone. A separate class-action suit was filed by Veterans for Common Sense and Veterans

United for Truth on behalf of hundreds of thousands of veterans who have been denied medical benefits.

Jeffrey Lucey's suicide note begins, "Dear Mom and Dad, I cannot express my apologies in words for the pain I have caused you but I beg for your forgiveness. I want you to know that I loved you both and still do but the pain of life was too much for me to deal with."

Supporting the troops means taking care of them when they return home.

WINTER SOLDIER MARCHES AGAIN

Last weekend, in the lead-up to the fifth anniversary of the invasion of Iraq, a remarkable gathering occurred just outside Washington, D.C., called Winter Soldier, Iraq and Afghanistan: Eyewitness Accounts of the Occupations. Hundreds of veterans of these two wars, along with active-duty soldiers, came together to offer testimony about the horrors of war, including atrocities they witnessed or committed themselves.

The name, Winter Soldier, comes from a similar event in 1971, when hundreds of Vietnam veterans gathered in Detroit, and is derived from the opening line of Thomas Paine's pamphlet, *The Crisis*, published in 1776: "These are the times that try men's souls: The summer soldier and the sunshine patriot will, in this crisis, shrink from the service of their country; but he that stands it now, deserves the love and thanks of man and woman."

This Winter Soldier was organized by the group Iraq Veterans Against the War. Kelly Dougherty, an Iraq veteran from the Colorado Army National Guard and IVAW's executive director, opened the proceedings, saying, "The voices of veterans and service members, as well as civilians on the ground, need to be heard by the American people, and by the people of the world, and also by other people in the military and other veterans so they can find their voice to tell their story, because each of our individual stories is crucially important and needs to be heard if people are to understand the reality and the true human cost of war and occupation."

What followed were four days of gripping testimony, ranging from firsthand accounts of the murder of Iraqi civilians, the dehumanization of Iraqis and Afghanis that undergirds the violence of the occupations, to the toll that violence takes on the soldiers themselves and the inadequate care they receive upon returning home.

Jon Michael Turner, who fought with the 3rd Battalion, 8th Marines, tore his medals off his chest. He said,

> On April 18, 2006, I had my first confirmed kill. This man was innocent. I don't know his name. I called him "the fat man." He was walking back to his house, and I shot him in front of his friend and his father. The first round didn't kill him, after I had hit him up here in his neck area. And afterward he started screaming and looked right into my eyes. So I looked at my friend, who I was on post with, and I said, "Well, I can't let that happen." So I took another shot and took him out. He was then carried away by the rest of his family. It took seven people to carry his body away.
>
> We were all congratulated after we had our first kills, and that happened to have been mine. My company commander personally congratulated me, as he did everyone else in our company. This is the same individual who had stated that whoever gets their first kill by stabbing them to death will get a four-day pass when we return from Iraq.

Hart Viges was with the 82nd Airborne, part of the invasion in March 2003. He described a house raid where they arrested the wrong men:

> We never went on a raid where we got the right house, much less the right person. Not once. I looked at my sergeant, and I was like, "Sergeant, these aren't the men that we're looking for." And he told me, "Don't worry. I'm sure they would have done something anyways." And this mother, all the while, is crying in my face, trying to kiss my feet. And, you know, I can't speak Arabic. I can speak human. She was saying, "Please, why are you taking my sons? They have done nothing wrong." And that made me feel very powerless. You know, 82nd Airborne Division, Infantry, with Apache heli-

copters, Bradley fighting vehicles and armor and my M4—I was powerless. I was powerless to help her.

Former Staff Sergeant Camilo Mejía also spoke. After serving in Iraq, he refused to return there. He was court-martialed and spent almost a year in prison. Mejía is now the chairman of IVAW. After he finished the testimony of his experience in Iraq, he laid out the group's demands:

> We have over a million Iraqi dead. We have over five million Iraqis displaced. We have close to 4,000 dead [Americans]. We have close to 60,000 injured. That's not even counting the post-traumatic stress disorder and all the other psychological and emotional scars that our generation is bringing home with them. War is dehumanizing a whole new generation of this country and destroying the people in the country of Iraq. In order for us to reclaim our humanity as a military and as a country, we demand the immediate and unconditional withdrawal of all troops from Iraq, care and benefits for all veterans, and reparations for the Iraqi people so they can rebuild their country on their terms.

As we enter the sixth year of the war in Iraq, more time than the United States was involved in World War II, we should honor the veterans of Iraq and Afghanistan, by listening to them.

BODY OF WAR

We just passed the grim milestone of 4,000 U.S. military members killed in Iraq since the invasion five years ago. Still, the death toll climbs.

Typically unmentioned alongside the count of U.S. war dead are the tens of thousands of wounded (not to mention the Iraqi dead). The Pentagon doesn't tout the number of U.S. injured, but the website icasualties.org reports an official number of more than 40,000 soldiers requiring medical airlifts out of Iraq, a good indicator of the scale of major injuries. That doesn't include many others. Dr. Arthur Blank, an expert on post-traumatic stress disorder (PTSD), estimates that 30 percent of Iraq veterans will suffer from PTSD.

Tomas Young was one of those injured, on April 4, 2004, in Sadr City. Young is the subject of a new feature documentary by legendary TV talk-show host Phil Donahue and filmmaker Ellen Spiro, called *Body of War*. In it, Young describes the incident that has left him paralyzed from the chest down: "I only managed to spend maybe five days in Iraq until I got picked to go on my first mission. There were 25 of us crammed into the back of a two-and-a-half-ton truck with no covering on top or armor on the sides. For the Iraqis on the top of the roof, it just looked like, you know, ducks in a barrel. They didn't even have to aim."

The film documents his struggle, coping with severe paralysis and life in a wheelchair, its impact on his psyche, his wrecked marriage, his family, and his political development from military enlistee into a member of Iraq Veterans Against the War.

Donahue has his own personal link to the anniversary of the invasion of Iraq. It was just weeks before the invasion that his nightly program, MSNBC's top-rated show, was canceled. As revealed shortly thereafter in a leaked memo, Donahue presented a "difficult public face for NBC in a time of war. He seems to delight in presenting guests who are anti-war, anti-Bush and skeptical of the administration's motives ... at the same time that our competitors are waving the flag at every opportunity."

Tomas Young enlisted in the military soon after September 11, 2001. Earlier this week, Vice President Dick Cheney said, "The president carries the biggest burden, obviously. He's the one who has to make the decision to commit young Americans, but we are fortunate to have a group of men and women, an all-volunteer force, who voluntarily put on the uniform and go in harm's way for the rest of us."

Young, speaking to me from Kansas City, Missouri, where he lives, responded to Cheney: "From one of those soldiers who volunteered to go to Afghanistan after September 11, which was where the evidence said we needed to go, to [Cheney], the master of the college deferment in Vietnam: Many of us volunteered with patriotic feelings in our heart, only to see them subverted and bastardized by the administration and sent into the wrong country."

Body of War depicts the personal cost of war. In one of the most moving scenes in the film, Young meets Senator Robert Byrd, the longest-serving senator, with the most votes cast in Senate history (more than 18,000). Byrd said his "no" vote on the Iraq war resolution was the most important of his life. Young helps him read the names of the 23 senators who voted against the war resolution. Byrd reflects: "The immortal 23. Our founders would be so proud." Turning to Young, he says, "Thank you for your service. Man, you've made a great sacrifice. You served your country well." Young replies, "As have you, sir."

WHISTLE-BLOWER POINTS TO
TARGET LIST IN U.S. ATTACK ON HOTEL

More than five years have passed since the invasion of Iraq, since President Bush stood under the "Mission Accomplished" banner on that aircraft carrier. While these fifth anniversaries got some notice, another did not: the shelling of the Palestine Hotel in Baghdad by a U.S. Army tank on April 8, 2003. The tank attack killed two unembedded journalists, Reuters cameraman Taras Protsyuk and José Couso, a cameraman for the Spanish television network Telecinco. Couso recorded his own death. He was filming from the balcony and caught on tape the distant tank as it rotated its turret and fired on the hotel. A Spanish court has charged three U.S. servicemen with murder, but the U.S. government refuses to hand over the accused soldiers. The story might have ended there, just another day of violence and death in Iraq, were it not for a young U.S. military intelligence veteran who has just decided to blow the whistle.

Adrienne Kinne is a former army sergeant who worked in military intelligence for ten years, from 1994 to 2004. Trained in Arabic, she worked in the army translating intercepted communications. She told me in an interview this week that she saw a target list that included the Palestine

Hotel. She knew that it housed journalists, since she had intercepted calls from the Palestine Hotel between journalists there and their families and friends back home (illegally and unconstitutionally, she thought).

Said Kinne:

> [W]e were listening to journalists who were staying in the Palestine Hotel. And I remember that, specifically because during the buildup to "shock and awe" ... we were given a list of potential targets in Baghdad, and the Palestine Hotel was listed. [P]utting one and one together, I went to my officer in charge, and I told him that there are journalists staying at this hotel who think they're safe, and yet we have this hotel listed as a potential target, and somehow the dots are not being connected here, and shouldn't we make an effort to make sure that the right people know the situation? And unfortunately, my officer in charge ... basically told me that it was not my job to analyze ... someone somewhere higher up the chain knew what they were doing.

She said the officer in charge was Warrant Officer John Berry.

Kinne's account directly contradicts the official line of the U.S. government. On May 2, 2003, Colin Powell, then secretary of state and a former general in the army, visited Spain. He said of the Palestine Hotel: "We knew about the hotel. We knew that it was a hotel where journalists were located, and others, and it is for that reason it was not attacked during any phase of the aerial campaign."

If Powell was telling the truth, then why was the hotel included on the list of targets that Kinne says she read in a secure e-mail? Or was he just parsing words by saying it wasn't a target during the "aerial campaign"? Kinne also revealed that the military was spying on nongovernmental organizations like Doctors Without Borders and the International Red Cross, listening in on these groups—also illegal—and justifying the pretense on the grounds that they might by chance report on a cache of weapons of mass destruction, or their satellite phone might get stolen by terrorists. She also received and translated a fax from the Iraqi National Congress, the CIA-funded group of Iraqi exiles who were funneling false information about WMDs to the U.S. government in order to bolster the case for war. The intel was considered high value and was sent directly to the White House.

Kinne has shown great courage and taken great risks to bring these revelations to light, to blow the whistle. She follows in the tradition of Daniel Ellsberg, who leaked the Pentagon Papers during the Vietnam War. Ellsberg has called on government workers to blow the whistle:

> It's a great, great risk to have the amount of secrecy we do have right now that enabled the president to lie us into this war and is heading us toward a war that will be even more disastrous in Iran. And this is the time for unauthorized disclosures, which are the only kind that are going to tell us the truth about what's happening, and they should be done, in my opinion, on a scale that will indeed risk or even ensure that the person doing it will be identified.

The brother of José Couso, Javier, has tirelessly pursued justice for his brother, traveling globally to make the story known and pushing the case in the Spanish courts. Kinne's revelations created a stir in Spain, where the jurisdiction of the case against the three U.S. Army members is being challenged. The video of Kinne's disclosures was downloaded and quickly translated for presentation the next day to the court in Madrid.

The Bush White House, we now know, used retired generals with ties to the Pentagon and to military contractors to deceive the U.S. public. Unembedded journalists in Iraq were a thorn in the side of the Pentagon spin masters. Might that April 8 attack have been a message to them? Thanks to former Army Sergeant Adrienne Kinne, we may be closer to finding out.

THREATS, LIES, AND AUDIOTAPE

It was like an action movie. A young man held at night in a hotel, threatened with prison. He is to be shipped off to war in the morning. His friends are desperately trying to find him. The "down" button on the elevator had been disabled. He considers jumping from the window. When his friends arrive, they encounter military personnel patrolling the grounds. One sneaks in, gets his friend out, and they drive off into the night. This was real life for 17-year-old Eric Martinez, a student at Aldine High School in a poor neighborhood of Houston. He responded to an army recruitment pitch called the delayed enlistment program.

But then, as 17-year-olds are wont to do, Eric changed his mind. When the recruiter came to his house and threatened his mother, she went to the recruiting station to meet with the officer in charge:

"She talked to Sergeant Marquette and told him that I didn't want to go, and that's it. And Marquette said that I had to go, and if I didn't, that I'd have a warrant for my arrest, and I wouldn't be able to get no government loans or nothing like that. So, my mom doesn't really know anything about it, so she believed it, and she told me. And I believed it, too, because I didn't know much about it either." It was then that they took Eric to the hotel.

Martinez's friend, Irving Gonzalez, knew he was next. He had signed up for the same program. As the oldest of four children of a single mother, Irving's impulse was to help his family survive, get the signing bonus, and gain access to a college education. He then wanted to get out of the program, to pursue college directly. He called the recruiter, Sergeant Glenn Marquette. Desperate, he had the call recorded.

Sergeant Marquette:

> This is what will happen. You want to go to school? You will not get no loans, because all college loans are federal and government loans. So you'll be black-marked from that. As soon as you get pulled over for a speeding ticket or anything with the law, they're gonna see that you're a deserter. Then they're going to apprehend you, take you to jail … you will do your time, as you deserve. All that lovey-dovey "I want to go to college" and all this? Guess what. You just threw it out the window, because you just screwed your life.

Irving and two others were the ones who sneaked Eric out of the hotel.

After the story broke, Marquette was suspended, and the military says it is conducting an investigation, but neither Martinez nor Gonzalez has been contacted. Recent history does not bode well. In 2005, Sergeant Thomas Kelt, who like Marquette worked at the Greenspoint Recruiting Station in Houston, left a phone message for potential recruit Chris Monarch, saying if he didn't show up at the recruiting station that afternoon, "We'll have a warrant, OK? So give me a call back." The story went national. The military conducted a daylong "stand down" on recruitment to retrain their recruiters. They said they removed Kelt. In fact, he was promoted to head up a nearby recruiting center.

I asked Douglas Smith, spokesman for the U.S. Army Recruiting Command in Kentucky, about why Kelt wasn't punished. Smith replied that Kelt had received a "negative administrative action … just because someone has done something wrong doesn't mean that they get the death penalty."

But there's a difference between the death penalty and a promotion. When I asked Smith what the penalty was, he replied, "I'm not allowed to tell you." Smith and the rest of the military may dodge reporters' questions, but they can be subpoenaed before Congress to testify under oath.

Texas Congressman Ted Poe, a Republican, said, "Our country cannot deceive its citizens. Since the army hasn't taken the initiative, now Congress may have to get involved." Another Texas congressman, Democrat Gene Greene, whose kids went to Aldine High and whose wife taught there for years, agrees. With no end in sight in Afghanistan and Iraq, recruiters must be prevented from using desperate and aggressive measures to lure our nation's young people—the poorest and most vulnerable—into the line of fire.

INVASION OF THE SEA-SMURFS

A little-noticed story surfaced a couple of weeks ago in the *Army Times* newspaper about the Third Infantry Division's First Brigade Combat Team. "Beginning Oct. 1 for 12 months," reported *Army Times* staff writer Gina Cavallaro, "the 1st BCT will be under the day-to-day control of U.S. Army North, the Army service component of Northern Command, as an on-call federal response force for natural or man-made emergencies and disasters, including terrorist attacks." Disturbingly, she writes that "they may be called upon to help with civil unrest and crowd control" as well.

The force will be called the chemical, biological, radiological, nuclear, or high-yield explosive Consequence Management Response Force. Its acronym, CCMRF, is pronounced "sea-smurf." These "sea-smurfs," Cavallaro reports, have "spent 35 of the last 60 months in Iraq patrolling in full battle rattle," in a combat zone, and now will spend their 20-month "dwell time"—time troops are required to spend to "reset and regenerate after a deployment"—armed and ready to hit the U.S. streets.

The *Army Times* piece includes a correction stating that the forces would not use nonlethal weaponry domestically. I called Air Force Lieutenant Colonel Jamie Goodpaster, a public-affairs officer for Northern Command. She told me that the overall mission was humanitarian, to save lives and help communities recover from catastrophic events. Nevertheless, the military forces would have weapons on-site, "containerized," she said—that is, stored in containers—including both lethal and so-called nonlethal weapons. They would have mostly wheeled vehicles but would also, she said, have access to tanks. She said that any decision to use weapons would be made at a higher level, perhaps at the secretary-of-defense level.

Talk of trouble on U.S. streets is omnipresent now, with the juxtaposition of Wall Street and Main Street. The financial crisis we face remains obscure to most people; titans of business and government officials assure us that the financial system is "on the brink," that a massive bailout is necessary, immediately, to prevent a disaster. Conservative and progressive members of Congress, at the insistence of constituents, blocked the initial plan. If the economy does collapse, if people can't go down to the bank to withdraw their savings, or get cash from an ATM, there may be serious "civil unrest," and the "sea-smurfs" may be called upon sooner than we imagine to assist with "crowd control."

The political and financial establishments seem completely galled that people would actually oppose their massive bailout, which rewards financiers for gambling. Normal people worry about paying their bills, buying groceries and gas, and paying rent or a mortgage in increasingly uncertain times. No one ever offers to bail them out. Wall Street's house of cards has collapsed, and the rich bankers are getting little sympathy from working people.

That's where the sea-smurfs come in. Officially formed to respond to major disasters, like a nuclear or biological attack, this combat brigade falls under the U.S. Northern Command, a military structure formed on October 1, 2002, to "provide command and control of Department of Defense homeland defense efforts." Military participation in domestic operations was originally outlawed with the Posse Comitatus Act in 1878. The John Warner National Defense Authorization Act for Fiscal Year 2007, however, included a section that allowed the president to deploy the armed forces to "restore public order" or to suppress "any insurrection."

While a later bill repealed this, President Bush attached a signing statement that he did not feel bound by the repeal.

We are in a time of increasing economic disparity, with the largest gap between rich and poor of any wealthy industrialized country. We are witnessing a crackdown on dissent, most recently with $100 million spent on "security" at the Democratic and Republican national conventions. The massive paramilitary police forces deployed at the RNC in St. Paul, Minnesota, were complete overkill, discouraging protests and conducting mass arrests (National Guard troops just back from Fallujah were there). The arrest there of almost 50 journalists (myself included) showed a clear escalation in attempting to control the message (akin to the ban on photos of flag-draped coffins of soldiers). There are two ongoing, unpopular wars that are costing lives and hundreds of billions of dollars. Nobel Prize–winning economist Joe Stiglitz estimates that Iraq alone will cost more than $3 trillion.

In December 2001, in the midst of restricted access to bank accounts due to a financial crisis, respectable, middle-class Argentines rose up, took to the streets, smashed bank windows, and ultimately forced the government out of power, despite a massive police crackdown and a failed attempt to control the media. Here in the United States, with the prospect of a complete failure of our financial system, the people have spoken and do not want an unprecedented act of corporate welfare. We don't know how close the system is to collapse, nor do we know how close the people are to taking to the streets. The creation of an active-duty military force, the sea-smurfs, that could be used to suppress public protest here at home is a very bad sign.

OBAMA'S AFGHAN TRAP

President Barack Obama on Monday night held his first prime-time news conference. When questioned on Afghanistan, he replied, "This is going to be a big challenge." He also was asked whether he would change the Pentagon policy banning the filming and photographing of the flag-draped coffins of soldiers killed in Iraq and Afghanistan. He said he was reviewing it. The journalist who asked the question pointed out that it was Joe Biden several years ago who accused the Bush administration of suppressing the images to avoid public furor over the deaths of U.S. service members. Now, Vice President Joe Biden predicts that a surge in U.S. troops in Afghanistan will mean more U.S. casualties: "I hate to say it, but yes, I think there will be. There will be an uptick."

Meanwhile, the Associated Press recently cited a classified report drafted by the Joint Chiefs of Staff recommending a shift in strategy from democracy-building in Afghanistan to attacking alleged Taliban and al-Qaeda strongholds along the Afghanistan-Pakistan border.

And the campaign has clearly begun. Days after his inauguration, Obama's first (known) military actions were two missile strikes inside

Pakistan's frontier province, reportedly killing 22 people, including women and children.

Cherif Bassiouni has spent years going back and forth to Afghanistan. He is a professor of law at DePaul University and the former United Nations human rights investigator in Afghanistan. In 2005, he was forced out of the United Nations under pressure from the Bush administration, days after he released a report accusing the U.S. military and private contractors of committing human rights abuses. I asked Bassiouni about Obama's approach to Afghanistan. He told me, "There is no military solution in Afghanistan. There is an economic-development solution, but I don't see that coming … Right now, the population has nothing to gain by supporting the U.S. and NATO. It has everything to gain by being supportive of the Taliban."

Bassiouni's scathing 2005 UN report accused the U.S. military and private military contractors of "forced entry into homes, arrest and detention of nationals and foreigners without legal authority or judicial review, sometimes for extended periods of time, forced nudity, hooding and sensory deprivation, sleep and food deprivation, forced squatting and standing for long periods of time in stress positions, sexual abuse, beatings, torture, and use of force resulting in death."

I also put the question of the military surge to former President Jimmy Carter. He responded, "I would disagree with Obama as far as a surge that would lead to a more intense bombing of Afghan villages and centers and a heavy dependence on military. I would like to see us reach out more, to be accommodating, and negotiate with all of the factions in Afghanistan."

Carter should know. He helped create what his national security adviser, Zbigniew Brzezinski, called "the Afghan trap," set for the Soviets. This was done by supporting Islamic mujahedeen in the late 1970s against the Soviets in Afghanistan, thereby creating what evolved into the Taliban. Brzezinski told the French newspaper *Le Nouvel Observateur* in 1998, "What is most important to the history of the world? The Taliban or the collapse of the Soviet empire? Some stirred-up Muslims or the liberation of Central Europe and the end of the Cold War?" More than 14,000 Soviet troops were killed, and the Afghan toll exceeded one million. Osama bin Laden got his start with the help of the CIA-funded Afghan operation.

Bassiouni suggests that a military solution is doomed to failure, noting that the Taliban "realized they could not defeat the American forces, so they went underground. They put their Kalashnikovs under the mattresses, and they waited. A year ago, they resurfaced again. They can do the same thing. They can go back in the mountains, push the Kalashnikovs under the mattress, wait out five years. They have been doing that since the 1800s with any and every foreign invader."

As Carter told me, "To offer a hand of friendship or accommodation, not only to the warlords but even to those radicals in the Taliban who are willing to negotiate would be the best approach, [rather] than to rely exclusively on major military force."

Have we learned nothing from Iraq? "When it comes to the war in Iraq, the time for promises and assurances, for waiting and patience is over. Too many lives have been lost and too many billions have been spent for us to trust the president on another tried-and-failed policy." That was Senator Barack Obama in January 2007. With his joint chiefs now apparently gunning for more fighting and less talk in Afghanistan, President Obama needs to be reminded of his own words.

MARCH 3, 2009

OBAMA'S COALITION OF THE UNWILLING

President Barack Obama met recently with the prime ministers of Canada and Britain. This week's meeting with Britain's Gordon Brown, who was pitching a "global New Deal," created a minor flap when the White House downsized a full news conference to an Oval Office question-and-answer session, viewed by some in Britain as a snub. The change was attributed to the weather, with the Rose Garden covered with snow.

It might have actually related not to snow cover, but to a snow job, covering up the growing divide between Afghanistan policies.

U.S. policy in Afghanistan includes a troop surge, already under way, and continued bombing in Pakistan using unmanned drones. Escalating civilian deaths are a certainty. The United Nations estimates that more than 2,100 civilians died in 2008, a 40 percent jump over 2007.

The occupation of Afghanistan is in its eighth year, and public support in many NATO countries is eroding. Joe Stiglitz, winner of the 2001 Nobel Memorial Prize in Economics, told me: "The move into Afghanistan is going to be very expensive ... Our European NATO partners are getting disillusioned with the war. I talked to a lot of the people in Europe, and they really feel this is a quagmire."

Forty-one nations contribute to NATO's 56,000-troop presence in Afghanistan. More than half of the troops are from the United States. The United Kingdom has 8,300 troops, Canada just under 3,000. Maintaining troops is costly, but the human toll is greater. Canada, with 111 deaths, has suffered the highest per capita death rate for foreign armies in Afghanistan, since its forces are based in the south around Kandahar, where the Taliban is strong.

Last Sunday on CNN, Canadian Prime Minister Stephen Harper said, "We're not going to win this war just by staying ... we are not going to ever defeat the insurgency." U.S. Defense Secretary Robert Gates recently wrote in *Foreign Affairs* magazine, "The United States cannot kill or capture its way to victory." Yet it's Canada that has set a deadline for troop withdrawal at the end of 2011. The United States is talking escalation.

Anand Gopal, Afghanistan correspondent for the *Christian Science Monitor*, described the situation on the ground: "A lot of Afghans that I speak to in these southern areas where the fighting has been happening say that to bring more troops, that's going to mean more civilian casualties. It'll mean more of these night raids, which have been deeply unpopular amongst Afghans ... Whenever American soldiers go into a village and then leave, the Taliban comes and attacks the village." Afghan Parliamentarian Shukria Barakzai, a woman, told Gopal: "Send us 30,000 scholars instead. Or 30,000 engineers. But don't send more troops—it will just bring more violence."

Women in Afghanistan play a key role in winning the peace. A photographer wrote me, "There will be various celebrations across Afghanistan to honor International Women's Day on Sunday, March 8. In Kandahar there will be an event with hundreds of women gathering to pray for peace, which is especially poignant in a part of Afghanistan that is so volatile." After returning from an international women's gathering in Moscow, feminist writer Gloria Steinem noted that the discussion centered around getting the media to hire peace correspondents to balance the war correspondents. Voices of civil society would be amplified, giving emphasis to those who wage peace. In the U.S. media, there is an equating of fighting the war with fighting terrorism. Yet on the ground, civilian casualties lead to tremendous hostility. Mary Robinson, former president of Ireland, recently told me, "I've been saddened and shocked by virulent anti-American responses to those wars [in Iraq and Afghanistan]. They're seen as occupations … I think it's very important we learn from mistakes of sounding war drums." She added, "There's such a connection from the Middle East to Afghanistan to Pakistan which builds on strengths of working with neighbors."

Barack Obama was swept through the primaries and into the presidency on the basis of his antiwar message. Prime ministers like Brown and Harper are bending to growing public demand for an end to war. Yet in the United States, there is scant debate about sending more troops to Afghanistan, and about the spillover of the war into Pakistan.

CLIMATE
CHANGE

GLOBAL WARRING, GLOBAL WARMING, GLOBAL WARNING

We begin this year with many milestones. 2006 was among the hottest years in recorded history. In Britain, it was the hottest year since they started keeping records in 1659. Ten of the hottest years in recorded history have occurred in the past 12 years. Snow has yet to fall in New York's Central Park. This hasn't happened in more than 100 years. And other records have been broken. ExxonMobil profits were slated to be the greatest ever. On December 31, the Pentagon announced another grim milestone: 3,000 U.S. soldiers killed in Iraq. It was a year of global warming, global warring, and global warning.

ExxonMobil is the world's largest publicly traded company. It is also the most profitable corporation in history. The Union of Concerned Scientists (UCS) just issued a report documenting how ExxonMobil has implemented tobacco-industry tactics in its efforts to fight the movement to accept global warming as truth and to require massive regulation to help slow its onset.

According to the UCS, ExxonMobil "manufactures uncertainty" with a sophisticated and well-funded campaign. They funded a network of 43 "grass-roots" organizations with $16 million, recruited scientists willing to publish non-peer-reviewed articles that challenge established science, and flooded the media with these "experts," creating the essential "echo chamber." A critical part of ExxonMobil's strategy involves lavish spending on electoral campaigns and lobbying to ensure that Congress and the White House follow the line on questioning human-caused climate change.

While the rest of the world accepts the reality of global warming, the United States, the world's largest producer of greenhouse gases, has been stymied by the disinformation campaigns of the oil industry. Let's hope the new 110th Congress shifts climate-change policy at a glacial pace— the rapidly receding twenty-first–century glaciers, that is. Key committees will be chaired by Senator Barbara Boxer, D-CA, and Representative John Dingell, D-MI. Replacing chairman Senator James Inhofe, R-OK, who describes global warming as a hoax, Boxer is bullish on fighting greenhouse gases. Dingell, from the heart of the auto industry in Michigan, is less direct and hedges on his willingness, for example, to push for better fuel efficiency in cars.

The flip side of oil consumption is oil production. That is where the warring comes in.

The *Independent* of London reported this week in a piece titled "SpOILs of War" that the Iraqi Parliament is rushing to pass a law that will open Iraq's oil reserves to exploitation by foreign corporations. The law would allow these foreign companies to retain 75 percent of the profits until they recouped their initial drilling investments, thereafter to retain 20 percent, which is about double the take normally allowed. It would be the first opening for such companies since the Iraqi oil industry was nationalized in 1972. This comports with the recommendation of the business-friendly Iraq Study Group report of James Baker III. One underreported item was the recommendation to privatize the oil industry. Recall that the initial "Shock and Awe" bombing campaign in March 2003 specifically spared the Iraqi Oil Ministry building.

As global temperatures surge, so do oil-company profits, and U.S. soldiers in Iraq. President Bush, despite plummeting to his all-time low popularity in the polls on his handling of Iraq, forces tens of thousands more young Americans to march lockstep into another year's deployment into the turmOIL of Iraq. As for Iraqis, the British medical journal *The Lancet* published a study by the Johns Hopkins University School of Public Health that an estimated 650,000 Iraqi civilians have been killed since the March 2003 invasion.

As for warning, the alarm has sounded: we need a sane energy policy that decreases our oil consumption (the Germans and French, "Old Europe," use half as much per capita as we do in the United States). The potential for environmental disaster, and the prospects of protracted wars for oil, demand no less.

MCKIBBEN:
HOLD POLITICIANS' FEET TO THE FIRE

Fires rage through Southern California. Massive rainstorms drench New Orleans. The Southeast United States, from Tennessee across the Carolinas and into Georgia, is in the midst of what could be the worst drought on record there. Atlanta could run out of water. While the press does an admirable job bringing us live images of extreme weather, it doesn't explain why these events are happening. What links these crises? Global warming. Two words that have all too often been vacuumed off government websites and erased from government scientific studies.

If the press isn't making the connection, Bill McKibben is. In 1989, he wrote the book *The End of Nature*, one of the first books to describe global warming as an emerging environmental crisis. Now, almost 20 years later, he is leading a campaign to draft mass grass-roots participation to publicize the potential catastrophe of climate change and to demand federal action to "Step It Up." The first Step It Up day of action, April 14, 2007, organized in local communities through a central website, saw 1,400 coordinated activities pulled together in just three months. The second day of action is planned for November 3, organized through the website stepitup2007.org.

"What's important to remember and the reason that we spend all our time organizing now, trying to change all this, is that so far human beings have raised the temperature of the planet about one degree Fahrenheit," says McKibben. "The computer modeling makes it very clear that before the century is out, unless we take very strong action, indeed, we're going to raise the temperature of the planet another five degrees Fahrenheit. So, take whatever you see now, multiply it by five, and then toss in all those cascading effects that come, as we exceed one threshold after another."

The cascade effect is what is so important to understand. How could one degree Fahrenheit make such a big difference? One immediate, measurable impact of that seemingly slight temperature rise, according to University of Arizona scientist Tom Swetnam, is the increase in the frequency and duration of large wildfires in the U.S. West. Swetnam and his team have linked a warming, drying trend since the 1980s to the incidence of fires, like the more than a dozen that are raging out of control in Southern California.

The predictions are not good. Trees take in carbon dioxide, the main greenhouse gas, releasing oxygen. In his August 2006 *Science* article, Swetnam reports that western U.S. forests remove 20 to 40 percent of the carbon dioxide in the United States. As forests burn, McKibben notes, carbon is released into the atmosphere. Fewer trees then remain to take carbon dioxide out of the atmosphere, making warmer conditions, supporting more and longer fires, and so on, creating a positive feedback loop. A central warning of the scientific community is this: at some point, if Earth's temperature rises much more, maybe three degrees, maybe six degrees, an irreversible feedback loop will overwhelm the planet's climate, with cascading impacts leading to a warmer and warmer planet.

Corporate America is feeling the heat. Carbon-emitting industries like the oil companies, chastened by the experience of Big Tobacco and asbestos, see that in the future they might be held accountable—especially since they are funding junk science and "astroturf" (i.e., fake grass-roots) groups to cast doubt about the effects of global warming. Insurance companies can't afford to ignore the consequences of global warming, as extreme weather causes billions of dollars in damage.

McKibben and the Step It Up campaign lay out three basic demands:

—Green jobs now, for all: five million green jobs conserving 20 percent of our energy by 2015. Green jobs are those created by transforming the economy from a coal- and oil-burning one to a sustainable economy built on a new set of energy sources, ensuring that the same people left behind by the last economy are not left behind again.

—Cut carbon 80 percent by 2050: freeze climate pollution levels now and cut at least 80 percent by 2050, and 30 percent by 2020.

—No new coal: a moratorium on new coal-fired power plants.

McKibben explains, "We need a movement as strong, as willing to sacrifice, as morally urgent, as passionate as the civil rights movement was a generation ago. If we don't get it soon—and we have a real time limit here—if we don't get it soon, then we're not going to be able to force the changes that we need over the power of the very strong vested interests that would like to keep things the way they are, even though it's now destabilizing the planet in the most powerful and most tragic ways."

People are taking action. On Monday, 60 people were arrested in Washington, D.C., as part of the No War, No Warming days of action, linking the war in Iraq, post-Katrina recovery, and climate change, and demanding action from Congress, holding elected officials' feet to the fire. Humans are causing global warming. For a short time, we have a chance to limit the damage. But time is running out. Step it up.

FROM OIL WARS TO WATER WARS

The Nobel Peace Prize was awarded this week in Oslo, Norway. Al Gore shared the prize with the United Nations' Intergovernmental Panel on Climate Change (IPPCC) which represents more than 2,500 scientists from 130 countries. The solemn ceremony took place as the United States is blocking meaningful progress at the UN Climate Change Conference in Bali, Indonesia, and the Republicans in the U.S. Senate have derailed the energy bill passed by the House of Representatives, which would have accelerated the adoption of renewable energy sources at the expense of big-oil and coal corporations.

Gore set the stage:

So, today, we dumped another 70 million tons of global-warming pollution into the thin shell of atmosphere surrounding our planet, as if it were an open sewer. And tomorrow, we will dump a slightly larger amount, with the cumulative concentrations now trapping more and more heat from the sun.

As a result, the Earth has a fever. And the fever is rising. The experts have told us it is not a passing affliction that will heal by itself. We asked for a second opinion. And a third. And a fourth. And the consistent conclusion, restated with increasing alarm, is that something basic is wrong. We are what is wrong, and we must make it right.

He went on: "Last September 21, as the Northern Hemisphere tilted away from the sun, scientists reported with unprecedented distress that the north polar ice cap is 'falling off a cliff.' One study estimated that it could be completely gone during summer in less than 22 years. Another new study, to be presented by U.S. Navy researchers later this week, warns it could happen in as little as seven years. Seven years from now."

How will climate-change skeptics explain that one? (Already, big business is celebrating the breakup of the polar ice cap, as a northern sea route from the Atlantic to the Pacific is opening, creating a cheaper route for more needless shipping.) It is hard to imagine the North Pole, the storied, frozen expanse of ice and snow, completely gone in just a few years. Lost as well will be the vast store of archeological data trapped in the ice: thousands of years of the Earth's climate history are told in the layers of ice that descend for miles there. Scientists are just now learning how to read and interpret the history. The great meltdown will surely have catastrophic effects on the ecosystem in the north, with species like the polar bear already edging toward extinction.

Rajendra Pachauri, an Indian scientist, accepted for the IPCC. He is a careful scientist with the political finesse to chair the work of the IPCC despite the enduring antagonism of the United States. He pointed to the disproportionate effect of climate change on the world's poor: "[T]he impacts of climate change on some of the poorest and the most vulnerable communities in the world could prove extremely unsettling ... in terms of access to clean water, access to sufficient food, stable health conditions, ecosystem resources, security of settlements."

Pachauri predicts water wars and mass migrations. "Migration, usually temporary and often from rural to urban areas, is a common response to calamities such as floods and famines."

Gore invoked the memory of Mohandas Gandhi, saying he "awakened the largest democracy on earth and forged a shared resolve with what he called 'Satyagraha'—or 'truth force.' In every land, the truth—once known—has the power to set us free." Satyagraha, as Gandhi practiced it, is the disciplined application of nonviolent resistance, which is exactly what Ted Glick is doing back in Washington, D.C.

Glick heads up the Climate Emergency Council. On his 99th day of a liquids-only fast, the day after the Nobel ceremony, he joined with 20 people in the office of Senate Minority Leader Mitch McConnell for a sit-in. The Senate Republicans are now blocking a federal energy bill that would create funding for the development of renewable energy sources in the United States, while stripping away billions of dollars worth of tax breaks for big oil and coal.

Glick told me, "We have to be willing to go to jail. Al Gore, himself, a couple of months ago talked about how young people need to be sitting in in front of the coal plants to prevent coal plants from being built. That's true. Young people need to be doing that. Middle-aged people need to be doing that. Older people need to be doing that. And Al Gore needs to be doing that. Let's get serious about this crisis."

While Glick was sitting in, news reports began to circulate about Republican presidential candidate Rudolph Giuliani's law firm's lobbying activities against the energy bill. According to Bloomberg news, Bracewell & Giuliani LLP was hired by energy giant Southern Co. to defeat the bill. At a $1,000-a-plate fundraiser last August, addressing members of the coal industry, Giuliani said, "We have to increase our reliance on coal."

As Giuliani's coffers get fat with money from big oil, gas, and coal, Glick has lost more than 40 pounds, and the Earth's temperature continues to rise.

WEATHER REPORTS
ARE MISSING THE STORY

The floodwaters are rising, swamping cities, breaching levees. Tens of thousands are displaced. Many are dead. No, I am not talking about Hurricane Katrina, but about the Midwest United States. As the floodwaters head south along the Mississippi, devastating communities one after another, the media are overflowing with televised images of the destruction.

While the TV meteorologists document "extreme weather" with their increasingly sophisticated toolbox, from Doppler radar to 3-D animated maps, the two words rarely uttered are its cause: global warming. I asked former Energy Department official Joseph Romm, senior fellow at the Center for American Progress, about the disconnect:

> Part of the reason is that the people who write about global warming for most newspapers and TV are not the same people as those who tend to cover weather. In general, the media is covering this as all sort of unconnected events, just regular weather maybe gone a little wacky. But, in fact, the scientific community has predicted for more than two decades now that as we pour more heat-trapping greenhouse gases into the atmosphere, the planet will heat up, and that would redistribute water. If you heat up the

planet ... you evaporate more water, and areas that are wetter will tend to see more intense rainfall and deluges and earlier snowmelts, and all that will lead to flooding. So what we're seeing is exactly what scientists have been telling us would happen because of human emissions.

Perry Beeman is an award-winning investigative reporter for the *Des Moines Register*, and former president of the Society of Environmental Journalists. From his flood-wracked city of Des Moines, he told me,

Not even a few weeks before this all happened, we were in the middle of doing a climate-change series that's going to run over the year. We had a two-page graphic talking about the different things that would happen [in Iowa as a result of climate change] and pointing out ... that you would expect more torrential rains. What has happened here is consistent with many scientists' view of what global warming will mean in the Midwest.

So if the disasters that follow one another, from hurricanes to tornadoes to flooding, are consistent with global warming, why aren't the networks, the weather reporters, making the link? Dr. Heidi Cullen, a climate expert on the Weather Channel, created a stir in late 2006 when she wrote in her Weather Channel blog:

If a meteorologist can't speak to the fundamental science of climate change, then maybe the AMS [American Meteorological Society] shouldn't give them a Seal of Approval. If a meteorologist has an AMS Seal of Approval, which is used to confer legitimacy to TV meteorologists, then meteorologists have a responsibility to truly educate themselves on the science of global warming.

As reporters stood in waist-high water in the flooded downtowns of major American cities, President George Bush basked in the sunlight in Washington, D.C., urging Congress to lift the ban on offshore oil drilling and on oil shale drilling, and to open up the Arctic National Wildlife Refuge to oil drilling. While regular people are getting hit in the wallet at the gas pump, paying now more than $4 per gallon for gasoline, the oil, coal, and gas industries are reaping huge rewards, and applying pressure to open up protected spaces for resource extraction.

One of the candidates to replace Bush has a solution. When I asked Ralph Nader about global warming this week, he said, "We've got to have a national mission of converting our economy, and the example for the world is solar energy, four billion years of supply. It is environmentally benign, decentralized, makes us energy-independent, and replaces the ExxonMobil/Peabody Coal/uranium complex. That is why we have got to go for economic, political, health, and safety reasons."

Nader understands how the levers of power and influence operate in Washington, but also how flooding can devastate a community. He grew up in Winsted, Connecticut, where the Mad River and Still River flooded in 1955, where another Nader confronted another Bush. Ralph Nader's mother, Rose, shook the hand of Bush's grandfather, Senator Prescott Bush, R-CT, and refused to let go until he agreed to build a dry dam. The dry dam got built, and Winsted hasn't flooded since. A half-century later, our global warming problems have gotten far worse. Citizen activists need to shake not hands but the system, holding to account those with power and influence, from politicians to the personalities who report the weather on TV.

DON'T DRINK THE NUCLEAR KOOL-AID

While the presidential candidates trade barbs and accuse each other of flip-flopping, they agree with President Bush on their enthusiastic support for nuclear power.

Senator John McCain has called for 100 new nuclear power plants. Senator Barack Obama, in a July 2007 Democratic candidate debate, answered a pro–nuclear power audience member, "I actually think that we should explore nuclear power as part of the energy mix." Among Obama's top contributors are executives of Exelon Corp., a leading nuclear power operator in the nation. Just this week, Exelon released a new plan, called "Exelon 2020: A Low-Carbon Roadmap." The nuclear power industry sees global warming as a golden opportunity to sell its insanely expensive and dangerous power plants.

But nuclear power is not a solution to climate change—rather, it causes problems. Amory Lovins is the cofounder and chief scientist of Rocky Mountain Institute in Colorado. He makes simple, powerful points against nuclear: "The nuclear revival that we often hear about is not actually happening. It is a very carefully fabricated illusion ... there are no buyers. Wall

Street is not putting a penny of private capital into the industry, despite 100-plus percent subsidies." He adds, "Basically, we can have as many nuclear plants as Congress can force the taxpayers to pay for. But you won't get any in a market economy."

Even if nuclear power were economically viable, Lovins continues,

the first issue to come up for me would be the spread of nuclear weapons, which it greatly facilitates. If you look at places like Iran and North Korea ... how do you think they're doing it? Iran claims to be making electricity vital to its development ... The technology, materials, equipment, skills are applicable to both ... The president is absolutely right in identifying the spread of nuclear weapons as the gravest threat to our security, so it's really puzzling to me that he's trying to accelerate that spread every way he can think of ... It's just an awful idea unless you're really interested in making bombs. He's really triggered a new Mideast arms race by trying to push nuclear power within the region.

Along with proliferation, there are terrorist threats to existing nuclear reactors, like Entergy's controversial Indian Point nuclear plant just 24 miles north of New York City. Lovins calls these "about as fat a terrorist target as you can imagine. It is not necessary to fly a plane into a nuclear plant or storm a plant and take over a control room in order to cause that material to be largely released. You can often do it from outside the site boundary with things the terrorists would have readily available."

Then there is the waste: "It stays dangerous for a very long time. So you have to put it someplace that stays away from people and life and water for a very long time ... millions of years, most likely ... So far, all the places we've looked turned out to be geologically unsuitable, including Yucca Mountain." Testifying at a congressional hearing this week, Energy Department official Edward Sproat said the price of a nuclear dump in Nevada's Yucca Mountain has climbed to $90 billion. Slated to go on line a decade ago, its opening is now projected for the year 2020. And even that's optimistic. Representative Jim Matheson, D-UT, wants to block nuclear waste from passing through Utah entirely, and most Nevadans oppose the Yucca waste plan.

The presidential candidates are wrong on nuclear power. Wind, solar, and microgeneration (generating electricity and heat at the same time, in smaller plants), on the other hand, are taking off globally, gaining billions of dollars in private investments. Lovins summarizes, "One of the big reasons we have an oil problem and a climate problem today is we spent our money on the wrong stuff. If we had spent it on efficiency and renewables, those problems would've gone away, and we would've made trillions of dollars' profit on the deal because it's so much cheaper to save energy than to supply it."

The answer is blowing in the wind.

LESSONS OF THE *EXXON VALDEZ*

Twenty years ago, the *Exxon Valdez* supertanker spilled at least 11 million gallons of oil into Alaska's pristine Prince William Sound. The consequences of the spill were epic and continue to this day, impacting the environment and the economy. Instead of seeing it as just a pollution story, Riki Ott considers the *Exxon Valdez* disaster to be a fundamental threat to U.S. democracy.

Ott, a marine toxicologist and commercial salmon "fisherma'am" from Cordova, Alaska, opens her book on the disaster, *Not One Drop*, with the words of Albert Einstein: "No problem can be solved from the same consciousness that created it."

The massive spill stretched 1,200 miles from the accident site, and covered 3,200 miles of shoreline and an incredible 10,000 square miles overall. Early on March 24, 1989, Ott, who was on the board of the Cordova District Fishermen United, was airborne, surveying the scene:

> [I]t was a surreal scene. It was just drop-dead gorgeous, March, sunrise, pink mountains glistening with the sunrise. And all of a sudden we come on the scene, where there's this red deck of this oil tanker that's three football

fields long; flat, calm water, dark blue; and there's this inky-black stain that's just stretching with the tide.

News of the spill went global, and people poured into Valdez, Alaska, to start the cleanup. Sea life was devastated. Ott says up to half a million sea birds died, along with 5,000 sea otters, 300 or so harp seals, and billions of young salmon, fish eggs, and young juvenile fish. The death of the fish eggs created a long-term but delayed impact on the herring and salmon fisheries in Prince William Sound. By 1993, the fisheries had collapsed. Families lost their livelihoods after taking huge loans to buy boats and expensive fishing permits. While the salmon fishery has improved, the herring have never come back.

This economic disruption is one basis of legal action against Exxon-Mobil, the biggest oil corporation in the world. Complex litigation has dragged on for two decades, and ExxonMobil is winning. There are 22,000 plaintiffs suing ExxonMobil. A jury awarded the plaintiffs $5 billion in damages, equal to what was, at the time, a year's worth of Exxon profits. This was cut in half by a U.S. appeals court, then finally lowered to just over $500 million by the Supreme Court. During the 20 years of court battles, 6,000 of the original plaintiffs have died. ExxonMobil, with its billions in annual profits and armies of lawyers, can tie up the *Valdez* case in the courts for decades, while the injured commercial fishers slowly die off.

The power of ExxonMobil to battle tens of thousands of citizens has pushed Ott to join a growing number of activists who want to put corporations back in their place by stripping them of their legal status as "persons." A 19th-century U.S. Supreme Court decision gave corporations the same status as people, with access to the protections of the Bill of Rights. Ironically, this comes from the Fourteenth Amendment's "equal protection clause," adopted to protect freed slaves from oppressive state laws after the Civil War. Corporations were historically chartered by states to conduct their business. States could revoke a corporation's charter if it broke the law or acted beyond its charter.

Corporations' "free speech" is interpreted to include making campaign contributions and lobbying Congress. People who break laws can be locked up; when a corporation breaks the law—even behaving criminally negligently, causing death—rarely are the consequences greater than a fine, which the corporation can write off on its taxes. As Ott put it, "If 'three strikes and you're out' laws can put a person in prison for life, why not a corporation?" So-called tort reform in U.S. law is eroding an individual's ability to sue corporations and the ability for courts to assess damages that would actually deter corporate wrongdoing.

Ott and others have drafted a "Twenty-Eighth Amendment" to the Constitution that would strip corporations of their personhood, subjecting them to the same oversight that existed for the first 100 years of U.S. history.

With the global economic meltdown and welling public outrage over the excesses of executives at AIG as well as over other bailout beneficiaries, now just might be the time to expand public engagement over the imbalance of power between people and corporations that has undermined our democracy.

TORTURE

RUMSFELD'S MOUNT MISERY

Frederick Douglass, the renowned abolitionist, began life as a slave on Maryland's Eastern Shore. When his owner had trouble with the young, unruly slave, Douglass was sent to Edward Covey, a notorious "slave breaker." Covey's plantation, where physical and psychological torture were standard, was called Mount Misery. Douglass eventually fought back, escaped to the North and went on to change the world. Today Mount Misery is owned by Donald Rumsfeld, the outgoing secretary of defense.

It is ironic that this notorious plantation run by a practiced torturer would now be owned by Rumsfeld, himself accused as the man principally responsible for the U.S. military's program of torture and detention.

Rumsfeld was recently named along with 11 other high-ranking U.S. officials in a criminal complaint filed in Germany by the New York–based Center for Constitutional Rights (CCR). The center is requesting that the German government conduct an investigation and ultimately a criminal prosecution of Rumsfeld and company. CCR President Michael Ratner says U.S. policy authorizing "harsh interrogation techniques" is in fact a torture program that Secretary of Defense Rumsfeld authorized himself, passed down through the chain of command, and was implemented by one of the other defendants, Major General Geoffrey Miller. The complaint represents victims of torture at Abu Ghraib prison and the U.S. prison at Guantánamo. Says Ratner, "I think it is important to make it very clear that CCR's suit is not just saying Rumsfeld is a war criminal because he tops the chain of command, but that he personally played a central role in one of the worst interrogations at Gitmo."

Ratner is referring to Saudi citizen Mohammed al-Qahtani. An internal military report as well as leaked interrogation logs show how the Guantánamo prisoner was systematically tortured.

His attorney, CCR's Gita Gutierrez, described his ordeal on my TV/radio news hour *Democracy Now!*:

He was subjected to approximately 160 days of isolation, 48 days of sleep deprivation, which was accompanied by 20 hour-long interrogations consecutively. During that period of time, he was also subjected to sexual humiliation, euphemistically called "invasion of space by a female" at times when MPs would hold him down on the floor and female interrogators would straddle him and molest him.

Gutierrez added, "At one point in Guantánamo, his heart rate dropped so low that he was at risk of dying and was rushed to the military hospital there and revived, then sent back to interrogations the following day and was actually interrogated in the ambulance on the way back to his cell."

The complaint follows one filed in 2004, which was dismissed. The 2006 complaint differs principally with Rumsfeld's departure as secretary of defense. Without the immunity of government office shielding him, Rumsfeld now falls under the jurisdiction of the German courts. Germany is among several nations that employ the concept of universal jurisdiction, which states that crimes against humanity or war crimes can be prosecuted by a state (such as Germany) regardless of the jurisdiction where the crimes were committed or the nationality of the accused. If an indictment follows, then Rumsfeld will have to be very careful when traveling abroad, as are former Chilean dictator Augusto Pinochet and former U.S. Secretary of State Henry Kissinger.

Torture is a noxious, heinous practice and should not be tolerated. Slavery was once legal and tolerated in the United States (it is still practiced in some parts of the world). But people fought back, organized, and formed the abolition movement. Pioneering legal and human rights organizations, such as CCR, aggressively and creatively are working to stop torture, and to hold the torturers and their superiors accountable. Ultimately, it will be the U.S. populace—not the German courts, not the U.S. Congress—that stops the U.S. torture program. Frederick Douglass summed it up most eloquently—in 1849:

> If there is no struggle, there is no progress. Those who profess to favor freedom, and yet depreciate agitation, are men who want crops without plowing up the ground. They want rain without thunder and lightning. They want the ocean without the awful roar of its many waters. Power concedes nothing without a demand. It never did and it never will.

The owner of Mount Misery should take heed.

UP TO DEMOCRATS
TO INVESTIGATE TORTURE

The new head of the Senate Judiciary Committee was angry. Senator Patrick Leahy was questioning U.S. Attorney General Alberto Gonzales about a man named Maher Arar.

Arar is a Canadian citizen the United States detained without charge, then sent to Syria in 2002. Leahy fumed, "We knew damn well, if he went to Canada, he wouldn't be tortured. He'd be held. He'd be investigated. We also knew damn well, if he went to Syria, he'd be tortured."

Leahy was responding to Alberto Gonzales' comments that "there were assurances sought that he would not be tortured from Syria." Assurances? From the country that President Bush recently described as the "crossroads for terrorism"? From the country that Bush has vilified and threatened to attack? But before we point the finger at other countries, we have to look here at home.

Gonzales knows about torture. Arar was detained less than two months after Gonzales' office produced the notorious "Torture Memo," which has served as the legal basis for the Bush administration's brutal torture methods such as "waterboarding" (holding a victim's head underwater until unconscious) that are increasingly well-known and globally despised.

The U.S. government also engages in "extraordinary rendition." This Orwellian phrase describes how foreigners are grabbed off the street or from their home and secretly delivered to some other place, outside the United States (in Arar's case, Syria), where illegal and brutal interrogations can take place beyond the reach of Congress and the courts.

Arar's Kafkaesque nightmare began September 26, 2002. He was returning to Canada from a family vacation, with a plane change at New York's JFK Airport. There he was pulled aside, searched, questioned, and imprisoned. Two weeks later, U.S. authorities sent Arar to Syria.

Arar spent the next ten months enduring brutal beatings and psychological torture, kept in a cell the size of a grave. Arar was accused of being connected to al-Qaeda, and of having been to a training camp in Afghanistan. Neither was true, but after weeks of beatings, he admitted to everything. Worse than the beatings, Arar said on *Democracy Now!*, was how he suffered while isolated in the dank, windowless cell: "The psychological torture that I endured during this 10-month period in the underground cell is really beyond human imagination. I was ready to confess to anything. I would just write anything so that they could only take me from that place and put me in a place where it is fit for a human being."

As inexplicably as Arar was kidnapped to Syria, he was released home to Canada, a broken man. Canada just finished a thorough inquiry that completely exonerated him and supported his request for financial damages. Conservative Canadian Prime Minister Stephen Harper, a Bush ally, has asked Bush to "come clean" on the Arar case.

Leahy is demanding action: "The Bush administration has yet to renounce the practice of sending detainees to countries that torture prisoners, and it has yet to offer even the hint of an apology to Mr. Arar for what he endured with our government's complicity."

The Bush policies of war, occupation, torture, and rendition are having a cumulative effect on global opinion. A recent BBC poll of more than 26,000 people found that 75 percent oppose the U.S. role in Iraq, two-thirds oppose the handling of prisoners at Guantánamo, and 52 percent feel that the United States has an overall negative effect on the planet. Citizens just protested the fifth anniversary of the prison at Guantánamo. Legislators in North Carolina are demanding an investigation into Aero Contractors, a firm based there that supplies Gulfstream jets to the CIA to execute these "extraordinary renditions." And tens of thousands are expected in Washington, D.C., and around the country on January 27 to protest the war.

Democrats criticized the Republican-controlled "rubber-stamp Congress," which failed to provide adequate oversight of the Bush administration. Now that the Democratic Party has control of Congress, the onus is upon them to restore law and order, to investigate the use of torture, and to demand prosecution of those who engaged in it.

HYPOCRITICAL OATH:
PSYCHOLOGISTS AND TORTURE

First, do no harm. This tenet of medicine applies equally to psychologists, yet they are increasingly implicated in abusive interrogations, dare we say torture, at U.S. military detention facilities like Guantánamo. While the American Medical Association and the American Psychiatric Association both have passed resolutions prohibiting members from participating in interrogations, the American Psychological Association refuses to, despite the outrage of many of its members.

Now, with the declassification of a report by the Pentagon's inspector general detailing psychologists' role in military interrogations, the U.S. Senate Committee on Armed Services announced it will investigate.

Leonard Rubenstein, executive director of Physicians for Human Rights, says such an "investigation into the development of torture techniques by the United States" would be "very significant ... It should get into ... the use of psychologists in the development of the techniques, what is happening now, and how this can be avoided in the future."

Two years ago, after a leaked report from the International Committee of the Red Cross criticizing the role of health professionals in U.S.

interrogations, the American Psychological Association formed its Presidential Task Force on Psychological Ethics and National Security (PENS). There were nine voting members. Six of them were connected to the military. At the time, the identities of the panelists were secret. The PENS panel endorsed the continued participation of psychologists in military interrogations.

Of the three nonmilitary voting members, one, Dr. Michael G. Wessells of Randolph-Macon College, resigned, and another, Dr. Jean Maria Arrigo, recently called for the PENS report to be annulled. "I'm an oral historian, maybe even before a psychologist, and I always take notes. And I was told very sharply by one of the military psychologists not to take notes." She took notes anyway. She archived the group's entire e-mail list-serv, including months of e-mails from before and after the sole two-day PENS meeting. She went on, "I came later to realize that the entire report had been orchestrated. I no longer felt bound by that confidentiality agreement." She recently handed over all her materials to the Senate Armed Services Committee. The third, Dr. Nina Thomas, told me, "I don't think I was, in fact, critically aware of what Morgan Banks' role was at the time of the meetings themselves. I knew the outline of his background, but I didn't know the meaning of his background. So it disturbs me."

Colonel Morgan Banks, as Mark Benjamin of Salon.cóm first reported, is "the senior Army Survival, Evasion, Resistance and Escape psychologist, responsible for the training and oversight of all Army SERE psychologists, who include those involved in SERE training. He provides technical support and consultation to all Army psychologists providing interrogation support." Another task-force member, Captain Bryce Lefever, served at the Navy SERE school from 1990 to '93, then became the "Special Forces Task Force psychologist to Afghanistan in 2002, where he lectured to interrogators and was consulted on various interrogation techniques."

Also included was R. Scott Shumate, who was the chief operational psychologist for the CIA's counterterrorism center until 2003. He then became head of the Pentagon Counterintelligence Field Activity's Behavioral Sciences directorate, overseeing psychologist participation in the interrogation process at Guantánamo.

SERE includes sensory and sleep deprivation, isolation, cultural and sexual humiliation, "stress" positions (like forced standing), extended subjection to light, loud noise, extremes of heat and cold, and "waterboarding," wherein a subject has their face covered with a cloth that then has water poured over it, giving the feeling of suffocation. The goal of SERE is to train U.S. military members to resist torture they might experience if captured. As first reported by Jane Mayer of the *New Yorker*, the SERE techniques were "reverse engineered." In other words, they were used against the prisoners.

The upcoming APA Annual Convention, taking place August 17–20, promises to be hotly contested. An unknown number of members are withholding dues. Some have quit. Physicians for Human Rights' Rubenstein summed it up:

> Even the army surgeon general's report ... said it was the role of psychologists to tell interrogators when to increase the pressure, how to exploit vulnerabilities. So I think we really do have to end this as a nation, not just as professional associations ... We're talking about ... ending complicity in torture by a profession that has an enormous amount to contribute to the good of humanity and should not be involved in the destruction of people.

HIGH SCHOOL STUDENTS TEACH THE
PRESIDENT A LESSON ABOUT TORTURE

President Bush got a lesson from a group of recent high school graduates. They were Presidential Scholars, a program designed "to recognize and provide leadership development experiences for some of America's most outstanding graduating high-school seniors."

The 141 Presidential Scholars were being honored at the White House. One of them, Mari Oye, from Wellesley, Massachusetts, describes what happened:

 The president walked in and gave us a short speech saying that as we went on into our careers, it was important to treat others as we would like to be treated. And he told us that we would have to make choices we would be able to live with for the rest of our lives. And so, I said to the president, "Several of us made a choice, and we would like you to have this," and handed him the letter.

It was a letter Mari had handwritten. It read:

 As members of the Presidential Scholars class of 2007, we have been told that we represent the best and brightest of our nation. Therefore, we believe

82

we have a responsibility to voice our convictions. We do not want America to represent torture. We urge you to do all in your power to stop violations of the human rights of detainees, to cease illegal renditions and to apply the Geneva Convention to all detainees, including those designated enemy combatants.

The letter was signed by close to 50 of the students, more than a third of the Presidential Scholars.

Mari described Bush's reaction to the letter: "He read down the letter. He got to the part about torture. He looked up, and he said, 'America doesn't torture people.' And I said, 'If you look specifically at what we said, we said, we ask you to cease illegal renditions. Please remove your signing statement to the McCain anti-torture bill.'

"At that point, he just said, 'America doesn't torture people' again."

In fact, after Bush signed the bill that outlawed the torture of detainees last year, he quietly issued a "signing statement" reserving the right to bypass the law, as he has more than 1,100 times, issuing more signing statements than all other U.S. presidents combined.

Mari knows a little bit about detention. Not high school detention, but detention Guantánamo-style. Mari recounted this to the president: "I said that for me personally, the issue of detainee rights also had a lot of importance, because my grandparents had been interned during World War II for being Japanese American." The government has since apologized for imprisoning more than 100,000 Japanese Americans during the war.

Mari said she was also inspired to act by her mother, Willa Michener. She, too, was a Presidential Scholar—40 years ago, in 1968—and had wanted to confront President Lyndon Johnson with her opposition to the Vietnam War. She deferred to a teacher who, Mari said, "stressed it was important to stay quiet when you're in the presence of the president." Willa Michener has regretted it since, Mari said.

Mari called her mother as soon as she left the White House to tell her what she had done.

She was actually in the Holocaust Museum in the last room when I called her to say that we had given the letter. She didn't know there was a letter beforehand … And she said that she walked out into the bright sunlight with tears streaming down her face, but since a lot of people walk out of the Holocaust Museum that way, you know, no one noticed anything out of the ordinary.

Another Presidential Scholar, Leah Anthony Libresco, from Long Island, New York, helped write the letter. She, like Mari, is remarkably eloquent. "If I'm going to be in the room with the president, I've got to say something, because silence betokens consent, and there's a lot going on I don't want to consent to." Her middle name, Anthony, comes from the famous suffragist Susan B. Anthony.

Afraid that Mari's letter would be confiscated before she was able to deliver it to the president, Leah had a handwritten copy of it—yes, up her sleeve. She handed it to a reporter, as she said later in a blog post, "at the No Child Left Behind photo op for which the Scholars were apparently supposed to be a backdrop."

With young leaders like Mari Oye and Leah Anthony Libresco speaking truth to power at so young an age, and demonstrating such eloquence, courage, and discipline, the only thing that looks likely to get left behind are politicians like George Bush and his torture policies.

PSYCHOLOGISTS IN DENIAL
ABOUT TORTURE

Last weekend, the American Psychological Association rejected a moratorium that would have prevented its member psychologists from participating in interrogations at U.S. detention centers at places like Guantánamo Bay and secret CIA "black sites" around the world. Instead, the 148,000-member organization passed a resolution at its annual meeting in San Francisco banning psychologists from participating in interrogations that employ certain harsh techniques. Many psychologists within the APA feel the resolution did not go far enough.

The issue of torture and interrogations has become a sore spot for the APA, the world's largest group of psychologists. The American Medical Association and the American Psychiatric Association both outright prohibit their members from participating in interrogations at locations where basic human rights are not guaranteed, like Guantánamo. These groups have been joined by others, like the American Translators Association and the Society for Ethnomusicology (since translation is essential in interrogations, and sustained, blaring music has been used as a form of torture).

Central to the debate is the question "Are psychologists participating in torture?" While the Bush administration repeatedly denies that it uses torture, a leaked report of the International Committee of the Red Cross says certain U.S. methods used are "tantamount to torture."

At a fiery APA town hall meeting after the vote, Dr. Steven Reisner, one of the leading proponents of a moratorium, demanded, "I want to know if passing this resolution prohibits psychologists from being involved in the enhanced interrogation techniques that the president of the United States authorized can take place at CIA black sites."

Defenders of the APA's position are clear: psychologists need to be present at these interrogations to protect the prisoners, to ensure that the interrogators do not go over the line. Critics argue that psychologists are there to help interrogators push the line further and further, to consult with the interrogators on how best to break the prisoners.

Dr. Jeffrey Kaye, a psychologist with Survivors International, a torture survivors group, says there is a loophole: psychologists cannot participate in harsh interrogations, but they can participate in harsh detention conditions. He said, "You see, they don't use sleep deprivation while they're interrogating you, they use it before they interrogate you, as part of the conditions of detention, to soften you up for the interrogation. So the winner today, and I'm sure their lawyers are very happy, is the CIA."

As the convention began, Anthony Romero of the American Civil Liberties Union issued a letter to the APA, urging a moratorium, warning that psychologists faced legal liability or even prosecution. "We have found troubling evidence of the collusion of medical psychologists in the development and implementation of procedures intended to inflict psychological harm on prisoners at Guantánamo Bay and other facilities."

In a surreal moment at the opening APA session on ethics and interrogations, a Pentagon interrogator, "Dr. Katherine Sherwood" (she appeared to be using a pseudonym), wanted the audience to know that the interrogations were conducted professionally. She said she was denied access to prisoner medical records:

> I like to bake at home for the detainees and bring home-baked goods to our sessions. I needed to know whether or not a detainee had a peanut allergy,

and that could be very serious. There was a process in place where … the liaison could ask the medical personnel, and they could choose whether or not to give a response.

Her baking gives new meaning to the term BSCT (pronounced "biscuit") psychologists, which stands for Behavioral Science Consultation Team. They were the psychologists who helped develop the harsh interrogation techniques, and who the International Committee of the Red Cross report said conveyed information about detainee "mental health and vulnerabilities," to help break them down psychologically.

Romero's ACLU letter ended by saying,

The history of torture is inexorably linked to the misuse of scientific and medical knowledge. As we move fully into the 21st century, it is no longer enough to denounce or to speak out against torture; rather, we must sever the connection between healers and tormentors once and for all. As guardians of the mind, psychologists are duty bound to promote the humane treatment of all people.

A VOTE FOR MUKASEY
IS A VOTE FOR TORTURE

Judge Michael Mukasey admits waterboarding is repugnant, but refuses to say whether it amounts to torture. Yet Democratic Senators Charles Schumer and Dianne Feinstein voted for his confirmation as U.S. attorney general anyway. Mukasey, Schumer, and Feinstein should talk to French journalist Henri Alleg. An editor of a paper in Algeria, he was waterboarded by the French military in 1957, when the French were trying to crush the Algerian independence movement. The 86-year-old journalist spoke to me from his home in Paris:

> I was put on a plank, on a board, fastened to it, and taken to a tap [water faucet]. And my face was covered with a rag. Very quickly, the rag was completely full of water. You have the impression of being drowned. And the water ran all over my face. I couldn't breathe. It's a terrible, terrible impression of torture and of death, being near death.

Journalist Stephen Grey, whose documentary *Extraordinary Rendition* airs on PBS stations this week, told me, "I, like many journalists, should issue a correction, an apology really, because we all reported waterboarding as a simulated drowning. It is clear from those who did it, this is actual drowning ... this is something that shocks the conscience and therefore is torture."

In a remarkable demonstration of commitment to his job, former acting Assistant Attorney General Daniel Levin, according to ABC News, underwent waterboarding when tasked by the White House to rework its official position on torture in 2004. Concluding that waterboarding is torture, he was forced out of his job.

On Monday, November 5, anti-torture activists engaged in an actual demonstration of waterboarding outside the Department of Justice. Twenty-six-year-old actor Maboud Ebrahimzadeh volunteered to be the victim. After the session, he was near tears: "It is the most terrifying experience I have ever had. And although this is a controlled environment, when water goes into your lungs and you want to scream and you cannot, as soon as you do you will choke."

Four retired military judge advocates general wrote a letter to Senate Judiciary Committee Chairman Patrick Leahy stating, "Waterboarding is inhumane, it is torture, and it is illegal." Twenty-four former intelligence agents and analysts agreed with the JAGs, adding, "Whether or not the practice is currently in use by U.S. intelligence, it should in fact be easy for him to respond."

Yet Mukasey told the Senate Judiciary Committee, "I don't know what's involved in the technique, if waterboarding is torture."

In the judiciary hearing when the votes were cast, Leahy said, "No senator should abet this administration's legalistic obfuscations by those such as Alberto Gonzales, John Yoo, and David Addington by agreeing that the laws on the books do not already make waterboarding illegal. We have been prosecuting water torture for more than 100 years."

U.S. soldiers have been prosecuted for participating in waterboarding in the Philippines in 1901 and Vietnam in 1968. The United States imprisoned a Japanese officer in 1947 for using waterboarding against U.S. troops in World War II.

Senator Edward Kennedy added,

Make no mistake about it: Waterboarding is already illegal under United States law. It is illegal under the Geneva Conventions, which prohibit "outrages upon personal dignity," including cruel, humiliating and degrading treatment. It is illegal under the Torture Act, which prohibits acts "specifically intended to inflict severe physical or mental pain or suffering." It is illegal under the Detainee Treatment Act, which prohibits "cruel, inhuman or degrading treatment." And it violates the Constitution.

He went on,

Waterboarding is slow-motion suffocation with enough time to contemplate the inevitability of blackout and expiration—usually the person goes into hysterics on the board. For the uninitiated, it is horrifying to watch, and if it goes wrong, it can lead straight to terminal hypoxia. When done right, it is controlled death.

Republican Senator Arlen Specter, who voted for Mukasey's confirmation, said Congress should pass a law forbidding waterboarding, having received assurances from Mukasey that he would uphold such a law. What if President Bush vetoed the law, or if he issued one of his signing statements used to sidestep bills he signs into law?

Despite all this, Schumer's and Feinstein's votes for Mukasey mean the Judiciary Committee has voted 11 to 8 to recommend his appointment as attorney general to the full Senate. From war funding to torture, you have to ask, if the Republicans were in the majority, would there be any difference?

Now only the full Senate can block Mukasey's appointment. Maybe at least one senator will step up and filibuster the confirmation, just long enough for Mukasey to research and announce his opinion on whether waterboarding amounts to torture. If a U.S. citizen, soldier, or official were waterboarded somewhere overseas, would Americans hesitate for a moment to call it torture? A filibuster might give the Mukasey supporters like Schumer and Feinstein pause to reconsider. For starters, they should talk to Henri Alleg.

SURVIVING A CIA "BLACK SITE"

The kidnap and torture program of the Bush administration, with its secret CIA "black site" prisons and "torture taxi" flights on private jets, saw a little light of day this week. I spoke to Mohamed Farag Ahmad Bashmilah in his first broadcast interview. Bashmilah was a victim of the CIA's so-called extraordinary rendition program, in which people are grabbed from their homes, out of airports, off the streets, and are whisked away, far from the prying eyes of the U.S. Congress, the press, far from the reach of the courts, to countries where cruelty and torture are routine.

Bashmilah is being represented by the American Civil Liberties Union and by the New York University School of Law International Human Rights Clinic in a lawsuit with four other victims of CIA rendition. They are suing not the U.S. government, not the CIA, but a company called Jeppesen Dataplan Inc., a subsidiary of Boeing Corp. A former Jeppesen employee, Sean Belcher, entered an affidavit in support of Bashmilah, reporting that Jeppesen executive Bob Overby bragged, "We do all of the extraordinary rendition flights," further explaining to staff that he was speaking of "the torture flights," and that they paid very well.

Through a translator, over the phone from his home in Yemen, Bashmilah described how his ordeal began on October 21, 2003, when he was arrested in Amman, Jordan:

> It was approximately six days, but what I endured there is worth years. They wanted me to confess to having some connections to some individuals of al-Qaeda. They tried several times to get me to confess, and every time I said no, I would get either a kick, a slap, or a curse. Then they said that if I did not confess, they will bring my wife and rape her in front of me. And out of fear for what would happen to my family, I screamed and I fainted. After I came to, I told them that "please, don't do anything to my family. I would cooperate with you in any way you want."

After signing a false confession, he was told he was going to be released. In the process of being led through the Jordanian intelligence facility, he lifted his blindfold.

> I saw another man who had a Western look. He was white and somewhat overweight and had dark glasses on. I realized then that they were probably handing me over to some other agency, because during the interrogations I had with the Jordanians, one of the threats was that if I did not confess, they will hand me over to American intelligence.

He was prepared for transit, stripped

> completely naked. They started taking pictures from all directions. And they also started to beat me on my sides and also my feet. And then they put me in a position similar to the position of prostration in Muslim prayer, which is similar to the fetal position. And in that position, one of them inserted his finger in my anus very violently. I was in terrible pain, and I started to scream. When they started taking pictures, I could see that they were people who were masked. They were dressed in black from head to toe, and they were also wearing surgical gloves.

He says he was put in a diaper, had his eyes and ears covered, a bag was put over his head, and he had additional earphones put on his head to block noise. He was then flown to Kabul, Afghanistan, where he was held in solitary confinement for close to six months. He believed he was being held by Americans.

Some of the interrogators would come to me and interrogate me in the interrogation room, and they would tell me, "You should calm down and be comforted, because we'll send all this information to Washington." And they would say that in Washington, they will determine whether my answers are truthful or not.

Although kept isolated from other prisoners, he managed to overhear some of them speculating that they were being held at Bagram Air Base. He went on to say that he was kept awake with blaring music and was held in shackles that were removed only for periodic interrogations.

While Bashmilah was being interrogated and tortured, he was also visited by "psychiatrists." "[T]he therapy mainly consisted of trying to look at my thoughts and trying to interpret them for me, in addition to some tranquilizers."

Bashmilah attempted suicide three times, staged a hunger strike that was painfully ended with a feeding tube forced down his nose, and was denied access to a lawyer, to any human rights group, to the International Committee of the Red Cross. In effect, he was disappeared.

On May 5, 2005, he was transferred to a prison in Yemen, where he eventually gained access to his family. Amnesty International got involved. He was released in March 2006 with no charges relating to terrorism.

Mohamed Bashmilah said there were cameras in his cells and interrogation rooms. Perhaps tapes were made of his ordeal. Let's hope that the CIA doesn't destroy these, too.

TAXI TO THE DARK SIDE

On the Sunday following September 11, 2001, Vice President Dick Cheney told the truth. On NBC's *Meet the Press*, he said, regarding plans to pursue the perpetrators of that attack, "We have to work the dark side, if you will. We're going to spend time in the shadows." The grim, deadly consequences of his promise have, in the intervening six years, become the shame of our nation and have outraged millions around the world. President George Bush and Cheney, many argue, have overseen a massive global campaign of kidnapping, illegal detentions, harsh interrogations, torture, and kangaroo courts where the accused face the death penalty, confronted by secret evidence obtained by torture, without legal representation.

Cheney's shadows saw a moment of sunlight recently, as Alex Gibney won the Academy Award for the Best Documentary Feature for his film *Taxi to the Dark Side*. The film traces the final days of a young Afghan man, Dilawar (many Afghans use just one name), who was arrested in 2001 by the U.S. military and brought to the hellish prison at Bagram Air Base. Five days later, Dilawar was dead, beaten and tortured to death by the U.S. military. Gibney obtained remarkable eyewitness accounts of

Dilawar's demise from the very low-level soldiers who beat him to death. We see the simple village that was his lifelong home and hear from people there how Dilawar had volunteered to drive the taxi, which was an important source of income for the village.

Dilawar had never spent the night away from home. His first sleepover was spent with arms shackled overhead, subjected to sleep and water deprivation, receiving regular beatings, including harsh knee kicks to the legs that would render his legs "pulpified." He had been fingered as a participant in a rocket attack on the Americans by some Afghans who were later proved to be the attackers themselves. Gibney uses the tragic story of Dilawar to open up a searing and compelling indictment of U.S. torture policy from Bush and Cheney through Donald Rumsfeld and the author of the infamous "torture memo," now–University of California, Berkeley, law professor John Yoo.

The Oscar ceremony was bereft of serious mention of the war, until Gibney rose to accept his award. He said,

> Thank you very much, Academy. Here's to all doc filmmakers. And, truth is, I think my dear wife Anne was kind of hoping I'd make a romantic comedy, but honestly, after Guantánamo, Abu Ghraib, extraordinary rendition, that simply wasn't possible. This is dedicated to two people who are no longer with us: Dilawar, the young Afghan taxi driver, and my father, a Navy interrogator who urged me to make this film because of his fury about what was being done to the rule of law. Let's hope we can turn this country around, move away from the dark side and back to the light. Thank you very much.

Taxi to the Dark Side can be seen in movie theaters, and the Oscar will surely help open it up to more audiences. Gibney got a surprise, though, from the Discovery Channel, the television network that had bought the TV rights to the film. He told me,

> Well, it turns out that the Discovery Channel isn't so interested in discovery. I was told a little bit before my Academy Award nomination that they had no intention of airing the film, that new management had come in and they were about to go through a public offering, so it was probably too controversial for that. They didn't want to cause any waves. It turns out Discovery turns out to be the see-no-evil/hear-no-evil channel.

The Discovery Channel is owned by John Malone, the conservative mogul who owns Liberty Media, one of the largest media corporations on the planet. Malone is famous for his complex business deals that involve spinning off media properties with stock offerings that net him millions. He also has just gotten approval to swap his extensive stock holdings in News Corp., Rupert Murdoch's empire, for control of Murdoch's DirecTV satellite television system. When Discovery told Gibney they would not be airing *Taxi to the Dark Side*, Malone and Murdoch were awaiting approval for the DirecTV deal from the Bush administration's Federal Communications Commission. (It was approved on Monday, the day after the Oscars.)

HBO managed to buy the television rights to *Taxi to the Dark Side*, so the film will find its way to those households that subscribe to premium TV channels. As Discovery wrote to a critical member of the public, "In its first pay-TV window, HBO will debut the film in September 2008. We are proud that *Taxi to the Dark Side* will make its basic cable debut in 2009 on Investigation Discovery." So Discovery will show *Taxi* on one of its smaller side channels, after the election, after its business with the Bush administration is wrapped up.

In the meantime, films like *Taxi to the Dark Side* and Phil Donahue's excellent Iraq war documentary, *Body of War*, have to fight for distribution. Let's hope that Gibney's Oscar will help open the theaters and the TV airwaves to these truly consciousness-raising films to turn this country away from the dark side and back to the light.

A TORTURE DEBATE AMONG HEALERS

Imagine a candidate for president who, a year or so ago, no one would have considered electable. Now the person is the front-runner, with a groundswell of grass-roots support, threatening the sense of inevitability of the establishment candidates. No, I'm not talking about the U.S. presidential race, but the race for president of the largest association of psychologists in the world, the American Psychological Association (APA). At the heart of the election is a raging debate over torture and interrogations. While the other healing professions, including the American Medical Association and the American Psychiatric Association, bar their members from participating in interrogations, the APA leadership has fought against such a restriction.

Frustrated with the APA, a New York psychoanalyst, Dr. Steven Reisner, has thrown his hat into the ring. Last year, Reisner and other dissident psychologists formed the Coalition for an Ethical Psychology in an attempt to force a moratorium against participation by APA members in harsh interrogations. During the initial phase of this year's selection process, Reisner received the most nominating votes. He is running on a platform opposing the use of psychologists to oversee abusive and coercive interrogations of prisoners at Guantánamo, secret CIA "black sites," or anywhere else international law or the Geneva Conventions are said not to apply.

The issue came to a head at the 2007 APA annual convention. After days of late-night negotiations, the moratorium came up for a climactic vote. We saw a surreal scene on the convention floor: uniformed military were out in force. Men and women in desert camo and navy whites worked the APA Council of Representatives, and officers in crisp dress uniforms stepped to the microphones.

Military psychologists insisted that they help make interrogations safe, ethical, and legal, and cited instances where psychologists allegedly intervened to stop abuse. "If we remove psychologists from these facilities, people are going to die!" boomed Colonel Larry James of the U.S. Army, chief psychologist at Guantánamo Bay and a member of the APA governing body. Dr. Laurie Wagner, a Dallas psychologist, shot back, "If psychologists have to be there in order to keep detainees from being killed, then those conditions are so horrendous that the only moral and ethical thing to do is to protest by leaving."

The moratorium failed, and instead a watered-down resolution passed, outlining 19 harsh interrogation techniques that were banned, but only if "used in a manner that represents significant pain or suffering or in a manner that a reasonable person would judge to cause lasting harm." In other words, this loophole allowed, you can rough people up, just don't do permanent harm.

Immediately after the vote, Reisner spoke out at a packed town hall meeting: "If we cannot say, 'No, we will not participate in enhanced interrogations at CIA black sites,' I think we have to seriously question what we are as an organization and, for me, what my allegiance is to this organization, or whether we might have to criticize it from outside the organization at this point."

Reisner and others began withholding dues. Prominent APA members resigned, and the best-selling author of *Reviving Ophelia*, Mary Pipher, returned her APA Presidential Citation award. After several months of bad publicity and internal negotiations, an emergency committee redrafted

that resolution, removing the loopholes and affirming the outright prohibition of 19 techniques, like mock executions and waterboarding.

When I asked Dr. Reisner, the son of Holocaust survivors, why he
would want to head the organization that he has battled for several years,
he told me,

> If I have this opportunity to make a change, I have a responsibility to do it.
> I never had the intention of being involved, but the only way to ensure this
> be changed was by claiming the democratic process in the name of human
> rights and social-justice issues. I was hoping that mass withholding of dues
> and mass resignations would shame the APA to come to its senses. It made
> them take a big step but didn't go far enough.

He expanded, "American people are sick of the reputation of the
United States as torturers, as people who abuse prisoners. American people want to see a restoration of values from war to health care. I think what
happens in the APA should point to a direction for the whole country."

The APA's annual meeting is this summer, in Boston. Expect interro-
gation to be the major issue confronting the members gathered there.
Final voting for the APA president starts in October. The APA and the
United States will determine their next presidents at about the same time.
In both elections, a thorough debate on torture should be central.

TORTURERS SHOULD BE PUNISHED

SPOKANE, Wash.—George W. Bush insisted that the United States did not use torture.

But the four Bush-era Office of Legal Counsel (OLC) memos released last week by the Obama administration's Justice Department paint a starkly different picture. The declassified memos provided legal authorization for "harsh interrogation techniques" used by the Bush administration in the years following September 11, 2001. They authorized (as listed in the August 1, 2002, memo by then–Assistant Attorney General Jay Bybee) "walling ... facial slap, cramped confinement, wall standing, stress positions, sleep deprivation, insects placed in a confinement box, and the waterboard."

According to the American Civil Liberties Union, the OLC under Bush "became a facilitator for illegal government conduct, issuing dozens of memos meant to permit gross violations of domestic and international law."

The memos authorize what the International Committee of the Red Cross called, in a leaked report, "treatment and interrogation techniques ... that amounted to torture."

These torture techniques were developed by two psychologists based in Spokane, Washington: James Mitchell and Bruce Jessen. Their company, Mitchell Jessen & Associates, provided specialized training to members of the U.S. military to deal with capture by enemy forces. The training is called SERE, for Survival, Evasion, Resistance, Escape. Mitchell and Jessen, both psychologists, were contracted by the U.S. government to train interrogators with techniques they claimed would break prisoners.

They reverse-engineered the SERE training, originally developed to help people withstand and survive torture, to train a new generation of torturers.

The memos provide gruesome details of the torture. Waterboarding was used hundreds of times on a number of prisoners. The Bybee memo includes this Kafkaesque authorization: "You would like to place [Abu] Zubaydah in a cramped confinement box with an insect. You have informed us that he appears to have a fear of insects. In particular, you would like to tell Zubaydah that you intend to place a stinging insect into the box with him."

After President Barack Obama said there should be no prosecutions, he was received with great fanfare at the CIA this week. Mark Benjamin, the reporter who originally broke the Mitchell and Jessen story, said when I questioned him about Obama's position,

> If you look at the president's statements and you combine them with the statements of Rahm Emanuel, the chief of staff, and Eric Holder, the attorney general ... you will see that over the last couple of days the Obama administration has announced that no one, not the people who carried out the torture program or the people who designed the program or the people that authorized the program or the people who said that it was legal—even though they knew that it frankly wasn't—none of those people will ever face charges. The attorney general has announced that ... the government will pay the legal fees for anybody who is brought up on any charges anywhere in the world or has to go before Congress. They will be provided attorneys ... they have been given this blanket immunity ... in return for nothing.

Senate Intelligence Committee Chair Dianne Feinstein asked Obama to hold off on ruling out prosecutions until her panel finishes an investigation during the next six months. Though Obama promises to let the torturers go, others are pursuing them. Bybee is now a federal judge. A grass-roots movement, including Common Cause and the Center for Constitutional Rights, is calling on Congress to impeach Bybee. In Spain, Judge Baltasar Garzon, who got Chilean dictator Augusto Pinochet indicted for crimes against humanity, has named Bybee and five others as targets of a prosecution.

For years, people have felt they have been hitting their heads against walls (some suffered this literally, as the memos detail). On Election Day, it looked like that wall had become a door. But that door is open only a crack. Whether it is kicked open or slammed shut is not up to the president. Though he may occupy the most powerful office on Earth, there is a force more powerful: committed people demanding change. We need a universal standard of justice. Torturers should be punished.

HEALTH
CARE

SiCKO: MICHAEL MOORE'S PRESCRIPTION FOR CHANGE

Michael Moore screened his new film, *SiCKO*, on Father's Day at a special New York event honoring September 11 first responders. Moore spoke of their heroism and recognized their role in the film. *SiCKO* is about the broken U.S. health care system. Case in point: the 9/11 rescue workers.

Their stories of selfless courage, followed by years of creeping, chronic illnesses, from pulmonary fibrosis to cancer to post-traumatic stress, often exacerbated by poor or no health insurance, drive home Moore's point that the medical/pharmaceutical industry is failing Americans—not only the 40-plus million Americans with no health insurance, but the 250 million Americans who do have health insurance.

Moore doesn't like health insurance companies:

> They're the Halliburtons of the health industry. I mean, they really—they get away with murder. They charge whatever they want. There's no government control. And frankly, we will not really fix our system until we remove these private insurance companies. I mean, they literally have to be eliminated. They cannot be allowed to exist in this country.

Moore transports the ailing 9/11 heroes, unable to get care in the United States, to boats just offshore from the U.S. naval base at Guantánamo Bay. Moore shows clips of congressmen and generals assuring the public that Guantánamo prisoners receive excellent health care. Bullhorn in hand, Moore appeals to the navy for care for the 9/11 responders on board as well. Denied, they make their way to Havana Hospital, where a team of Cuba's world-renowned doctors administers much-needed treatment. Reggie Cervantes, coughing throughout her interview, is outraged to learn that an inhaler cartridge that she pays $120 for stateside sets her back only five cents in Cuba, and vows to "take back a suitcase full of them."

The U.S. Treasury Department is investigating Moore for possible violations of the trade embargo against Cuba (he has sent a copy of his film to Canada for safekeeping).

When Moore began his film, he put out a call for stories from his website and received more than 25,000 replies. In addition to neglected patients, Moore heard from hundreds of people within the industry blowing the whistle, like Dr. Linda Peeno. She testified before Congress, "I denied a man a necessary operation that would have saved his life and thus caused his death. No person and no group has held me accountable for this. Because, in fact, what I did was I saved a company a half a million dollars with this."

Moore knows that people who organize can fight back and win. *SiCKO* is more than a movie; it's a movement. The release of the film is being coordinated with an unprecedented, sophisticated, grass-roots action campaign. Oprah Winfrey will hold a town hall meeting on health care. YouTube is calling for people to post videos of their health care horror stories, and the California Nurses Association is leading a campaign to get one million nurses in the United States to see the film. Healthcare-NOW! is organizing leafleting and petitioning at all 3,000 theaters where *SiCKO* is debuting; Moveon.org and Physicians for a National Health Program are mobilizing. And Moore himself is heading to New Hampshire to challenge the Democratic presidential candidates.

SiCKO shows how Hillary Clinton tried to reform the health care system as first lady.

She was destroyed as a result of it. I mean, they put out I think well over $100 million to fight her. But to jump ahead here with Hillary, in last year's Congress, she was the second-largest recipient of health industry money. She may be No. 1 at this point, for all I know. It's very sad to see ... they're into her pocket, and she's into their pocket.

Moore continued, "By the time of the election, by the primaries, I'm sure all the Democrats are going to be using that word: 'universal' coverage. Their plans are going to take our tax dollars and put them into the pockets of these insurance companies. We need to cut out the middleman here. The government can run this program." This is called a single-payer system.

Taking on the multibillion-dollar health care industry is all in a day's work for Michael Moore. After several million people see *SiCKO*, the time just might be right for a prescription for change.

CHILDREN'S HEALTH CARE
IS A NO-BRAINER

Deamonte Driver had a toothache. He was 12 years old. He had no insurance, and his mother couldn't afford the $80 to have the decayed tooth removed. He might have gotten it taken care of through Medicaid, but his mother couldn't find a dentist who accepted the low reimbursements. Instead, Deamonte got some minimal attention from an emergency room, his condition worsened, and he died. Deamonte was one of nine million children in the United States without health insurance.

Congress is considering bipartisan legislation that will cover poor children in the United States.

The major obstacle? President Bush is vowing to veto the bill, even though Republican and Democratic senators reached bipartisan agreement on it. The bill adds $35 billion to the State Children's Health Insurance Program over the next five years by increasing federal taxes on cigarettes.

The conservative Heritage Foundation is against the tobacco tax to fund SCHIP (pronounced "s-chip"), saying that it "disproportionately burdens low-income smokers" as well as "young adults." No mention is made of any adverse impact on Heritage-funder Altria Group, the cigarette giant formerly known as Philip Morris.

According to the American Association for Respiratory Care, with every 10 percent rise in the cigarette tax, youth smoking drops by 7 percent and overall smoking declines by 4 percent. Marian Wright Edelman, founder of the Children's Defense Fund, says,

> It is a public health good in and of itself and will save lives to increase the tobacco tax. Cigarettes kill and cigarettes provoke lung cancer, and every child and every [other] human being we can, by increasing the cigarette tax, stop from smoking or slow down from smoking is going to have a public health benefit, save taxpayers money from the cost of the effects of smoking and tobacco.

Two programs serve as the health safety net for poor and working-class children: Medicaid and SCHIP. SCHIP is a federal grant program that allows states to provide health coverage to children of working families earning too much to be eligible for Medicaid but not enough to afford private health insurance when their employers do not provide it. It's the SCHIP funding that is now being debated in Congress.

The Children's Defense Fund has published scores of stories similar to Deamonte's. Children like Devante Johnson of Houston. At 13, Devante was fighting advanced kidney cancer. His mother tried to renew his Medicaid coverage, but bureaucratic red tape tied up the process. By the time Devante got access to the care he needed, his fate was sealed. He died at the age of 14, in Bush's home state, only miles from the M. D. Anderson Cancer Center, one of the world's leading cancer treatment and research facilities.

With children's lives at stake, Edelman has no patience for political gamesmanship:

> Why is this country, at this time, the richest in the world, arguing about how few or how many children they can serve? We ought to—this is a no-brainer. The American people want all of its children served. All children deserve health coverage, and I don't know why we're having such a hard time getting our president and our political leaders to get it, that children should have health insurance.

Republican Senator Gordon Smith originally introduced the SCHIP budget resolution in the Senate. Unlike Bush, who is not up for reelection,

Smith is defending his vulnerable Senate seat in 2008, in the blue state of Oregon. He, like other Republicans who are breaking with Bush on the war in Iraq, is sensitive to Bush's domestic policies. Georgetown University's Center for Children and Families just released a poll that says 91 percent of Americans support the expansion of SCHIP to cover more kids.

And the American people are willing to go much further. As demonstrated by the popularity of Michael Moore's latest blockbuster, *SiCKO*, the public, across the political spectrum, is ready to fix the U.S. health care system. How many more children like Deamonte and Devante have to die before the politicians, all with great health insurance themselves, take action?

FOR WHOM THE
BELL'S PALSY TOLLS

Bell's palsy. It hit suddenly a month ago. I had just stepped off a plane in New York, and my friend noticed the telltale sagging lip. It felt like novocaine. I raced to the emergency room. The doctors prescribed a weeklong course of steroids and antivirals. The following day it got worse. I had to make a decision: do I host *Democracy Now!*, our daily news broadcast, on Monday? I could speak perfectly well, and I'm tired of seeing women (and men) on TV who look like they just stepped off the set of *Dynasty*. Maybe if they see a person they trust to deliver the news, still there, but just looking a little lopsided, it might change their view of friends and family—or strangers, for that matter—who are struggling with some health issue.

Wikipedia, the popular online encyclopedia anyone can edit, stated that I had suffered a stroke. So on Tuesday I decided to tell viewers and listeners that I was suffering from a temporary bout of Bell's palsy, that it wasn't painful, and that "the doctors tell me I will be back to my usual self in the next few weeks. In the meantime, it just makes it a little harder to smile. But so does the world."

Bell's palsy affects 50,000 people in the United States every year. It is an inflammation of the seventh cranial nerve, which connects to the eye, nose, and ear. The inflammation causes temporary paralysis of the nerve. For some, the eye can't close, so they have to tape it shut at night, and some can't speak. George Clooney had it. Ralph Nader came down with it in the midst of a speaking tour. He was in Boston debating someone when his eye started to water and his mouth sagged. It didn't stop him. He continued his tour, just beginning each talk by saying, "At least you can't accuse me of speaking out of both sides of my mouth."

I was just in Santa Fe, New Mexico, interviewing Tim Flannery, voted 2007 Australian of the Year for his remarkable work as an explorer, paleontologist, zoologist, and climate-change scientist. Before we went on the stage, I apologized for my crooked smile. He said he knew the feeling, having had shingles, a more painful viral condition that affects one side of the face. I was beginning to feel less and less alone.

The next day we broadcast from the New Mexico State Legislature. The cameraman told me that Ambassador Joe Wilson, husband of Valerie Plame, had just been in. He had been doing an interview with his wife from a remote studio with Larry King. The cameraman told Wilson that I had Bell's palsy. He said that he, too, had suffered a bout of it. I caught up with Wilson after our morning broadcast. He described what happened to him. It was ten years ago. He had just gotten off Air Force One in Africa with President Clinton. He splashed some water on his face, looked in the mirror, and saw the telltale face sag, unblinking eye, and mouth droop; he thought he had had a stroke. Walter Reed Army Medical Center was called, and Wilson was diagnosed with Bell's palsy within a few minutes. Clinton sat him down and said that he had known a number of people who had had Bell's, and that he should just carry on. It would go away. Wilson flew off to Luanda and gave a speech on the tarmac. Later that day, he passed a television set and hardly recognized himself, with his mouth askew. He thought he looked like the actor Edward G. Robinson, a tough-talking gangster speaking out of the side of his mouth.

Even my neurologist once had Bell's palsy, and said I should just keep working, that, with the medication, it would heal itself. Just to make sure,

I visited an acupuncturist in New York's Chinatown, next to the offtrack betting parlor, hearing that the doctor was a good bet!

I'm happy to report the Bell's palsy is easing up, and I feel fortunate. Fortunate for the waves of support, from the hundreds of e-mails from strangers. A female marketing professor from a Houston business school wrote, "Watching you carry on with Bell's palsy has taught me a little bit about myself. In real life we encounter people with physical imperfections all the time. Why are we shielded from seeing people with flaws and imperfections on TV? Reporters and anchors on TV news, especially women, typically look as if they just won a beauty pageant or a modeling contest, which seems to add to the disingenuousness of their messages."

I feel fortunate to have good health insurance, yet feel unfortunate to live in a society where other people's access to health care is subject to the whims of fortune. The hardest part of this temporary bout has been how tough it is to smile. It has made me realize what a precious gift a smile is. It reminds me of the world's most famous smile—or, actually, half-smile—the Mona Lisa's. Perhaps even she had Bell's palsy.

NOTHING TO FEAR BUT
NO HEALTH CARE

Fifty million Americans are without health insurance, and 25 million are "underinsured." Millions being laid off will soon be added to those rolls. Medical bills cause more than half of personal bankruptcies in the United States. Desperate for care, the under- and uninsured flock to emergency rooms, often dealing with problems that could have been prevented.

The U.S. auto giants are collapsing in part due to extraordinary health care expenses, while they are competing with companies in countries that provide universal health care. Economist Dean Baker calculated how General Motors would fare if its health care costs were the same as costs in Canada: "GM would have had higher profits, making no other changes ... that would equal $22 billion over the course of the last decade. They wouldn't have to be running to the government for help." GM is sometimes referred to as a health care company that makes cars. Former Chrysler Chairman Lee Iacocca said in 2005, "It is a well-known fact that the U.S. automobile industry spends more per car on health care than on steel." He supports national health care.

Barack Obama said in a 2007 speech that "affordable, universal health care for every single American must not be a question of whether, it must be a question of how ... Every four years, health care plans are offered up in campaigns with great fanfare and promise. But once those campaigns end, the plans collapse under the weight of Washington politics."

Franklin Delano Roosevelt, in his March 1933 inaugural address, famously declared, "We have nothing to fear but fear itself ... This nation asks for action, and action now." Deep in the Great Depression, a flurry of ambitious policies followed, detailed by *New York Times* editorial writer Adam Cohen in his new book, *Nothing to Fear*. He writes that FDR developed the New Deal with key, visionary advisers and cabinet members who enacted bold policies, among them Frances Perkins, the United States' first woman cabinet member. Perkins, FDR's secretary of labor, pushed for a rapid, national relief program that formed the basis of the welfare system, and for regulations on the minimum wage and maximum hours and a ban on child labor.

But she failed to achieve universal health care. Cohen told me,

> She really was the conscience of the New Deal in many ways ... she chaired the Social Security committee. And she wanted it to go further ... to include national health insurance, but the AMA [American Medical Association], even back then, was very strong and opposed it. And she and a couple other progressives on the committee said, you know, "We better just settle for what we can get." They didn't want to lose the whole Social Security program.

Obama nominated former Senator Tom Daschle as secretary of health and human services and director of the new White House Office of Health Reform. Daschle's health care book, *Critical*, recalls historical failures to achieve universal care:

> Like Clinton, Truman had reason to be confident. His fellow Democrats controlled both houses of Congress, and polls showed that Americans were anxious about the high cost of health care and eager for change. But both presidents underestimated the strength of the forces arrayed against them ... [s]pecial-interest lobbyists—led by doctors in Truman's time, and insurance companies in Clinton's.

Obama knows the issue well—while his mother lay dying of cancer, she still had to battle the insurance industry. He said in that 2007 speech,

"Plans that tinker and halfway measures now belong to yesterday ... [W]e can't afford another disappointing charade ... [W]e need to look at ... how much of our health care spending is going toward the record-breaking profits earned by the drug and health care industry."

Yet Daschle proposes not much more than tinkering—improving Medicare, Medicaid, and the Veterans Health Administration, all examples of "single-payer health care" in which the government is the single payer for the health care—while preserving the inefficient, multipayer, for-profit insurance model. In December 2007, the American College of Physicians compared U.S. health care with other countries', writing, "Single-payer systems generally have the advantage of being more equitable, with lower administrative costs than systems using private health insurance, lower per capita health care expenditures, high levels of consumer and patient satisfaction."

Michael Moore, in his film *SiCKO*, includes a recording of John Ehrlichman speaking to Richard Nixon, discussing medical-insurance profits: "the less care they give 'em [patients], the more money they [the insurance companies] make." Obama is in charge now. Whom will he emulate—Nixon or FDR? People across the political and economic spectrum, from big business to the little guy, are dying to know.

TOXINS "R" US

Is your lipstick laden with lead? Is your baby's bottle toxic? The American Chemistry Council assures us that "we make the products that help keep you safe and healthy." But U.S. consumers are actually exposed to a vast array of harmful chemicals and additives embedded in toys, cosmetics, plastic water bottles, and countless other products. U.S. chemical and manufacturing industries have fought regulation, while Europe moves ahead with strict prohibitions against the most harmful toxins. The European Union says regulation is good for business, inspiring consumer confidence and saving money over the long term.

Most people would be surprised to learn that the cosmetics industry in the United States is largely unregulated. Investigative journalist Mark Schapiro is the author of *Exposed: The Toxic Chemistry of Everyday Products and What's at Stake for American Power*. In the absence of oversight, researchers and journalists like Schapiro and grass-roots organizations have stepped into the breach.

Schapiro told me, "Whether it is your nail polish, eye shadow, shampoo, essentially personal-care products [are] not regulated by the [Food and Drug Administration] ... Numerous times in the Senate, over the last 50 years, there have been efforts to expand the purview of the FDA, and it's been repeatedly beaten back by the cosmetics industry." Details on the toxins are hard to come by. Schapiro continued, "The reason I even know what kind of material is in cosmetics is not because the FDA has told us; it's actually because the European Union has taken the action to remove that stuff, and they have a list."

The Campaign for Safe Cosmetics lists numerous toxins that appear regularly in cosmetics and personal-care products, among them lead and phthalates. Phthalates are linked to birth defects, including disruption of genital development in boys, decreased sperm counts, and infertility. Lead appears in lipstick and hundreds of other products. The CSC reports that "lead ... is a proven neurotoxin—linked to learning, language and behavioral problems ... miscarriage, reduced fertility in both men and women, hormonal changes, menstrual irregularities and delays in puberty onset in girls." This is the stuff women and girls are putting on their lips all day, licking off, and reapplying.

The European Union, with 27 member nations representing almost half a billion people, is asserting itself on issues of toxins, using serious economic muscle. Stavros Dimas, European Union commissioner for the environment, explained the long-term benefits of regulation: "The medical expenses for chemical-related diseases will be less. Medicines will not be needed. We will not lose working hours, and productivity will be better. So the overall benefits will by far outweigh costs to the industry."

Interestingly, because European countries pay a far larger share of their citizens' health care costs than does the United States, they want to keep costs down and they expect to save upward of $50 billion in coming decades, says Schapiro, as a result of the improved health and environmental conditions brought about by stricter chemical regulations.

In the wake of the 2007 China toy recall in the United States (because of lead found in the toys), Congress passed, and President George W. Bush signed, the Consumer Product Safety Improvement Act. A key provision, mandating a ban of phthalate- and lead-containing products intended for children 12 years of age and younger, went into effect February 10. If you bought a plastic toy before that date, beware: after the law passed last summer, some stores stuffed their shelves with tainted toys and sold them at fire-sale prices to unload their inventory.

Safe alternatives for toys, cosmetics, shampoos, and other products are becoming increasingly available as demand for organic products grows. The difference between market forces limiting toxins and a law doing it, Schapiro says, is "if you have a law, it makes it far more equitable, because everybody gets the same protections, whether you have the resources or the knowledge to pursue the alternatives."

That is where the EU comes in, with its expansive and world-leading regulatory system in place (called "REACH," for Registration, Evaluation, Authorization, and restriction of CHemical substances). Schapiro notes, "The European-led revolution in chemical regulation requires that thousands of chemicals finally be assessed for their potentially toxic effects on human beings and signals the end of American industry's ability to withhold critical data from the public."

Tough regulations on toxins are not only essential to saving lives; they also make good business sense. The United States now has an opportunity to catch up to our European partners—and make changes that are more than just cosmetic.

PUT SINGLE-PAYER ON THE TABLE

President Barack Obama promises health care reform, but he has taken single-payer health care off the table. Single-payer is the system that removes private insurance companies from the picture; the government pays all the bills, but health care delivery remains private. People still get their choice of which doctor to go to and what hospital to use. Single-payer reduces the administrative costs and removes the profit that insurance companies add to health care delivery. Single-payer solutions, however, get almost no space in the debate.

A study just released by Fairness and Accuracy in Reporting, a media watchdog group, found that in the week before Obama's health care summit, of the hundreds of stories that appeared in major newspapers and on the networks, "only five included the views of advocates of single-payer—none of which appeared on television." Most opinion columns that mentioned single-payer were written by opponents.

Congress is considering H.R. 676, "Expanded and Improved Medicare for All," sponsored by John Conyers, D-MI, with 64 cosponsors. Yet even when Representative Conyers directly asked Obama at a Congressional

Black Caucus meeting if he could attend the White House health care summit, he was not immediately invited. Nor was any other advocate for single-payer health care.

Conyers had asked to bring Dr. Marcia Angell, the first woman editor in chief of the *New England Journal of Medicine*, the most prestigious medical journal in the country, and Dr. Quentin Young. Young is perhaps the most well-known single-payer advocate in America. He was Martin Luther King Jr.'s doctor when King lived in Chicago. "My 15-minute house calls would stretch into three hours," he told me.

But he came to know Barack Obama even better. Though his medical partner was Obama's doctor, Young was his neighbor, friend, and ally for decades. "Obama supported single-payer, gave speeches for it," he said.

This past weekend, hundreds turned out to honor the 85-year-old Young, including the Illinois governor and three members of Congress, but the White House's response to Conyers' request that Young be included in the summit? A resounding no. Perhaps because Obama personally knows how persuasive and committed Young is.

After much outcry, Conyers was invited. Activist groups like Physicians for a National Health Program (pnhp.org) expressed outrage that no other single-payer advocate was to be among the 120 people at the summit. Finally, the White House relented and invited Dr. Oliver Fein, president of PNHP. Two people out of 120.

Locked out of the debate, silenced by the media, single-payer advocates are taking action. Russell Mokhiber, who writes and edits the *Corporate Crime Reporter*, has decided that the time has come to directly confront the problem of our broken health care system. He's going to the national meeting of the American Health Insurance Plans and is joining others in burning their health insurance bills outside in protest. Mokhiber told me, "The insurance companies have no place in the health care of American people. How are we going to beat these people? We have to start the direct confrontation." Launching a new organization, Single Payer Action (singlepayeraction.org), Mokhiber and others promise to take the issue to the insurance industry executives, the lobbyists, and the members of Congress directly, in Washington, D.C., and their home district offices.

Critical mass is building behind a single-payer system, from Nobel Laureate in Economics Joe Stiglitz, who told me, "I've reluctantly come to the view that it's the only alternative," to health care providers themselves, who witness and endure the system's failure firsthand. Geri Jenkins of the newly formed, 150,000-nurses-strong United American Nurses-National Nurses Organizing Committee (nnoc.net) said, "It is the only health-care-reform proposal that can work ... We are currently pushing to have a genuine, honest policy debate, because we'll win ... the health insurers will collapse under the weight of their own irrelevance."

Dr. Young has now been invited to a Senate meeting along with the "usual suspects": health-insurance providers, Big Pharma, and health-care-reform advocates. I asked Young what he thought of the refrain coming from the White House, as well as from the leading senator on the issue, Max Baucus, that "single-payer is off the table." "It's repulsive," sighed Young. "We are very angry." But not discouraged. I asked him what he thought about Burn Your Health Insurance Bill Day. "Things are heating up," he chuckled. "When things are happening that you have nothing to do with, you know it's a movement."

BAUCUS' RAUCOUS CAUCUS

Barack Obama appeared this week with health-industry bigwigs, proclaiming light at the end of the health care tunnel. Among those gathered were executives from HMO giants Kaiser Foundation Health Plan and Health Net Inc., and the health-insurance lobbying group America's Health Insurance Plans; from the American Hospital Association and the American Medical Association; from medical-device companies; and from the pharmaceutical industry, including the president and CEO of Merck and former Representative Billy Tauzin, now president and CEO of PhRMA, the massive industry lobbying group. They have pledged to voluntarily shave some $2 trillion off of U.S. health care costs over ten years. But these groups, which are heavily invested in the U.S. health care status quo, have little incentive to actually make good on their promises.

This is beginning to look like a replay of the failed 1993 health care reform efforts led by then–first lady Hillary Rodham Clinton. Back then, the business interests took a hard line and waged a PR campaign, headlined by a fictitious middle-class couple, Harry and Louise, who feared a government-run health care bureaucracy.

Still absent from the debate are advocates for single-payer, often referred to as "Canadian-style" health care. Single-payer health care is not "socialized medicine." According to Physicians for a National Health Program, single-payer means "the government pays for care that is delivered in the private (mostly not-for-profit) sector."

A February CBS News poll found that 59 percent in the United States say the government should provide national health insurance.

Single-payer advocates have been protesting in Senate Finance Committee hearings, chaired by Democratic Montana Senator Max Baucus. Last week, at a committee hearing with 15 industry speakers, not one represented the single-payer perspective. A group of single-payer advocates, including doctors and lawyers, filled the hearing room and, one by one, interrupted the proceedings.

Protester Adam Schneider yelled, "We need to have single-payer at the table. I have friends who have died, who don't have health care, whose health care did not withstand their personal health emergencies ... Single-payer now!"

Baucus gaveled for order, guffawing, "We need more police." The single-payer movement has taken his words as a rallying cry. At a hearing Tuesday, five more were arrested. They call themselves the "Baucus 13."

One of the Baucus 13, Kevin Zeese, recently summarized Baucus' career campaign contributions: "From the insurance industry: $1,170,313; health professionals: $1,016,276; pharmaceuticals/health-products industry: $734,605; hospitals/nursing homes: $541,891; health services/HMOs: $439,700."

That's almost $4 million from the very industries that have the most to gain or lose from health care reform.

Another of the Baucus 13, Russell Mokhiber, cofounder of SinglePayer-Action.org, has been charged with "disruption of Congress."

He was quick to respond: "I charge Baucus with disrupting Congress. It once was a democratic institution; now it's corrupt, because of people like him. He takes money from the industry and does their bidding. He won't even defuse the situation by seating a single-payer advocate at the table."

As I traveled through Montana recently, from Missoula to Helena to Bozeman, health care activists kept referring to Baucus as the "money man."

Montana State Senator Christine Kaufmann sponsored an amendment to the Montana Constitution, granting everyone in Montana "the right to quality health care regardless of ability to pay," or health care as a human right. It died in committee.

Wisconsin Senator Russ Feingold, a single-payer advocate, said his position will not likely prevail in Washington: "I don't think there's any possibility that that will come out of this Congress." That's if things remain business as usual.

Mario Savio led the Free Speech Movement on the UC Berkeley campus. In 1964, he said, "There comes a time when the operation of the machine becomes so odious, makes you so sick at heart, that you can't take part, you can't even passively take part, and you've got to put your bodies upon the gears and upon the wheels, upon all the apparatus, and you've got to make it stop. And you've got to indicate to the people who run it, the people who own it, that unless you're free, the machine will be prevented from working at all."

"Unless you're free," the Baucus 13 might add, "to speak." The current official debate has locked single-payer options out of the discussion, but also escalated the movement—from Healthcare-NOW! to Single Payer Action—to shut down the orderly functioning of the debate, until single-payer gets a seat at the table.

CONGRE$$, HEAL THYSELF

As the Obama administration pushes for a vote on health care reform before Congress recesses in August, has health industry money too thoroughly polluted the process for anything good to come of it?

Senator Max Baucus, D-MT, chairs the Senate Finance Committee, key to any health care reform. Baucus has held several high-profile Senate committee hearings on health care, with no single-payer advocates. They were present, though, until Baucus had them arrested—for standing up one by one in the audience, protesting the exclusion of a single-payer representative on the panel. Baucus is only parroting President Barack Obama's pledge that "single-payer is off the table." Yet single-payer health care has significant support among the U.S. public, and increasingly among health care providers. With single-payer, the government pays the bills, but people still choose which doctors to see. Private health insurance companies and HMOs—the profiteers—go out of business.

Mike Dennison, a reporter for the *Montana Standard*, found that Baucus has received more campaign money from health and insurance industry interests than any other member of Congress. Dennison told me,

"We're talking about the health insurance industry and ... HMOs, hospitals, physicians, pharmaceutical companies—that's probably where the bulk of his money has come from ... out of about almost $15 million he's raised in the last six years, both for his campaign and his leadership PAC, 23 percent of that came from insurance and health interests ... which we believe is probably more than any other member has received."

At a public forum in New Mexico, Linda Allison asked Obama about Baucus' finances: "[S]o many people go bankrupt using their credit cards to pay for health care. Why have they taken single-payer off the plate? And why is Baucus on the Finance Committee discussing health care when he has received so much money from the pharmaceutical companies? Isn't it a conflict of interest?"

Obama dodged the issue of Baucus, but did admit, "If I were starting a system from scratch, then I think that the idea of moving towards a single-payer system could very well make sense. That's the kind of system that you have in most industrialized countries around the world."

Allison's concern about bankruptcy is timely. According to a recent Harvard Medical School study, "62.1 percent of all bankruptcies in 2007 were medical." Many of these people are not from the 50 million or so uninsured Americans, but from among the estimated 25 million who are underinsured. That a person can have health insurance and still be driven to bankruptcy over hospital bills and pharmaceutical costs is a national disgrace.

Just days before Obama addressed the American Medical Association this week, the AMA announced that it would oppose a public health option.

In response, at least one doctor canceled his membership. In his resignation letter, Dr. Chris McCoy of the Mayo Clinic in Rochester, Minnesota, wrote that the AMA

> couldn't get through the second paragraph before bringing up the issue of physician reimbursement ... the AMA represents a physician-centered and self-interested perspective rather than honoring the altruistic nature of my profession ... I advocate first for what is best for my patients and believe that as a physician, as long as I continue to maintain the trust and integrity of the profession, I will earn the respect of my community. The appropriate financial compensation for my endeavors will follow in kind.

Recent congressional financial disclosures show that many key members have major investments in the health care industry. The *Washington Post* reported this week that almost 30 members of Congress who hold key committee memberships that will impact the health care debate also have significant investments in health care companies. The bipartisan group of investors includes Senate Majority Leader Harry Reid, D-NV; Senator Judd Gregg, R-NH; the family of Representative Jane Harman, D-CA; Senator Johnny Isakson, R-GA; Senator John Kerry, D-MA; Senator Michael Crapo, R-ID—in all, amounting to between $11 million and $27 million (the number is imprecise, since the disclosure forms allow some ambiguity).

According to the Associated Press, Jackie Clegg Dodd, wife of Senator Chris Dodd, D-CT, serves on the boards of four health-related companies and earned more than $200,000 last year. Senator Dodd is sitting in as chair of the Senate Health, Education, Labor, and Pensions Committee, in place of Senator Ted Kennedy, D-MA.

Congress will soon break for its "summer recess," with members going back to their home districts to raise money, of course, and, perhaps, to visit their hometown health care provider—paid for by their publicly funded congressional health care plan.

HEALTH INSURANCE WHISTLE-BLOWER
KNOWS WHERE THE BODIES ARE BURIED

Wendell Potter is the health insurance industry's worst nightmare. He's a whistle-blower. Potter, the former chief spokesperson for insurance giant CIGNA, recently testified before Congress, "I saw how they confuse their customers and dump the sick—all so they can satisfy their Wall Street investors."

Potter was deeply involved in CIGNA and industrywide strategies for maintaining their profitable grip on U.S. health care. He told me, "The thing they fear most is a single-payer plan. They fear even the public insurance option being proposed; they'll pull out all the stops they can to defeat that to try to scare people into thinking that embracing a public health insurance option would lead down the slippery slope toward socialism ... putting a government bureaucrat between you and your doctor. They've used those talking points for years, and they've always worked."

In 2007, CIGNA denied a California teenager, Nataline Sarkisyan, coverage for a liver transplant. Her family went to the media. The California Nurses Association joined in. Under mounting pressure, CIGNA finally granted coverage for the procedure. But it was too late. Two hours later, Nataline died.

While visiting family in Tennessee, Potter stopped at a "medical expedition" in Wise, Virginia. People drove hours for free care from temporary clinics set up in animal stalls at the local fairground. Potter told me that weeks later, flying on a CIGNA corporate jet with the CEO, "I realized that someone's premiums were helping me to travel that way ... paying for my lunch on gold-trimmed china. I thought about those men and women I had seen in Wise County ... not having any idea [how] insurance executives lived." He decided he couldn't be an industry PR hack anymore.

Insurance executives and their Wall Street investors are addicted to massive profits and double-digit annual rate increases. To squeeze more profit, Potter says, if a person makes a major claim for coverage, the insurer will often scrutinize the person's original application, looking for any error that would allow it to cancel the policy. Likewise, if a small company's employees make too many claims, the insurer, Potter says, "very likely will jack up the rates so much that your employer has no alternative but to leave you and your coworkers without insurance."

This week, as the House and Senate introduce their health care bills, Potter warns, "One thing to remember is that the health insurance industry has been anticipating this debate on health care for many years ... they've been positioning themselves to get very close to influential members of Congress in both parties." Montana Senator Max Baucus chairs the Senate Finance Committee, key for health care reform. Potter went on, "[T]he insurance industry, the pharmaceutical industry, and others in health care have donated ... millions of dollars to his campaigns over the past few years. But aside from money, it's relationships that count ... the insurance industry has hired scores and scores of lobbyists, many of whom have worked for members of Congress, and some who are former members of Congress."

The insurance industry and other health care interests are lobbying hard against a government-sponsored, nonprofit, public health insurance option, and are spending, according to the *Washington Post*, up to $1.4 million per day to sway Congress and public opinion.

Don't be fooled. Profit-driven insurance claim denials actually kill people, and Wendell Potter knows where the bodies are buried. His whistle-blowing may be just what's needed to dump what's sick in our health care system.

GLOBAL
ECONOMIC MELTDOWN

TICKER TAPE AIN'T SPAGHETTI

Food riots are erupting around the world. Protests have occurred in Egypt, Cameroon, the Philippines, Burkina Faso, Ivory Coast, Mauritania, and Senegal. Sarata Guisse, a Senegalese demonstrator, told Reuters, "We are holding this demonstration because we are hungry. We need to eat, we need to work, we are hungry. That's all. We are hungry." United Nations Secretary-General Ban Ki-moon has convened a task force to confront the problem, which threatens, he said, "the specter of widespread hunger, malnutrition and social unrest on an unprecedented scale." The World Food Program has called the food crisis the worst in 45 years, dubbing it a "silent tsunami" that will plunge 100 million more people into hunger.

Behind the hunger, behind the riots, are so-called free-trade agreements, and the brutal emergency-loan agreements imposed on poor countries by financial institutions like the International Monetary Fund. Food riots in Haiti have killed six, injured hundreds, and led to the ousting of Prime Minister Jacques-Edouard Alexis. The Reverend Jesse Jackson just returned from Haiti and writes that "hunger is on the march here.

Garbage is carefully sifted for whatever food might be left. Young babies wail in frustration, seeking milk from a mother too anemic to produce it." Jackson is calling for debt relief so that Haiti can direct the $70 million per year it spends on interest to the World Bank and other loans into schools, infrastructure, and agriculture.

The rise in food prices is generally attributed to a perfect storm caused by increased food demand from India and China, diminished food supplies caused by drought and other climate-change-related problems, increased fuel costs to grow and transport the food, and the increased demand for bio-fuels, which has diverted food supplies like corn into ethanol production.

This week, the United Nations' special rapporteur on the right to food, Jean Ziegler, called for the suspension of biofuels production: "Burning food today so as to serve the mobility of the rich countries is a crime against humanity." He's asked the UN to impose a five-year ban on food-based biofuels production. The Consultative Group on International Agricultural Research, a group of 8,000 scientists globally, is also speaking out against biofuels. The scientists are pushing for a plant called switch-grass to be used as the source for biofuels, reserving corn and other food plants to be used solely as food.

In a news conference this week, President Bush defended food-based ethanol production: "The truth of the matter is it's in our national inter-ests that our farmers grow energy, as opposed to us purchasing energy from parts of the world that are unstable or may not like us." One part of the world that does like Bush and his policies are the multinational food corporations. International nonprofit group Genetic Resources Action International (GRAIN) has just published a report called "Making a Killing from Hunger." In it, GRAIN points out that major multinational corporations are realizing vast, increasing profits amid the rising misery of world hunger. Profits are up for agribusiness giants Cargill (86 percent) and Bunge (77 percent), and Archer Daniels Midland (which dubs itself "the supermarket to the world") enjoyed a 67 percent increase in profits.

GRAIN writes, "Is this a price blip? No. A food shortage? Not that either. We are in a structural meltdown, the direct result of three decades of neolib-eral globalization ... We have allowed food to be transformed from some-thing that nourishes people and provides them with secure livelihoods into a commodity for speculation and bargaining." The report states, "The amount of speculative money in commodities futures … was less than $5 billion in 2000. Last year, it ballooned to roughly $175 billion."

There was a global food crisis in 1946. Then, as now, the UN convened a working group to deal with it. At its meeting, the head of the UN Relief and Rehabilitation Administration, former New York City Mayor Fiorello La-Guardia said, "Ticker tape ain't spaghetti." In other words, the stock market doesn't feed the hungry. His words remain true today. We in the United States aren't immune to the crisis. Wal-Mart, Sam's Club, and Costco have placed limits on bulk rice purchases. Record numbers of people are on food stamps, and food pantries are seeing an increase in needy people.

Current technology exists to feed the planet in an organic, locally based, sustainable manner. The large corporate food and energy interests, and the U.S. government, need to recognize this and change direction or the food riots in distant lands will soon be coming to their doors.

WALL STREET SOCIALISTS

The financial crisis gripping the United States has the largest banks and insurance companies begging for massive government bailouts. The banking, investment, finance, and insurance industries, long the foes of taxation, now need money from working-class taxpayers to stay alive. Taxpayers should be in the driver's seat now. Instead, decisions that will cost people for decades are being made behind closed doors, by the wealthy, by the regulators, and by those they have failed to regulate.

Tuesday, the Federal Reserve and the U.S. Treasury Department agreed to a massive, $85 billion bailout of AIG, the insurance giant. This follows the abrupt bankruptcy of Lehman Brothers, the 158-year-old investment bank; the distressed sale of Merrill Lynch to Bank of America; the bailout of both Fannie Mae and Freddie Mac; the collapse of retail bank IndyMac; and the federally guaranteed buyout of Bear Stearns by JPMorgan Chase. AIG was deemed "too big to fail," with 103,000 employees and more than $1 trillion in assets. According to regulators, an unruly collapse could cause global financial turmoil. U.S. taxpayers now own close to 80 percent of AIG, so the orderly sale of AIG will allow the taxpayers to recoup their money, the theory goes.

It's not so easy.

The financial crisis will most likely deepen. More banks and giant financial institutions could collapse. Millions of people bought houses with shady subprime mortgages and have already lost or will soon lose their homes. The financiers packaged these mortgages into complex "mortgage-backed securities" and other derivative investment schemes. Investors went hog-wild, buying these derivatives with more and more borrowed money.

Nomi Prins used to run the European analytics group at Bear Stearns and also worked at Lehman Brothers. "AIG was acting not simply as an insurance company," she told me. "It was acting as a speculative investment bank/hedge fund, as was Bear Stearns, as was Lehman Brothers, as is what will become Bank of America/Merrill Lynch. So you have a situation where it's [the U.S. government] ... taking on the risk of items it cannot even begin to understand."

She went on:

> It's about taking on too much leverage and borrowing to take on the risk and borrowing again and borrowing again, 25 to 30 times the amount of capital ... They had to basically back the borrowing that they were doing ... There was no transparency to the Fed, to the SEC, to the Treasury, to anyone who would have even bothered to look as to how much of a catastrophe was being created, so that when anything fell, whether it was the subprime mortgage or whether it was a credit complex security, it was all below a pile of immense interlocked, incestuous borrowing, and that's what is bringing down the entire banking system.

As these high-rolling gamblers are losing all their banks' money, it comes to the taxpayer to bail them out. A better use of the money, says Michael Hudson, professor of economics at the University of Missouri, Kansas City, and an economic adviser to Representative Dennis Kucinich, would be to "save these four million homeowners from defaulting and being kicked out of their houses. Now they're going to be kicked out of the houses. The houses will be vacant. The cities are going to [lose] property taxes, they're going to have to cut back local expenditures, local infrastructure. The economy is being sacrificed to pay the gamblers."

Prins elaborated, "You're nationalizing the worst portion of the banking system ... You're taking on risk you won't be able to understand. So it's even more dangerous." I asked Prins, in light of all this nationalization, to comment on the prospect of nationalizing health care into a single-payer system. She responded, "You could actually put some money into something that preempts a problem happening and helps people get health care."

The meltdown is a bipartisan affair. Presidential contenders John Mc-Cain and Barack Obama each have received millions of dollars from these very companies that are collapsing and are receiving the corporate welfare. President Clinton and his treasury secretary, Robert Rubin (now an Obama economic adviser), presided over the repeal in 1999 of the Glass-Steagall Act, passed after the 1929 start of the Great Depression to curb speculation that caused that calamity. The repeal was pushed through by former Republican Senator Phil Gramm, one of McCain's former top advisers. Politicians are too dependent on Wall Street to do anything. The people who vote for them, and whose taxes are being handed over to these failed financiers, need to show their outrage and demand that their leaders truly put "country first" and bring about "change."

WORKERS LAID OFF,
EXECUTIVES PAID OFF,
BERNARD MADOFF

The global financial crisis deepens, with more than ten million in the United States out of work, according to the Department of Labor. Unemployment hit 6.7 percent in November. Add the 7.3 million "involuntary part-time workers," who want to work full time but can't find such a job. Jobless claims have reached a 26-year high, while 30 states reportedly face potential shortfalls in their unemployment-insurance pools. The stunning failure of regulators like the Securities and Exchange Commission was again highlighted, as former NASDAQ head Bernard Madoff (you got it, pronounced "made off") was arrested for allegedly running the world's largest criminal pyramid scheme, with losses expected to be $50 billion, dwarfing those from the Enron scandal. The picture is grim—unless, that is, you are a corporate executive.

The $700 billion financial bailout package, TARP (Troubled Assets Relief Program), was supposed to mandate the elimination of exorbitant executive compensation and "golden parachutes." As U.S. taxpayers pony up their hard-earned dollars, high-flying executives and corporate boards are now considering whether to give themselves multimillion-dollar bonuses.

According to the *Washington Post*, the specific language in the TARP law that forbade such payouts was changed at the last minute, with a small but significant one-sentence edit made by the Bush administration. The *Post* reported, "The change stipulated that the penalty would apply only to firms that received bailout funds by selling troubled assets to the government in an auction."

Read the fine print. Of the TARP bailout funds to be disbursed, only those that were technically spent "in an auction" would carry limits on executive pay. But Treasury Secretary Henry Paulson and his former Goldman Sachs colleague Neel Kashkari (yes, pronounced "cash carry"), who is running the program, aren't inclined to spend the funds in auctions. They prefer their Capital Purchase Program, handing over cash directly. Recall Paulson's curriculum vitae: he began as a special assistant to John Ehrlichman in the Nixon White House and then went on to work for a quarter-century at Goldman Sachs, one of the largest recipients of bailout funds and chief competitor to Lehman Brothers, the firm that Paulson let fail.

The Government Accountability Office issued a report on TARP December 10, expressing concerns about the lack of oversight of the companies receiving bailout funds. The report states that "without a strong oversight and monitoring function, Treasury's ability to ensure an appropriate level of accountability and transparency will be limited." The nonprofit news organization ProPublica has been tracking the bailout program, reporting details that remain shrouded by the Treasury Department. As of Tuesday, 202 institutions had obtained bailout funds totaling close to $250 billion.

House Speaker Nancy Pelosi said recently, "The Treasury Department's implementation of the TARP is insufficiently transparent and is not accountable to American taxpayers." Barney Frank, D-MA, chair of the House Financial Services Committee, said earlier, "Use of these funds ... for bonuses, for severance pay, for dividends, for acquisitions of other institutions, etc. ... is a violation of the terms of the act."

Republican Senator Charles Grassley of Iowa said of the loophole, "The flimsy executive-compensation restrictions in the original bill are now all but gone." Put aside for the moment that these three all voted for the legislation. The law clearly needs to be corrected before additional funds are granted.

The sums these titans of Wall Street are walking away with are staggering. In their annual "Executive Excess" report, the groups United for a Fair Economy and the Institute for Policy Studies reported 2007 compensation for Lloyd Blankfein, CEO of Goldman Sachs (Paulson's replacement), at $54 million and that of John Thain, CEO of Merrill Lynch, at a whopping $83 million. Merrill has since been sold to Bank of America, after losing more than $11 billion this year—yet Thain still wants a $10 million bonus.

Paulson, Kashkari, and their boss, President George W. Bush, might not be the best people to spend the next $350 billion tranche of U.S. taxpayer money, with just weeks to go before the new Congress convenes January 6 and Barack Obama assumes the presidency January 20. As Watergate leaker Deep Throat was said to have told Bob Woodward, back when Paulson was just starting out, "Follow the money." The U.S. populace, its representatives in Congress, and the new Obama administration need to follow the money, close the executive-pay loophole, and demand accountability from the banks that the public has bailed out.

TOO BIG TO FAIL, TOO BIG TO JAIL

Karl Rove recently described George W. Bush as a book lover, writing, "There is a myth perpetuated by Bush critics that he would rather burn a book than read one." There will be many histories written about the Bush administration. What will they use for source material? The Bush White House was sued for losing e-mails and for skirting laws intended to protect public records. A federal judge ordered White House computers scoured for e-mails just days before Bush left office. Three hundred million e-mails reportedly went to the National Archives, but 23 million e-mails remain "lost." Vice President Dick Cheney left office in a wheelchair due to a back injury suffered when moving boxes out of his office. He has not only hobbled a nation in his attempt to sequester information—he hobbled himself. Cheney also won court approval to decide which of his records remain private.

Barack Obama was questioned by George Stephanopoulos about the possibility of prosecuting Bush administration officials. Obama said,

> We're still evaluating how we're going to approach the whole issue of interrogations, detentions and so forth ... I don't believe that anybody is above

the law. On the other hand, I also have a belief that we need to look forward as opposed to looking backwards ... [W]hat we have to focus on is getting things right in the future, as opposed to looking at what we got wrong in the past.

Legal writer Karen Greenberg notes in *Mother Jones* magazine, "The list of potential legal breaches is, of course, enormous; by one count, the administration has broken 269 laws, both domestic and international."

Torture, wiretapping, and "extraordinary rendition"—these are serious crimes that have been alleged. President Obama now has, more than anyone else, the power to investigate.

John Conyers, chair of the House Judiciary Committee, has just subpoenaed Karl Rove while investigating the politicization of the Justice Department and the political prosecution of former Alabama Governor Don Siegelman. Rove previously invoked executive privilege to avoid congressional subpoenas. Conyers said in a press release, "I will carry this investigation forward to its conclusion, whether in Congress or in court ... Change has come to Washington, and I hope Karl Rove is ready for it."

House Speaker Nancy Pelosi, who blocked impeachment hearings, is at least now calling for an investigation. She told Fox News, "I think that we have to learn from the past, and we cannot let the politicizing of the— for example, the Justice Department—to go unreviewed ... I want to see the truth come forth."

Why not take it a step further?

Dennis Kucinich, D-OH, who led the charge in Congress for impeachment of Bush and Cheney, has called for "the establishment of a National Commission on Truth and Reconciliation, which will have the power to compel testimony and gather official documents to reveal to the American people not only the underlying deception which has divided us, but in that process of truth-seeking set our nation on a path of reconciliation."

Millions have served time in U.S. prisons for crimes that fall far short of those attributed to the Bush administration. Some criminals, it seems, are like banks judged too big to fail: too big to jail, too powerful to prosecute. What if we apply President Obama's legal theory to the small guys? Why look back? Crimes, large or small, can be forgiven, in the spirit of unity. But few would endorse letting muggers, rapists, or armed robbers of convenience stores off scot-free. So why the different treatment for those potentially guilty of torture, widespread illegal spying, and leading a nation into wars that have killed untold numbers?

Which brings us back to George Bush and books. Ray Bradbury's novel *Fahrenheit 451* is one of the titles in the National Endowment for the Arts' "The Big Read." This ambitious program is "designed to restore reading to the center of American culture." Cities, towns, even entire states choose a book and encourage everyone to read it. In *Fahrenheit 451* (the temperature at which paper spontaneously combusts), books are outlawed. Firemen don't put out fires, they start them, burning down houses that contain books. Bradbury said, "You don't have to burn books to destroy a culture. Just get people to stop reading them." The secretive Bush administration is out of power; the transparency-proclaiming Obama administration is in. But transparency is useful only when accompanied by accountability.

Without thorough, aggressive, public investigations of the full spectrum of crimes alleged of the Bush administration, there will be no accountability, and the complete record of this chapter of U.S. history will never be written.

PRODUCE THE NOTE

Marcy Kaptur of Ohio is the longest-serving Democratic congresswoman in U.S. history. Her district, stretching along the shore of Lake Erie from west of Cleveland to Toledo, faces an epidemic of home foreclosures and 11.5 percent unemployment. That heartland region, the Rust Belt, had its heart torn out by the North American Free Trade Agreement (NAFTA), with shuttered factories and struggling family farms. Kaptur led the fight in Congress against NAFTA. Now, she is recommending a radical foreclosure solution from the floor of the U.S. Congress: "So I say to the American people, you be squatters in your own homes. Don't you leave."

She criticizes the bailout's failure to protect homeowners facing foreclosure. Her advice to "squat" cleverly exploits a legal technicality within the subprime mortgage crisis. These mortgages were made, then bundled into securities and sold and resold repeatedly, by the very Wall Street banks that are now benefiting from TARP (the Troubled Asset Relief Program). The banks foreclosing on families very often can't locate the actual loan note that binds the homeowner to the bad loan. "Produce the note," Kaptur recommends those facing foreclosure demand of the banks.

[P]ossession is nine-tenths of the law," Representative Kaptur told me.

Therefore, stay in your property. Get proper legal representation … [if] Wall Street cannot produce the deed nor the mortgage audit trail … you should stay in your home. It is your castle. It's more than a piece of property … Most people don't even think about getting representation, because they get a piece of paper from the bank, and they go, "Oh, it's the bank," and they become fearful, rather than saying: "This is contract law. The mortgage is a contract. I am one party. There is another party. What are my legal rights under the law as a property owner?"

If you look at the bad paper, if you look at where there's trouble, 95 to 98 percent of the paper really has moved to five institutions: JPMorgan Chase, Bank of America, Wachovia, Citigroup and HSBC. They have this country held by the neck.

Kaptur recommends calling the local Legal Aid Society, bar association, or (888) 995-HOPE for legal assistance.

The onerous duty of physically evicting people and dragging their possessions to the curb typically falls on the local sheriff. Kaptur conditions her squatting advice, saying, "If it's a sheriff's eviction, if it's reached that point, that [staying in the home] is almost impossible." Unless the sheriff refuses to carry out the eviction, as Sheriff Warren Evans of Wayne County, Michigan, has decided to do. Wayne County, including Detroit, has had more than 46,000 foreclosures in the past two years.

After reviewing TARP, Sheriff Evans determined that home foreclosures would conflict with TARP's goal of reducing foreclosures, and that he'd be violating the law by denying foreclosed homeowners the chance at potential federal assistance. "I cannot in clear conscience allow one more family to be put out of their home until I am satisfied they have been afforded every option they are entitled to under the law to avoid foreclosure," he said.

Bruce Marks of the Boston-based Neighborhood Assistance Corporation of America (NACA) is taking the fight to the homes of the banks' CEOs. Last October, as the TARP bailout was shaping up to benefit Wall Street and not Main Street, NACA blockaded the entrance of mortgage giant Fannie Mae until it got a meeting with executives there. Now NACA is working with Fannie Mae to restructure mortgages. Marks is organizing a nationwide, three-day "Predator's Tour," going to the CEOs' homes to demand meetings with them. He told me, "This is what we're going to do with thousands of homeowners, go to their [the CEOs'] home and say: 'I want you to meet my family. I want you to see who you're foreclosing on.' ... If they're going to take our homes, we're going to go to their homes, and we're going to tell them, 'No more.'"

Before the inauguration, Larry Summers, the chair of President Barack Obama's National Economic Council, promised congressional Democratic leaders to "implement smart, aggressive policies to reduce the number of preventable foreclosures by helping to reduce mortgage payments for economically stressed but responsible homeowners, while also reforming our bankruptcy laws and strengthening existing housing initiatives."

According to a report by RealtyTrac, "Foreclosure filings were reported on 2.3 million U.S. properties in 2008, an increase of 81 percent from 2007 and up 225 percent from 2006." As the financial crisis deepens, people facing foreclosure should take Kaptur's advice and tell their bankers, "Produce the note."

MEDIA

DEATH IN OAXACA

Bradley Will captured a murder on video: his own. Will was in the southern Mexican city of Oaxaca (pronounced "wuh-HAH-kuh"), documenting the ongoing protests against the state government there. He was an unembedded journalist, reporting from the front lines of a mass nonviolent movement, and he was shot in broad daylight before a crowd, by plainclothes paramilitaries. Will's murder is just one of too many in the growing list of journalists killed while doing their job. His death on October 27, 2006, and the deaths of three others that day, is proving to be a flash point in Oaxaca.

In May of 2006, the teachers of Oaxaca went on strike, demanding higher wages. The almost annual strike has traditionally obtained a pay hike without conflict. This year, however, the Oaxacan governor, Ulises Ruiz, called out local, state, and federal police and attempted to crush the strike.

The attack prompted a cross section of Oaxacan society to join in the protests, first by occupying the historic central square in Oaxaca City, the Zócalo, then by occupying government buildings and taking over radio and television stations. They were tired of being misrepresented by the media.

They formed an umbrella group, the Popular Assembly of the Peoples of Oaxaca (APPO). For the past four months, the APPO has led a broad movement fighting not only to remove the governor, but also to construct a new form of direct democracy. In response to nightly attacks by police and paramilitaries, hundreds of barricades have been set up throughout the city. Will was documenting the efforts to protect a key barricade in the town of Santa Lucia del Camino when he was killed.

Brad's final video was recovered and posted on the Internet. In it, you can walk with him through his final hours, interviewing the poor but determined protesters, scrambling for cover amid intermittent gunfire directed at them. We see the shooters and Brad's careful balance of protecting himself but documenting the violence against the unarmed protesters. We hear the fatal shot and his cry of pain as he falls to the ground with two bullets in his abdomen, the camera still recording. U.S. Ambassador to Mexico Tony Garza criticized the murder, but said Will died in a "shootout." As Brad's video shows, and to which witnesses attest, the protesters were unarmed. There was no shootout. The Associated Press reported that Santa Lucia del Camino Mayor Manuel Martinez Feria said the suspected shooters have been identified from a photo, all connected to local government or police.

In his sadly prescient final written piece posted to indymedia.org, Brad described the sense of the movement following the murder of a man maintaining a barricade by plainclothes paramilitaries. Just ten days before his death, Brad wrote the following: "What can you say about this movement—this revolutionary moment—you know it is building, growing, shaping—you can feel it—trying desperately for a direct democracy."

This past weekend, claiming to restore order, Mexican President Vicente Fox sent in thousands of federal police, using the death of the American journalist as a pretext. They retook the city square. On *Democracy Now!* on Monday morning, I interviewed Gustavo Esteva, a columnist for the Mexican newspaper *La Jornada*:

> It is not the people themselves who have created disorder in the city. That is
> the alibi of President Fox, using the police to support this governor in a very
> peculiar structure of cynicism and complicity. It is a combination that is

forcing the people of Oaxaca to pay a very heavy price for a democratic, peaceful struggle.

The police, yes, can kill us. The police can come and occupy with all their weapons, with all their tanks. They can occupy one plaza. They can occupy one specific point, but they cannot control the city. They cannot govern the city. They cannot govern our lives and our conscience. We are in control of the city and in control of our lives. And we will surround these police with our bare hands, and we will still control our lives, not the police.

While Congress and President Bush build a wall along the U.S.–Mexico border in a vain denial of our inextricably linked realities, Oaxaca's coalescence of popular grass-roots groups is reaching a critical moment. The federal government has moved in. Will they slaughter the protesters as they did the students in Mexico City in 1968? Will the suppression of the civic demands result in an armed insurrection akin to that of the Zapatistas of 1994? These momentous events will go less well understood by people in the United States, denied the insights and reporting of yet another journalist murdered for the crime of reporting the truth.

SHOOTING THE MESSENGER
IS A WAR CRIME

The Committee to Protect Journalists recently released its 2006 report on threats to journalists. Iraq is by far the deadliest place for the fourth year in a row, with 32 journalists killed this year. Sad to say, the violence follows a trend that started with the U.S. invasion of Iraq.

When you step off the elevator at the Reuters news offices in Washington, D.C., you see a large book sitting on a wooden stand. Each entry describes a Reuters journalist killed in the line of duty. Such as Taras Protsyuk. The veteran Ukrainian cameraman was killed on April 8, 2003, the day before the United States seized Baghdad. Protsyuk was on the balcony of the Palestine Hotel when a U.S. tank positioned itself on the al-Jumhuriyah bridge and, as people watched in horror, unleashed a round into the side of the building. The hotel was known for housing hundreds of unembedded reporters. Protsyuk was killed instantly. José Couso, a cameraman for the Spanish network Telecinco, was filming from the balcony below. He was also killed.

The difference between the responses by the mainstream media in the United States versus Europe was stunning. While in this country there was hardly a peep of protest, Spanish journalists engaged in a one-day strike. From the elite journalists down to the technicians, they laid down their cables, cameras, and pens. They refused to record the words of then–Spanish Prime Minister José María Aznar, who joined British Prime Minister Tony Blair and President Bush in supporting the war. When Aznar came into parliament, they piled their equipment at the front of the room and turned their backs on him. Photographers refused to take his picture and instead held up a photo of their slain colleague. At a news conference in Madrid with British Foreign Secretary Jack Straw, Spanish reporters walked out in protest. Later, hundreds of journalists, camerapeople, and technicians marched on the U.S. embassy in Madrid, chanting "Murderer, murderer."

About four hours before the U.S. military opened fire on the Palestine Hotel, a U.S. warplane strafed Al-Jazeera's Baghdad office. Reporter Tareq Ayyoub was on the roof. He died almost instantly.

When interviewed after his death, Ayyoub's wife, Dima, said, "Hate breeds hate. The United States said they were doing this to rout out terrorism. Who is engaged in terrorism now?" This summer, she sued the U.S. government.

The family of José Couso has also taken action. They know the names of the three U.S. servicemen who fired on the Palestine Hotel. On December 5, 2006, the Spanish Supreme Court said the men could be tried in Spanish courts, opening the possibility for indictments against the U.S. soldiers.

The military response to the journalists' deaths? Pentagon spokeswoman Victoria "Torie" Clarke, who has since become a news consultant for CNN and ABC, said at the time that Baghdad "is not a safe place. They should not be there."

David Schlesinger, global managing editor of Reuters, said: "It seems in my interactions with the U.S. military—to paraphrase, basically—if you are not embedded, we cannot do anything to protect you. Journalists need to be accorded the rights under the Geneva Convention, of civilians not to be shot at willy-nilly, not to be harassed in doing their professional jobs."

The UN Security Council agrees. On December 23, it passed a unanimous resolution insisting on the protection of journalists in conflict zones.

More than 120 reporters and other media workers have been killed in Iraq since the invasion. In August 2003, Reuters cameraman Mazen

Dana was filming outside Abu Ghraib prison when a machine-gun bullet tore through his chest. The Pentagon said the soldiers had "engaged a cameraman."

Not long before his death, Dana won the International Press Freedom Award. "We carry a gift," he said. "We film and we show the world what is going on. We are not part of the conflict." In receiving his award, Dana reflected, "Words and images are a public trust, and for this reason I will continue with my work regardless of the hardships and even if it costs me my life."

But it shouldn't have. The Pentagon should adopt the UN standard and send a clear message to its ranks: shooting the messenger is a war crime that will not be tolerated.

NAB-BING THE ELECTION

As the TV pundits on the networks gab about the tens of millions of dollars raised by the top presidential candidates, what they don't talk about is where that money is going: to their own networks. Money is now considered the single most important factor in our electoral process. Ideas and issues take a backseat to the bottom line. This prostitution of our electoral process has one key culprit: television advertising.

Political advertising makes or breaks candidates, and it takes a huge amount of money to implement a national advertising strategy. Now more than 20 states are piling onto February 5, 2008, as their primary day, including states like California and New York with large, expensive media markets. The early, deciding role of money and television advertising in determining who gets to run for president is secure.

The costs of running for federal office have been skyrocketing. More than $880 million was raised by the 2004 presidential campaigns. The 2008 election is predicted to cost more than $1 billion. Sixty percent will be spent on advertising.

Citizens are the losers, and the broadcasters and elite political consultants are the winners. We ought to turn this around. The public owns the airwaves that are being used by the big corporate broadcasters. The broadcasters, like NBC, ABC, and CBS, have an obligation to use those airwaves "in the public interest, convenience and necessity." These profitable corporations take these public airwaves for free, then peddle them for exorbitant advertising rates.

We have to ask, as U.S. servicemen and -women are being killed overseas ostensibly in defense of democracy, why are our airwaves—the single most important method by which Americans get information about choosing the future president—being held hostage by corporate broadcasters?

The answer: the NAB, or the National Association of Broadcasters, which convenes its annual NAB trade show in Las Vegas next week, is one of Washington's largest and most influential lobbying groups representing the owners of TV and radio stations. For the tens of millions of lobbying and campaign contributions they dole out annually, broadcasters get back billions in corporate welfare, in the form of legislation that protects their ability to sell ads over the public airwaves.

Some bold members of Congress have tried throughout the decades to end this stranglehold on the process. Senator Bill Bradley tried in the 1990s. He said then, "Today's Senate campaigns function as collection agencies for broadcasters. You simply transfer money from contributors to television stations." In 2003, Senator Russ Feingold, along with Senators Richard Durbin, Jon Corzine, and John McCain, submitted the Our Democracy, Our Airwaves Act, which proposed a system of advertising vouchers for candidates. Feingold said at the time, "The public owns the airwaves and licenses them to broadcasters. Broadcasters pay nothing for their use of this scarce and very valuable public resource. Their only 'payment' is a promise to serve the public interest, a promise that often goes unfulfilled."

They wanted to close a loophole allowing broadcasters to extract top dollar for desirable ad slots. Existing law compels broadcasters to give candidates the lowest ad rate for a given market, but then the broadcasters threaten to relegate the ad to the middle of the night. So candidates pony up. A 2002 study by the Alliance for Better Campaigns even showed that stations were hiking ad rates in the lead-up to elections by as much as 53 percent.

Now Durbin is taking another crack at the NAB. He has introduced the Fair Elections Now Act, which would both grant vouchers for broadcast ads and also mandate a 20 percent discount beyond the lowest unit cost of ads near primary and election times.

While the public airwaves are sold off to the highest campaign bidders (often to push negative ads, but that is another issue), the broadcasters fail miserably to report on the campaigns. After all, if the broadcasters fulfilled their public-interest obligations and actually reported fully and consistently on the various candidates and their issues, and not just on the campaign horse race, then there would be less need for campaigns to buy ads in the first place.

More than $2 billion will be poured into the broadcasters' coffers in the 2008 election cycle, almost all for use of the airwaves that the public owns. Imagine what could be done with that money—to register and educate voters, to fully equip polling stations with functioning voting machines, to produce many vigorous debates and public forums. The American public is being robbed by the National Association of Broadcasters—it's time to take back the airwaves.

CBS SILENCES GENERAL DISSENT

Listening to retired U.S. Army Major General John Batiste, you sense his intense loyalty to the military. He commanded the army's First Infantry Division in Iraq, capping a 31-year army career. So why did CBS News fire him as a paid news consultant? A straight answer from CBS seems as elusive as those Iraqi weapons of mass destruction.

The short answer: Batiste appeared in a television advertisement sponsored by VoteVets.org, a nonpartisan group that advocates for veterans. In the 30-second spot, he said, in part, "Mr. President, you did not listen. You continue to pursue a failed strategy that is breaking our great army and Marine Corps. I left the army in protest in order to speak out. Mr. President, you have placed our nation in peril."

Batiste is one of the six retired generals who called for the resignation of then–Secretary of Defense Donald Rumsfeld in the spring of 2006. Of those generals, he alone both served at a high level in the Pentagon and commanded 22,000 troops in Iraq. Despite a promised promotion to three-star general, which would have made him the second-highest-ranking officer in Iraq, Batiste made the difficult decision to retire and speak out.

In his book and documentary *War Made Easy*, media critic Norman

Solomon explains the impact these retired TV generals have on the national debate:

> In the run-up to the war in Iraq, the failure of mainstream news organizations to raise legitimate questions about the government's rush to war was compounded by the networks' deliberate decision to stress military perspectives before any fighting had even begun. CNN's use of retired generals as supposedly independent experts reinforced the decidedly military mindset even as serious questions remained about the wisdom and necessity about going to war.

In 1999, when the United States was bombing Yugoslavia, I asked Frank Sesno, vice president of CNN, "Why pay these generals? And have you ever considered putting peace activists on the payroll? Or inviting them into the studio to respond to the drumbeat for war?" He replied, "We've talked about this. But no, we wouldn't do that. Because generals are analysts, and peace activists are advocates."

That's not far from the reason CBS gave for firing Batiste. According to a cbsnews.com blog, CBS News Vice President Linda Mason explained, "We ask that people not be involved in advocacy." Generals, it seems, are analysts when they agree with the war plan, and advocates when they oppose it. Political blog the Horse's Mouth reported that CBS News consultant Michael O'Hanlon clearly advocated for President Bush's troop surge but didn't get tossed. O'Hanlon, a senior fellow at the Brookings Institution, told the Horse's Mouth he "would be personally gratified to see Batiste back on CBS."

CBS is not alone in icing out perspectives critical of the Iraq war, especially when it mattered. Fairness and Accuracy in Reporting, a media watchdog group, did a study analyzing the major nightly newscasts for the two weeks surrounding then–Secretary of State Colin Powell's speech for war before the United Nations on February 5, 2003. On the major evening newscasts on ABC, CBS, NBC, and PBS, FAIR found 393 interviews on the issue of war, of which only three were with antiwar leaders. This when a majority in the United States either opposed war or supported more time for inspections. This is not a mainstream media, but an extreme media, beating the drums for war.

When I spoke with Batiste, he shied away from political commentary. He was focused on the issues: the safety of the troops, the situation in Iraq. He says we need "a comprehensive national strategy," including "tough diplomatic, political, and economic measures." Instead, he says, the United States is "depending on our military almost entirely to accomplish this ill-fated mission in Iraq."

Batiste is a lifelong Republican. His father and both his grandfathers were in the military. "You see, we got this war terribly wrong. I'm not antiwar at all." Moveon.org circulated an online petition demanding CBS restore Batiste, which more than 230,000 people signed.

Batiste's crime is obvious: he dared to dissent, directly contradicting the endlessly repeated assurances reported by the network news that Bush takes his military advice from his generals on the ground, not from Congress or public-opinion polls.

CBS News has reached a new low when it censors even a pro-war Republican retired general merely for criticizing the president. The power that the broadcasters have amassed, their craven servility to the Bush administration and its failed wars, and their refusal to offer airtime to dissenters all amount to a direct threat to our democracy, a far greater threat than Saddam's imagined WMDs.

DECEMBER 4, 2007

THE DUBIOUS MR. DOBBS

Truth matters. History and context count. "You're entitled to your own opinions. You're not entitled to your own facts," the late Senator Daniel Patrick Moynihan famously observed. CNN's Lou Dobbs has migrated to a preeminent position in the debate on immigration in the United States. Since he identifies himself as a journalist, he has a special responsibility to rely on facts and to correct misstatements of fact. CNN, which purports to be a news organization, touting itself as the "Most Trusted Name in News," has an equally strong obligation to its audience to tell the truth.

Dobbs was best known for anchoring CNN's *Moneyline*, an early and influential program that helped create the televised financial-news genre. On *Moneyline*, Dobbs featured corporate CEOs and generally lauded them. About five years ago, Dobbs began changing his line, invoking populist rhetoric and championing the cause of the middle class. He thematically titled his coverage "War on the Middle Class" and "Broken Borders." Dobbs' signature issue of undocumented immigrants, or, as he calls them, illegal aliens, has tremendous influence on the debate nationally. So it matters if he is wrong.

On March 28, 2006, Dobbs said on his show, "And it's costing us, no one knows precisely how much, to incarcerate what is about a third of our prison population who are illegal aliens." As it turns out, the number of noncitizens incarcerated in the U.S. federal and state prisons is closer to 6 percent, not 33 percent. Note that the 6 percent includes legal immigrants as well.

On April 14, 2005, Lou Dobbs opened his show by saying, "The invasion of illegal aliens is threatening the health of many Americans. Highly contagious diseases are now crossing our borders decades after those diseases had been eradicated in this country." CNN correspondent Christine Romans filed a report, then told Dobbs, "There have been 7,000 [cases of leprosy] in the past three years." CBS' 60 Minutes later challenged the fact, pointing out that there had actually been 7,029 cases reported over 30 years. When Lesley Stahl confronted Dobbs on the statistic, he defended it, saying, "Well, I can tell you this. If we reported it, it's a fact."

Dobbs' reporter, Romans, said her source was "Dr. Madeleine Cosman, a respected medical lawyer and medical historian." Cosman, who died in March 2006, was a medical lawyer and staunch anti-immigrant activist. She was recorded saying publicly of Mexican men, "Recognize that most of these bastards molest girls under age 12, some as young as age 5, others aged 3, although, of course, some specialize in boys, some specialize in nuns, some are exceedingly versatile and rape little girls aged 11 and women up to age 79."

After I played the tape of Cosman for Dobbs, he conceded to me that his reporter's source, Cosman, was a "whack job."

On May 23, 2006, Dobbs aired a report on a state visit by Mexican President Vicente Fox. His correspondent, Casey Wian, called it a "Mexican military incursion" and displayed a map of the United States with the seven Southwest states highlighted as "Aztlan," which, Wian reported, "some militant Latino activists ... claim rightfully belongs to Mexico." The graphic came from the Council of Conservative Citizens (CCC), which the Southern Poverty Law Center(SPLC), a group that tracks hate groups, points out is the current incarnation of the old White Citizens' Councils of the 1950s and 1960s, which Thurgood Marshall referred to as "the uptown Klan." The SPLC has reported that several of Dobbs' guests and sources have had links to the CCC, such as Joe McCutchen of Protect Arkansas Now, part of the Minuteman vigilante movement, and Barbara Coe of the California Coalition for Immigration Reform. Another guest, Glenn Spencer, head of the anti-immigrant group American Patrol, speaks on the white-supremacist circuit. When CNN's Wolf Blitzer had Spencer on, Blitzer told his audience that the SPLC had designated American Patrol as a hate group. When Dobbs had him on, he never identified the connection.

In our conversation with Dobbs, *Democracy Now!* co-host Juan Gonzalez raised the issue of history, of how immigrants have been scapegoated: the Irish in the 1860s, the Chinese in the 1880s and, later, Southern Europeans. Dobbs rolled his eyes, saying, "Are you holding me responsible?" No, and Dobbs knows better. But he must be held responsible for not bringing a historical context to this crucial discussion of immigration reform. The immigration issue will not be solved by vilifying a population. The SPLC has just released a report on the upsurge in anti-immigrant, anti-Latino violence in the United States.

United Stations Radio Networks has just announced that Dobbs will soon be hosting a three-hour daily talk radio show. The website claims, "It's not about what's right and left ... it's about what's right and wrong." Let's hope that Lou Dobbs follows his own advice.

THE FCC'S CHRISTMAS GIFT
TO BIG MEDIA

On December 18, the five commissioners of the Federal Communications Commission met in Washington, D.C., and, by a 3 to 2 vote, passed new regulations that would allow more media consolidation. This, despite the U.S. public's increasing concern over the nation's media being controlled by a few giant corporations.

Dissident FCC Commissioner Michael Copps said of the decision:

> We generously ask big media to sit on Santa's knee, tell us what it wants for Christmas, and then push through whatever of these wishes are politically and practically feasible. No test to see if anyone's been naughty or nice. Just another big, shiny present for the favored few who already hold an FCC license—and a lump of coal for the rest of us. Happy holidays!

It was Bush-appointed FCC Chairman Kevin Martin, now just 41 years old, who rammed through the rule changes. He has served President Bush well. As deputy general counsel for the Bush-Cheney campaign in 2000, he was active during the Florida recount. Before that he worked for Kenneth Starr at the Office of Independent Counsel during the Monica Lewinsky scandal. Rumor has it that he may run for governor of his native North Carolina. His wife, Cathie Martin, was a spokeswoman for Vice President Dick Cheney in the midst of the scandal around the outing of CIA operative Valerie Plame. She now works on Bush's communications staff.

The federal regulation in question is the newspaper-broadcast cross-ownership ban. It has for decades prevented the same company from owning both a television or radio station in a town as well as a newspaper. Underlying this ban is the core concept of the public interest. Copps couldn't have been clearer: "Today's decision would make George Orwell proud. We claim to be giving the news industry a shot in the arm—but the real effect is to reduce total newsgathering." Mergers will result in newsroom layoffs and less, not more, coverage of local issues.

Martin's new rule is also going to hurt the diversity of the U.S. media. Juan Gonzalez, former president of the National Association of Hispanic Journalists, recently testified at a congressional hearing on media ownership. He said,

> Even as our nation has become ever more diverse racially and ethnically ... minority ownership of the broadcast companies ... has remained at shockingly low levels ... Direct experience has shown us that ownership matters when it comes to ... a diversity of voices and meeting the news and information needs of minority communities.

Gonzalez pointed out that the new rule will allow the 19 minority-owned TV stations in the country's top 20 cities to be targeted for takeovers by newspapers, further reducing minority ownership.

There is a reason that journalism is the sole profession explicitly protected in the U.S. Constitution. As a check and balance on government, it is essential to the functioning of a democratic society. As Thomas Jefferson famously stated, "Were it left to me to decide whether we should have a government without newspapers or newspapers without a government, I should not hesitate a moment to prefer the latter."

By eliminating the newspaper-broadcast cross-ownership ban, Martin claims to be saving newspapers. In a *New York Times* Op-Ed piece, he writes, "In many towns and cities, the newspaper is an endangered species ... If we don't act to improve the health of the newspaper industry, we will see newspapers wither and die." As Copps pointed out in his scathing dissent to the rule change, "We shed crocodile tears for the financial plight of newspapers—yet the truth is that newspaper profits are about double the S&P 500 average."

The problem facing Martin and his big media friends isn't that newspapers are unprofitable; it's that they are simply not as profitable as they used to be. This is in part because of the Internet. People no longer have to rely on the newspaper to post or read classified ads, for example, with free online outlets like Craigslist.

The media system in the United States is too highly concentrated and serves not the public interest but rather the interests of moguls like Rupert Murdoch and Sumner Redstone, who controls CBS/Viacom. Media corporations that will benefit from Martin's handout are the same ones that acted as a conveyor belt for the lies of the Bush administration about weapons of mass destruction in Iraq. We need a media that challenges the government, that acts as a fourth estate, not for the state. We need a diverse media. The U.S. Congress has a chance to overrule Martin and the FCC, and to keep the newspaper-broadcast cross-ownership ban in place. It should do so immediately, before the consolidated press leads us into another war.

THE BROADCASTERS' BIG PAYDAY

Hillary Clinton's surprise victory in New Hampshire guarantees a longer, more competitive Democratic primary season. It's like money in the bank for broadcasters, as the first billion-dollar presidential campaign continues.

While the world's oldest democracy, the United States, spends trillions of dollars claiming to bring democracy to Afghanistan and Iraq (through the barrel of a gun), what have we got here? A process driven by major donors shoveling huge sums of cash into the troughs of television broadcasters, who are holding the electoral process hostage through their control of the public airwaves. The same broadcasters arbitrarily exclude viable candidates from their so-called debates, elevating themselves to kingmaker.

According to TNS Media Intelligence/CMAG, a group that tracks political advertising, overall spending by the presidential candidates in Iowa topped $50 million. In 2004, spending was closer to $9 million. The group reported that spending on all campaign and issue ads, for all current races (presidential and others) in the United States, reached $715 million by the end of 2007. WMUR, New Hampshire's only statewide commercial television channel, raked in millions of dollars from political advertising this primary season. WMUR's headquarters is dubbed "The House That Forbes Built," after Steve Forbes spent so much on ads in his 1996 presidential run.

With the new, compressed, "front-loaded" primary schedule, with more and more states moving their primary dates closer to those first-in-nation events in Iowa and New Hampshire, the need for money is extreme. February 5, dubbed "Super-Duper Tuesday," will see primaries in more than 20 states, including huge media "markets" like New York, Illinois, and California. Barack Obama, Clinton, and John Edwards will have to continue to raise huge sums, only to hand most of it over to broadcasters, who, through their control of the public airwaves, dole out access to the electorate.

One way Fox News/News Corp. recently tried to influence the process was to exclude Ron Paul from a Republican candidate forum in New Hampshire, two days before that state's first-in-the-nation primary. Paul was the most successful fundraiser among Republican candidates in the fourth quarter of 2007; he decisively beat Rudy Giuliani in the Iowa caucus, with 10 percent of the vote versus Giuliani's 4 percent. Fox nixed Paul from the debate, while Giuliani was welcomed. The New Hampshire Republican Party pulled its support from the debate. Party chair Fergus Cullen said,

> The first-in-the-nation New Hampshire primary serves a national purpose by giving all candidates an equal opportunity on a level playing field. Lesser-known, lesser-funded underdogs have a fighting chance to establish themselves as national figures. [W]e believe all recognized major candidates should have an equal opportunity to participate in pre-primary debates and forums.

Paul appeared on NBC's *Tonight Show with Jay Leno* (which has restarted production despite the ongoing Writers Guild of America strike, which is keeping Democratic candidates away from the strikebreaking network shows). Leno asked him how he was responding to Fox's banning him: "I realized that they really had some property rights ability there, and I wasn't going to crash the party. And I thought, 'Well, maybe I ought to sue them.' I've decided what to sue them over, and that is for fraud, because of this 'fair and balanced' idea."

While threatening to sue the network for its fraudulent claim of being "Fair and Balanced" (a ludicrous motto for Fox), Paul neglects the key point: the airwaves are not the private property of Fox. Rupert Murdoch and his News Corp. profit from their use of the public airwaves, which comes with the responsibility to serve the public interest. If the electoral process itself, the nuts and bolts of democracy, does not rate as a public interest, what does?

ABC News pulled the same stunt on Dennis Kucinich, barring him from the debate it sponsored on Sunday night. Kucinich filed an emergency complaint with the Federal Communications Commission, saying, "ABC should not be the first primary." He noted that ABC "is a wholly owned subsidiary of Walt Disney Co., whose executives have contributed heavily to ... Senators Hillary Clinton and Barack Obama, former Senator John Edwards and Governor Bill Richardson." ABC limited the debate to those four by requiring participants to place at least fourth in the Iowa caucus to qualify. But the Kucinich campaign said it "bypassed the Iowa caucuses," preferring to focus resources on New Hampshire, then got shut out of the debate. Kucinich's key points, getting out of Iraq and promoting single-payer health care, went virtually unheard in New Hampshire.

The majority of the money that candidates are forced to raise is for TV ads. They are running to be the nation's top public servant. The networks should provide the airtime as a free public service. The airwaves belong to the public; they are a national treasure. They should be used to enrich our electoral process. Instead, they are exploited by highly profitable TV networks, forcing the candidates to rely on monied interests. This vicious cycle must be broken.

THE U.S. WAR ON JOURNALISTS

Sami al-Haj is a free man today, after having been imprisoned by the U.S. military for more than six years. His crime: journalism.

Targeting journalists, the Bush administration has engaged in direct assault, intimidation, imprisonment, and information blackouts to limit the ability of journalists to do their jobs. The principal target these past seven years has been Al-Jazeera, the Arabic television network based in Doha, Qatar.

In November 2001, despite the fact that Al-Jazeera had given the U.S. military the coordinates of its office in Kabul, U.S. warplanes bombed Al-Jazeera's bureau there, destroying it. An Al-Jazeera reporter covering the George Bush–Vladimir Putin summit in Crawford, Texas, in the same month was detained by the FBI because his credit card was "linked to Afghanistan." In spring 2003, the United States dropped four bombs on the Sheraton hotel in Basra, Iraq, where Al-Jazeera correspondents—the only journalists reporting from that city—were the lone guests. Another Al-Jazeera staffer showed his ID to a U.S. Marine at a Baghdad checkpoint, only to have his car fired upon by the marines. He was unhurt. That can't be said for Tareq Ayyoub, an Al-Jazeera correspondent who was on the roof of the network's bureau in Baghdad on April 8, 2003, when a U.S. warplane strafed it. He was killed. His widow, Dima Tahboub, lamented: "Hate breeds hate. The United States said they were doing this to rout out terrorism. Who is engaged in terrorism now?"

Then there is the story of Sami al-Haj. A cameraman for Al-Jazeera, he was reporting on the U.S. invasion of Afghanistan. On December 15, 2001, while in a Pakistani town near the Afghanistan border, Haj was arrested, then imprisoned in Afghanistan. Six months later, shackled and gagged, he was flown to the U.S. prison at Guantanamo Bay. Haj was held there for close to six years, repeatedly interrogated, and never charged with any crime, never tried in a court. He engaged in a hunger strike for more than a year, but was force-fed by his jailers with a feeding tube sent into his stomach through his nose. Haj was abruptly released this week. The U.S. government announced that he was being transferred to the custody of Sudan, his home nation, but the government of Sudan took no action against him. He was rushed to an emergency room, and soon was seen on his old network, Al-Jazeera:

> I'm very happy to be in Sudan, but I'm very sad because of the situation of our brothers who remain in Guantánamo. Conditions in Guantánamo are very, very bad, and they get worse by the day. Our human condition, our human dignity was violated, and the American administration went beyond all human values, all moral values, all religious values. In Guantánamo, you have animals that are called iguanas, rats that are treated with more humanity. But we have people from more than 50 countries that are completely deprived of all rights and privileges, and they will not give them the rights that they give to animals.

He described the desecration of the Quran as part of the effort to break him: "They hold the Quran in contempt, destroyed it several times and put their dirty feet on it. They also sat on the Quran while trying to get us angry. They repeatedly committed violations against our dignity and our sexual organs." At least one official in the Defense Department has denied the charges.

Asim al-Haj, Sami's brother, told me in an interview last January about the 130 interrogations: "During these times, the interrogations were all about Al-Jazeera and alleged relations between Al-Jazeera and al-Qaeda. They tried to induce him to spy on his colleagues at Al-Jazeera."

According to the Committee to Protect Journalists, ten journalists have been held for extended periods by the U.S. military and then released without charge. Just weeks ago in Iraq, the U.S. military released Pulitzer Prize–winning Associated Press photographer Bilal Hussein after holding him without charge for two years. The military had once accused Hussein of being a "terrorist media operative who infiltrated the AP."

The committee reports that 127 journalists and an additional 50 media workers have been killed in Iraq since 2003, well more than twice the number killed in World War II. We need to remind the Bush administration: don't shoot the messenger.

WHY WE WERE FALSELY ARRESTED

ST. PAUL, Minn.—Government crackdowns on journalists are a true threat to democracy. As the Republican National Convention meets in St. Paul, Minnesota, this week, police are systematically targeting journalists. I was arrested with my two colleagues, *Democracy Now!* producers Sharif Abdel Kouddous and Nicole Salazar, while reporting on the first day of the RNC. I have been wrongly charged with a misdemeanor. My coworkers, who were simply reporting, may be charged with felony riot.

The Democratic and Republican national conventions have become very expensive and protracted acts of political theater, essentially four-day-long advertisements for the major presidential candidates. Outside the fences, they have become major gatherings for grass-roots movements—for people to come, amid the banners, bunting, flags, and confetti, to express the rights enumerated in the Constitution's First Amendment: "Congress shall make no law respecting an establishment of religion, or prohibiting the free exercise thereof; or abridging the freedom of speech, or of the press, or the right of the people peaceably to assemble, and to petition the Government for a redress of grievances."

Behind all the patriotic hyperbole that accompanies the conventions, and the thousands of journalists and media workers who arrive to cover the staged events, there are serious violations of the basic right of freedom of the press. Here on the streets of St. Paul, the press is free to report on the official proceedings of the RNC, but not to report on the police violence and mass arrests directed at those who have come to petition their government, to protest.

It was Labor Day, and there was an antiwar march, with a huge turnout, with local families, students, veterans, and people from around the country gathered to oppose the war. The protesters greatly outnumbered the Republican delegates.

There was a positive, festive feeling, coupled with a growing anxiety about the course that Hurricane Gustav was taking, and whether New Orleans would be devastated anew. Later in the day, there was a splinter march. The police—clad in full body armor, with helmets, face shields, batons, and canisters of pepper spray—charged. They forced marchers, onlookers, and working journalists into a nearby parking lot, then surrounded the people and began handcuffing them.

Nicole was videotaping. Her tape of her own violent arrest is chilling. Police in riot gear charged her, yelling, "Get down on your face." You hear her voice, clearly and repeatedly announcing "Press! Press! Where are we supposed to go?" She was trapped between parked cars. The camera drops to the pavement amid Nicole's screams of pain. Her face was smashed into the pavement, and she was bleeding from the nose, with the heavy officer with a boot or knee on her back. Another officer was pulling on her leg. Sharif was thrown up against the wall and kicked in the chest, and he was bleeding from his arm.

I was at the Xcel Center on the convention floor, interviewing delegates. I had just made it to the Minnesota delegation when I got a call on my cell phone with news that Sharif and Nicole were being bloody arrested, in every sense. Filmmaker Rick Rowley of Big Noise Films and I raced on foot to the scene. Out of breath, we arrived at the parking lot. I went up to the line of riot police and asked to speak to a commanding officer, saying that they had arrested accredited journalists.

Within seconds, they grabbed me, pulled me behind the police line and forcibly twisted my arms behind my back and handcuffed me, the rigid plastic cuffs digging into my wrists. I saw Sharif, his arm bloody, his credentials hanging from his neck. I repeated we were accredited journalists, whereupon a Secret Service agent came over and ripped my convention credential from my neck. I was taken to the St. Paul police garage where cages were set up for protesters. I was charged with obstruction of a peace officer. Nicole and Sharif were taken to jail, facing riot charges.

The attack on and arrest of myself and the *Democracy Now!* producers was not an isolated event. A video group called I-Witness Video was raided two days earlier. Another video documentary group, the Glass Bead Collective, was detained, with its computers and video cameras confiscated. On Wednesday, I-Witness Video was again raided, forced out of its office location. When I asked St. Paul Police Chief John Harrington how reporters are to operate in this atmosphere, he suggested, "By embedding reporters in our mobile field force."

On Monday night, hours after we were arrested, after much public outcry, Nicole, Sharif, and I were released. That was our Labor Day. It's all in a day's work.

APRIL 14, 2009

PACIFICA RADIO AT 60:
A SANCTUARY OF DISSENT

Pacifica Radio, the oldest independent media network in the United States, turns 60 years old this week as a deepening crisis engulfs mainstream media. Journalists are being laid off by the hundreds, even thousands. Venerable newspapers, some more than a century old, are being abruptly shuttered. Digital technology is changing the rules, disrupting whole industries, and blending and upending traditional roles of writer, filmmaker, publisher, consumer. Commercial media are losing audience and advertising. People are exploring new models for media, including nonprofit journalism.

Pacifica Radio was founded by Lew Hill, a pacifist who refused to fight in World War II. When he came out of a detention camp after the war, he said the United States needed a media outlet that wasn't run by corporations profiting from war. Instead, he said, it needed one run by journalists and artists—not by "corporations with nothing to tell and everything to sell that are raising our children today," in the words of the late George Gerbner, one-time dean of the Annenberg School for Communication at the University of Pennsylvania. KPFA, the first Pacifica station, began in Berkeley,

178

California, on April 15, 1949. FM radio was in its infancy at the time, so KPFA had to make and give out FM radios in order for people to hear the station. Pacifica Radio tried something no one thought would work: building a network based on the voluntary financial support of individual listeners, a model later adopted by National Public Radio and public television.

The Pacifica network grew to five stations: KPFA in Berkeley, KPFK in Los Angeles, WBAI in New York, WPFW in Washington, D.C., and KPFT in Houston.

In 1970, in its first months of operation, KPFT became the only radio station in the United States whose transmitter was blown up. The Ku Klux Klan did it. The KKK's grand wizard described the bombing as his proudest act. I think it was because he understood how dangerous Pacifica was, as it allowed people to speak for themselves. When you hear someone speaking from his or her own experience—a Palestinian child, an Israeli mother, a grandfather from Afghanistan—it breaks down stereotypes that fuel the hate groups that divide society. The media can build bridges between communities, rather than advocating the bombing of bridges.

Pacifica is a sanctuary for dissent. In the 1950s, when the legendary singer and African-American leader Paul Robeson was "whitelisted" during Senator Joseph McCarthy's witch hunts, banned from almost every public space in the United States but for a few black churches, he knew he could go to KPFA and be heard. The great writer James Baldwin, debating Malcolm X about the effectiveness of nonviolent sit-ins in the South, broadcast over the airwaves of WBAI. I got my start in broadcast journalism in the newsroom of WBAI. Today, the Pacifica tradition is needed more than ever.

In this high-tech digital age, with high-definition television and digital radio, all we get is more static: that veil of distortions, lies, misrepresentations, and half-truths that obscures reality. What we need the media to give us is the dictionary definition of static: criticism, opposition, unwanted interference. We need a media that covers power, not covers for power. We need a media that is the fourth estate, not for the state. We need a media that covers the movements that create static and make history.

With more channels than ever, the lack of any diversity of opinion is breathtaking. Freedom of the press is enshrined in the Constitution, yet our media largely act as a megaphone for those in power. As we confront unprecedented crises—from global warming to global warring to a global economic meltdown—there is also an unprecedented opportunity for change.

Where will innovative thinkers, grass-roots activists, human rights leaders, and ordinary citizens come together to hash out solutions to today's most pressing problems?

For example, while there are many people in this country—in the peace movement as well as in the military—who oppose the "surge" in Afghanistan, as they did in Iraq, we see and hear virtually none of these dissenting voices in the U.S. media. While some polls indicate that a majority of Americans support single-payer health care, these voices are essentially ignored or disparaged in the newspapers and network-news programs.

While traveling the country, I was asked the other day what I thought about the mainstream media. I said I thought it would be a good idea. On this sixtieth anniversary of the Pacifica Radio Network, we should celebrate the tradition of dissent and the power of diverse voices to resolve conflict peacefully.

YOO'S VIEWS MAKE PHILLY NEWS

The *Philadelphia Inquirer*, one of that city's two major daily newspapers, is in the news itself these days after hiring controversial former Bush administration lawyer John Yoo as a monthly columnist.

Letters and e-mails critical of the *Inquirer* are pouring in. "How in the world could John Yoo's legal analysis of anything be informative?" wrote Lisa Ernst of Philadelphia. "What next? An investment advice column by Bernie Madoff?" Will Bunch of the rival *Philadelphia Daily News* wrote, "It's not about muzzling John Yoo from expressing his far-out-of-the-mainstream opinion in the many venues that are available to him, but whether a major American newspaper should give Yoo, his actions, and the notion of torture advocacy its implied endorsement by handing him a megaphone."

Yoo served from 2001 to 2003 as a deputy assistant attorney general in the Office of Legal Counsel in the Bush Justice Department, where he worked under Jay Bybee. There, Yoo authored or co-authored "torture memos," the legal advice given to the Bush White House authorizing harsh interrogation practices. Yoo defined torture in one memo: "The victim must experience intense pain or suffering of the kind that is equivalent to the pain that would be associated with serious physical injury, so severe that death, organ failure, or permanent damage resulting in a loss of significant body function will likely result."

Judge Baltasar Garzon of the Spanish National Court is moving ahead with an investigation of "The Bush Six," which includes Yoo and Bybee, as well as former Attorney General Alberto Gonzales; William J. Haynes II, then–general counsel to the Department of Defense; Douglas Feith, former undersecretary of defense for policy; and David Addington, the chief of staff under former Vice President Dick Cheney. These six could possibly face criminal charges in Spain for enabling torture at Guantánamo and elsewhere. They might think twice before traveling abroad to Spain or other European nations. Yoo, Bybee, and another Bush Justice Department attorney, Steven G. Bradbury, face an investigation into their conduct by the Justice Department's Office of Professional Responsibility. The Justice Department could forward the report to state bar associations, where the attorneys could be disciplined, possibly disbarred. Bybee, now a federal judge, could be impeached.

The disbarment strategy has been embraced by grass-roots activists as well. The group DisbarTortureLawyers.com stated, "On Monday, May 18, 2009, a broad coalition of organizations dedicated to accountable government, and representing over one million members, filed disciplinary complaints with state bar licensing boards against … twelve attorneys for advocating the torture of detainees during the Bush administration."

Disbarment would certainly be a problem for many of these people, perhaps costing them their jobs. But the detention and interrogation practices that gained their official sanction, from the highest level of the executive branch, have had much more serious and far-reaching consequences for hundreds, if not thousands, of people around the globe.

John Sifton is a human rights investigator who recently wrote a piece titled "The Bush Administration Homicides." He concludes that "an estimated 100 detainees have died during interrogations, some who were clearly tortured to death." He told me, "These aggressive techniques were not just limited to the high-value detainee program in the CIA. They spread to the military with disastrous results. They led to the deaths of human beings ... when there's a dead body involved, you can't just have a debate about policy differences and looking forward or looking backward."

Bunch told me, "Philadelphia is a city of four million people. John Yoo grew up here, but he doesn't even live here now. And to think this is a voice that's reflective of the community, frankly, [is] an insult to true conservatives that the best voice they can get on the editorial page is somebody who's famous for being a torture advocate."

I was in Philadelphia this past weekend and got to hear Grammy Award–winning soul singer John Legend give the commencement address at the University of Pennsylvania, his alma mater. He said in his speech:

> As a nation and as a world, we need more truth. Let me repeat that. We need more truth ... Too often, in business and in government, people are rewarded for having the answer that the person they report to wants them to have: "Yes, sir. We can provide mortgages to people who have no down payment and can't afford the monthly payments." ... "Yes, ma'am. I can write a legal brief to justify torture."

The students listened with rapt attention.

There are many Philadelphians who can write and inspire debate that leads people to action. John Yoo has done enough harm.

NEWS FROM THE
UNREPORTED WORLD

NOVEMBER 15, 2006

TIMOR:
BUSH HAS A CHANCE TO HOLD
TERRORISTS ACCOUNTABLE

The troops marched slowly, their U.S.-made M-16s raised. It was November 12, 1991, a day that would forever be seared into my memory, and into history. I was reporting in East Timor, a small island nation 300 miles north of Australia, brutally occupied by Indonesia since 1975. A third of the population—200,000 Timorese—had been killed in one of the worst genocides of the twentieth century.

Thousands marched that morning toward the Santa Cruz cemetery to remember Sebastião Gomes, yet another young Timorese killed by Indonesian soldiers. I was doing a documentary for Pacifica Radio. My colleague Allan Nairn was writing for the *New Yorker* magazine. In a land where there was no freedom of speech, press, or assembly, we asked people, "Why are you risking your lives by marching?"

"I'm doing it for my mother," one replied. "I'm doing it for my father," said another. "I'm doing it for freedom."

At the cemetery, we saw hundreds of Indonesian troops coming up the road, 12 to 15 abreast. The Indonesian military had committed many massacres in the past, but never in front of Western journalists. We walked to the front of the crowd, hoping that our presence could stop the attack. Children whispered behind us. I put on my headphones, took out my tape recorder, and held up my microphone like a flag. We wanted to alert the troops that this time they were being watched by the world.

The Timorese couldn't escape. They were trapped by the cemetery walls that lined both sides of the road. Without any warning, provocation, or hesitation, the soldiers swept past us and opened fire.

People were ripped apart. The troops just kept shooting, killing anyone still standing. A group of soldiers surrounded me. They started to shake my microphone in my face. Then they slammed me to the ground with their rifle butts and kicked me with their boots. I gasped for breath. Allan threw himself on top of me to protect me from further injury.

The soldiers wielded their M-16s like baseball bats, slamming them against his head until they fractured his skull. He lay in the road in spasm, covered in blood, unable to move. Suddenly, about a dozen soldiers lined up like a firing squad. They put the guns to our heads and screamed, "Politik! Politik!" They were accusing us of being involved in politics, a crime clearly punishable by death. They demanded, "Australia? Australia?" The Indonesians executed six Australian journalists during the 1975 invasion.

We shouted, "No, we're from America!" I threw my passport at them. When I regained my breath, I said again, "We're from America! America!" Finally, the soldiers lowered their guns from our heads. We think it was because we were from the same country their weapons were from. They would have to pay a price for killing us that they never had to pay for killing Timorese.

At least 271 Timorese died that day, in what became known as the Santa Cruz massacre. Indonesian troops went on killing for days. It was not even one of the larger massacres in East Timor, and it wouldn't be the last. It was simply the first to be witnessed by outsiders.

I write about the massacre this week not just to remember the 15th anniversary of that event and those who died that day. President Bush is headed to Indonesia on Monday. This will give the president and Congress an opportunity to show they are serious about holding terrorists accountable. If they were to cut all military aid to Indonesia until those responsible for the massacre and for the policy of genocide are held accountable, they would be showing the world that the United States stands on the side of justice. The U.S. Congress must hear the East Timor Commission for Reception, Truth, and Reconciliation's call for an international human rights tribunal and for reparations from the countries and corporations that supported the brutal occupation.

The definition of terrorism is the same in all languages, whether carried out by individuals or states, by al-Qaeda, or, in our name, by U.S.-supported governments abusing human rights. Sad to say, the Bush administration and Congress have so far ignored the call for justice. What we witnessed and survived 15 years ago was terrorism, pure and simple—the killing of innocent civilians.

DECEMBER 14, 2006

ASK KISSINGER ABOUT PINOCHET

As the world marked International Human Rights Day, one of the century's most notorious dictators, General Augusto Pinochet, died under house arrest in Chile at the age of 91. His 17-year reign left a deep scar on Chilean society. Yet Pinochet's legacy includes an ironic upside: his regime and the U.S. support for it galvanized the modern-day international human rights movement.

On September 11, 2001, as the planes hit the towers of the World Trade Center, on our daily broadcast of *Democracy Now!* we were looking at the connection between terrorism and September 11 ... 1973. It was on that day that the democratically elected government of Chilean President Salvador Allende was overthrown in a violent coup, and the forces of Pinochet rose to power. The coup was supported by the U.S. government. Henry Kissinger, national security adviser and U.S. secretary of state, summed up the policy this way: "I don't see why we need to stand by and watch a country go communist due to the irresponsibility of its own people. The issues are much too important for the Chilean voters to be left to decide for themselves."

As Pinochet seized power, first among the dead was the president himself, Allende. Then there were the thousands rounded up. Among them was Victor Jara, the legendary Chilean folk singer. Jara was beaten, tortured, then executed. His body was dumped on a Santiago street and found by his wife in the morgue.

Charles Horman was a U.S. journalist working in Chile. He, too, disappeared in those days following the coup. His body was found buried in a cement wall. His story was immortalized in the Academy Award–winning Constantin Costa-Gavras film *Missing*. His widow, Joyce Horman, sued not only Pinochet for the death of her husband, but also Kissinger and others at the U.S. State Department.

Pinochet's reign of terror extended beyond Chile's borders. On September 21, 1976, the former foreign minister of Chile, Orlando Letelier, and his American colleague, Ronni Moffitt, died in a car bombing, not in Chile, but on Embassy Row in Washington, D.C.

Then there was Chile's current president, Michelle Bachelet. Her father was a general under Allende and opposed the coup. He was arrested and died of a heart attack in prison. She and her mother were detained and tortured at the notorious Villa Grimaldi, a secret torture site in Santiago. Bachelet and her mother survived and went into exile. Her return to Chile and eventual election as president on the Socialist ticket has brought Chilean politics and history full circle. In October 2006, she returned to Villa Grimaldi. In November, Pinochet was placed under house arrest and charged with the kidnap and murder of prisoners there.

This was not the first time Pinochet was arrested. In 1998, while on a medical visit in London, he was put under house arrest after Spanish Judge Baltasar Garzon issued a warrant for his arrest for the torture and murder of Spanish nationals. After 18 months, Britain finally allowed Pinochet to return to Chile for health reasons, avoiding extradition to Spain.

Pinochet's death allows him to escape conviction. Kissinger, whose support for the Pinochet regime is increasingly well documented, is still alive and still of interest to those seeking justice. Kissinger has been sought for questioning by Judge Garzon and by French Judge Roger Le Loire, both investigating the death and disappearance of their citizens in Chile. While Kissinger is frequently questioned by the media in this country, he is almost never asked about his own record. Instead, he is treated like royalty.

Questions remain about the brutal regime of Pinochet. Kissinger likely holds many answers. If we are to have a uniform standard of justice, then answers need to be demanded of the genuine terrorism experts such as Henry Kissinger.

CHIQUITA'S SLIPPING APPEAL

What do Osama bin Laden and Chiquita bananas have in common? Both have used their millions to finance terrorism.

The Justice Department has just fined Chiquita Brands International $25 million for funding a terrorist organization ... for years. Chiquita must also cooperate fully with ongoing investigations into its payments to the ultra-right-wing Colombian paramilitary group Autodefensas Unidas de Colombia (AUC). Chiquita made almost monthly payments to the AUC from 1997 to 2004, totaling at least $1.7 million.

The AUC is a brutal paramilitary umbrella group, with an estimated 15,000 to 20,000 armed troops. It was named a terrorist organization by the United States on September 10, 2001. Among its standard tactics are kidnapping, torture, disappearance, rape, murder, beatings, extortion, and drug trafficking.

Chiquita claims it had to make the payments under threat from the AUC in order to protect its employees and property. Chiquita's outside lawyers implored them to stop the illegal payments, to no avail. The payments were made by check through Chiquita's Colombian subsidiary,

Banadex. When Chiquita executives figured out how illegal the payments were, they started delivering them in cash. Chiquita sold Banadex in June 2004 when the heat got too intense.

While the AUC was collecting U.S. dinero from Chiquita, it was butchering thousands of innocent people in rural Colombia. Chengue (pronounced "CHEN-gay") was a small farming village in the state of Sucre. About 80 AUC paramilitary members went into the town in the early hours of January 17, 2001. They rounded up the men and smashed their skulls with stones and a sledgehammer, killing 24 of them. One 19-year-old perpetrator confessed, naming the organizers of the mass murder, including police and navy officials. To date, he is the only one who has been punished. This is just one of hundreds of massacres carried out by AUC.

Chiquita has had a long history of criminal behavior. It was the subject of an extraordinary exposé in its hometown paper, the *Cincinnati Enquirer*, in 1998. The paper found that Chiquita exposed entire communities to dangerous U.S.-banned pesticides, forced the eviction of an entire Honduran village at gunpoint and its subsequent bulldozing, suppressed unions, unwittingly allowed the use of Chiquita transport ships to move cocaine internationally, and paid a fortune to U.S. politicians to influence trade policy. The lead reporter, Mike Gallagher, illegally accessed more than 2,000 Chiquita voice mails. The voice mails backed up his story, but his methods got him fired. The *Enquirer* issued a front-page apology and paid Chiquita a reported $14 million. The voice-mail scandal rocked the *Enquirer*, burying the important exposé.

Chiquita was formerly called the United Fruit Co., which, with the help of its former lawyer, Secretary of State John Foster Dulles, and his brother Allen Dulles' Central Intelligence Agency, overthrew the democratically elected president of Guatemala, Jacobo Arbenz Guzman, in 1954. And you can go back further. Colombian Nobel Laureate Gabriel García Márquez wrote in his classic *One Hundred Years of Solitude* about the 1928 Santa Marta massacre of striking United Fruit banana workers: "When the banana company arrived ... the old policemen were replaced by hired assassins."

While the United States is seeking extradition of Colombia-based Chiquita executives, the administration of President Alvaro Uribe in Colombia, with its own officials now linked to the right-wing paramilitaries, has countered that Colombia would seek the extradition of U.S.-based Chiquita executives. Colombian prosecutors are also seeking information in Chiquita's role in smuggling 3,000 AK-47 rifles and millions of rounds of ammunition to paramilitaries in November 2001.

A $25 million fine to a multibillion-dollar corporation like Chiquita is a mere slap on the wrist, the cost of doing business. Presidents like George W. Bush and Uribe, businessmen first, while squabbling over extraditions, would never lose track of their overarching shared goal of a stridently pro-corporate, military-supported, so-called free-trade regime. As long as that remains the same, union organizers and hard-working farmers, like the men of Chengue, will continue to be killed on behalf of Chiquita or some other multinational company.

That next organic, fair-trade banana you buy just might save a life.

GLOBAL CONSENSUS,
NOT GLOBAL CONQUEST

As world leaders gather this week to address the United Nations General Assembly, President Bush's refusal to negotiate on the two key issues of our day—war and global warming—has been stunning. And the media haven't helped. Focusing on whether Columbia University should have invited Iran's President Mahmoud Ahmadinejad to speak, the Bush administration's drumbeat for war with Iran goes unchallenged. Let this not be a reprise of the war on Iraq.

Former Federal Reserve Chairman Alan Greenspan says in his new memoir, "I am saddened that it is politically inconvenient to acknowledge what everyone knows: The Iraq War is largely about oil." I asked him to elaborate: "It's clear to me that were there not the oil resources in Iraq, the whole picture of how that part of the Middle East developed would have been different."

It is an obvious point. It's just too bad that he wasn't willing to admit this before the invasion; his every utterance during his tenure at the Fed influenced decision-makers around the world, particularly in his own backyard at the White House.

As Naomi Klein, the author of *The Shock Doctrine: The Rise of Disaster Capitalism*, listened to Greenspan, she pointed out, "Under international law ... it is illegal to wage wars to gain access to other countries', sovereign countries', natural resources."

Which brings us to Iran, another oil-rich country. As with Iraq, the Bush administration doesn't talk about Iran's oil, but rather claims that Iran is developing a nuclear bomb. Sound familiar? The answer isn't war; it's diplomacy. Earlier this week, I spoke with one of Israel's top political columnists, Akiva Eldar, with the Israeli newspaper *Haaretz*. He opposes an attack on Iran: "[T]he Middle East is going to be nuclearized in no time. I think that solution should be a regional agreement ... the Middle East should be nuclear free, including Israel. I think this has to be part of an agreement."

The UN gathering of world leaders is an ideal moment to hammer out agreements like Eldar recommends, as it is to take on the other crisis fueled by oil: climate change.

On the global-warming front, the opening of the UN General Assembly this week coincided with a major meeting on climate change, attended by more than 80 world leaders. As UN Secretary-General Ban Ki-moon kicked off the meeting, he said,

> We hold the future in our hands. Together we must ensure that our grandchildren will not have to ask why we have failed to do the right things and left them to suffer the consequences. So let us send a clear and collective signal to people everywhere. Today, let the world know that you are ready to shoulder this responsibility and that you will address this challenge head-on.

Yvo de Boer, a top UN climate expert, said, "The United States is still the largest emitter worldwide of greenhouse gases. For that reason and for a number of others, the participation of the U.S. is essential." Yet Bush did not participate in the global meeting. Instead, Bush is hosting an invitation-only gathering of "major economies" in Washington, D.C., to discuss voluntary caps on greenhouse gas emissions. This is simply not enough. Ban Ki-moon criticized the Bush meeting, saying, "The UN climate process is the appropriate forum for negotiating global action."

One of those leaders who came to address the UN General Assembly was Evo Morales, the first indigenous president of Bolivia. While the United States rarely looks south for leadership, Morales' example is worth considering. He has restored diplomatic relations with Iran. Against tremendous internal opposition, he nationalized Bolivia's natural gas fields, transforming the country's economic stability, and, interestingly, enriching the very elite that originally criticized the move. (Contrast this with the United States pressuring the Iraqi parliament to pass an oil law that would virtually hand over control of Iraq's oil to the major U.S. oil corporations.) President Morales told me, "Neither mother earth nor life are commodities. We are talking about a profound change of models and systems."

The twin crises of war and climate change, inexorably linked by our thirst for oil, need a concerted global solution—one that won't be obtained by cowboy diplomacy. The United States must pursue global consensus, not global conquest—before it is too late.

CHEVRON'S PIPELINE IS
THE BURMESE REGIME'S LIFELINE

The image was stunning: tens of thousands of saffron-robed Buddhist monks marching through the streets of Rangoon (also known as Yangon), protesting the military dictatorship of Burma. The monks marched in front of the home of Nobel Peace Prize winner Aung San Suu Kyi, who was seen weeping and praying quietly as they passed. She hadn't been seen for years. The democratically elected leader of Burma, Suu Kyi has been under house arrest since 2003. She is considered the Nelson Mandela of Burma, the Southeast Asian nation renamed Myanmar by the regime.

After almost two weeks of protest, the monks have disappeared. The monasteries have been emptied. One report says thousands of monks are imprisoned in the north of the country.

No one believes that this is the end of the protests, dubbed "The Saffron Revolution." Nor do they believe the official body count of ten dead. The trickle of video, photos, and oral accounts of the violence that leaked out on Burma's cellular phone and Internet lines has been largely stifled by government censorship. Still, gruesome images of murdered monks and other activists and accounts of executions make it out to the global public.

At the time of this writing, several unconfirmed accounts of prisoners being burned alive have been posted to Burma-solidarity websites.

The Bush administration is making headlines with its strong language against the Burmese regime. President Bush declared increased sanctions in his UN General Assembly speech. First Lady Laura Bush has come out with perhaps the strongest statements. Explaining that she has a cousin who is a Burma activist, Laura Bush said, "The deplorable acts of violence being perpetrated against Buddhist monks and peaceful Burmese demonstrators shame the military regime."

Secretary of State Condoleezza Rice, at the meeting of the Association of Southeast Asian Nations, said, "The United States is determined to keep an international focus on the travesty that is taking place." Keeping an international focus is essential, but should not distract from one of the most powerful supporters of the junta, one that is much closer to home. Rice knows it well: Chevron.

Fueling the military junta that has ruled for decades are Burma's natural gas reserves, controlled by the Burmese regime in partnership with the U.S. multinational oil giant Chevron, the French oil company Total, and a Thai oil firm. Offshore natural gas facilities deliver their extracted gas to Thailand through Burma's Yadana pipeline. The pipeline was built with slave labor, forced into servitude by the Burmese military.

The original pipeline partner, Unocal, was sued by EarthRights International for the use of slave labor. As soon as the suit was settled out of court, Chevron bought Unocal.

Chevron's role in propping up the brutal regime in Burma is clear. According to Marco Simons, U.S. legal director at EarthRights International, "Sanctions haven't worked because gas is the lifeline of the regime. Before Yadana went on line, Burma's regime was facing severe shortages of currency. It's really Yadana and gas projects that kept the military regime afloat to buy arms and ammunition and pay its soldiers."

The U.S. government has had sanctions in place against Burma since 1997. A loophole exists, though, for companies grandfathered in. Unocal's exemption from the Burma sanctions has been passed on to its new owner, Chevron.

Rice served on the Chevron board of directors for a decade. She even had a Chevron oil tanker named after her. While she served on the board,

Chevron was sued for involvement in the killing of nonviolent protesters in the Niger Delta region of Nigeria. Like the Burmese, Nigerians suffer political repression and pollution where oil and gas are extracted and they live in dire poverty. The protests in Burma were actually triggered by a government-imposed increase in fuel prices.

Human rights groups around the world have called for a global day of action on Saturday, October 6, in solidarity with the people of Burma. Like the brave activists and citizen journalists sending news and photos out of the country, the organizers of the October 6 protest are using the Internet to pull together what will probably be the largest demonstration ever in support of Burma. Among the demands are calls for companies to stop doing business with Burma's brutal regime.

CONGO:
THE INVISIBLE WAR

It's the deadliest conflict since World War II. More than five million people have died in the past decade, yet it goes virtually unnoticed and unreported in the United States. The conflict is in the Democratic Republic of Congo, in Central Africa. At its heart are the natural resources found in Congo and multinational corporations that extract them. The prospects for peace have slightly improved: a peace accord was just signed in Congo's eastern Kivu provinces. But without a comprehensive truth and reconciliation process for the entire country and a renegotiation of all mining contracts, the suffering will undoubtedly continue.

In its latest Congo mortality report, the International Rescue Committee found that a stunning 5.4 million "excess deaths" have occurred in Congo since 1998. These are deaths beyond those that would normally occur. In other words, a loss of life on the scale of September 11 occurring every two days, in a country whose population is one-sixth our own.

Just a little history: after supporting the allies in World War II, Congo gained independence and elected Patrice Lumumba, a progressive Pan-Africanist, as prime minister in 1960. He was assassinated soon after in a plot involving the CIA. The United States installed and supported Mobutu Sese Seko, who ruled tyrannically for more than 30 years, plundering the nation. Since his death, Congo has seen war, from 1996 to 2002, provoked by invasions by neighboring Rwanda and Uganda, and ongoing conflict since then.

A particularly horrifying aspect of the conflict is the mass sexual violence being used as a weapon of war. Congolese human rights activist Christine Schuler Deschryver told me about the hundreds of thousands of women and children subjected to rape: "We are not talking about normal rapes anymore. We are talking about sexual terrorism, because they are destroyed—you cannot imagine what's going on in Congo. We are talking about new surgery to repair the women, because they're completely destroyed." She was describing the physical damage done to the women, and to children, one, she said, as young as ten months old, by acts of rape that involve insertion of sticks, guns, and molten plastic. Deschryver was in the United States as a guest of V-Day, Eve Ensler's campaign to end violence against women, in an attempt to generate public awareness of this genocide and to support the Panzi Hospital in Deschryver's hometown of Bukavu.

Maurice Carney is executive director of Friends of the Congo, in Washington, D.C.:

> Two types of rape, basically, are taking place in the Congo: One is the rape of the women and children, and the other the rape of the land, natural resources. The Congo has tremendous natural resources: 30 percent of the world's cobalt, 10 percent of the world's copper, 80 percent of the world's reserves of coltan. You have to look at the corporate influence on everything that takes place in the Congo.

Among the companies Carney blames for fueling the violence are Cleveland-based OM Group, the world's leading producer of cobalt-based specialty chemicals and a leading supplier of nickel-based specialty chemicals, as well as Boston-based chemical giant Cabot Corp. Cabot produces coltan, also known as tantalum, a hard-to-extract but critical component of electronic circuitry, which is used in all cell phones and other consumer electronics. The massive demand for coltan is credited with fueling the

Second Congo War of 1998–2002. A former CEO of Cabot is none other than the Bush administration's current secretary of energy, Samuel Bodman. Phoenix-based Freeport-McMoRan, which took over the Phelps Dodge company's enormous mining concession in the Congo, is also in on the game.

The United Nations has issued several reports that are highly critical of illegal corporate exploitation of the Congo's minerals. A Congolese government review of more than 60 mining contracts call for their renegotiation or outright cancellation. Says Carney, "Eighty percent of the population live on 30 cents a day or less, with billions of dollars going out the back door and into the pockets of mining companies." An important question for us in the United States is: how could close to six million people die from war and related disease in one country in less than a decade and go virtually unnoticed?

COLOMBIA:
CELEBRATE THE RELEASE,
NOT THE REGIME

It is fantastic to see Ingrid Betancourt free. She was the Green Party candidate running for president of Colombia against Alvaro Uribe in 2002 when she was kidnapped by the Revolutionary Armed Forces of Colombia (FARC) just days after appealing to the FARC to stop its campaign of kidnapping. She was held hostage for more than six years and was released last week along with 14 others. The flamboyant rescue operation by the Colombian Army has been splashed across newspapers and TV screens globally, but the celebration of their release should not be confused with celebration of the Colombian government.

I reached Manuel Rozental at his home in Canada. He's a Colombian doctor and human rights activist who fled Colombia after receiving several threats on his life:

> We're talking about the regime with the worst human rights record in the continent and the army with the worst human rights record in the continent with the greatest U.S. support, including the contractors or mercenaries. So the fact that this regime was involved in this liberation does not and should not and cannot cover up the fact that it is a horrendous regime.

Colombia has been the largest recipient of U.S. foreign aid outside of Israel and Egypt. Amnesty International USA has called for a halt to all support for Colombia, saying "torture, massacres, 'disappearances' and killings of noncombatants are widespread, and collusion between the armed forces and paramilitary groups continues to this day. In 2006, U.S. assistance to Colombia amounted to an estimated $728 million, approximately 80 percent of which was military and police assistance."

John McCain was in Colombia on July 2, the day Betancourt was released along with U.S. military contractors and Colombian soldiers and police officers who were held. McCain's links to Colombia are worth noting. The Huffington Post reports that a McCain fundraising event was just given by billionaire Carl Lindner of Cincinnati, the former CEO of Chiquita Brands International. Chiquita, under Lindner's watch, paid and armed one of the most notorious right-wing paramilitary groups in Colombia, the United Self-Defense Forces of Colombia (AUC). The U.S. government fined Chiquita $25 million for its funding and arming of the AUC, designated a "foreign terrorist organization" by the U.S. State Department as early as 2001. One of the conditions of the deal was that Chiquita would not have to name the top executives involved.

The Huffington Post and the *New York Times* recently reported another McCain connection to Colombia. His top adviser, Charlie Black, resigned in March as chairman of the Washington, D.C., lobbying firm BKSH & Associates in order to work full time on the McCain campaign. Since 1998, BKSH has earned $1.8 million representing Occidental Petroleum, which has controversial oil operations in Colombia. Occidental worked with a military contractor and the Colombian military to counter pipeline attacks. In December 1998, the Colombian military dropped a bomb on the village of Santa Domingo, killing 11 adults and seven children. According to the *Los Angeles Times*, Occidental "supplied, directly or through contractors, troop transportation, planning facilities and fuel to Colombian military aircraft, including the helicopter crew accused of dropping the bomb."

It was a photographed hug that grabbed the attention of Inter Press Service, an independent global news agency. Soon after Betancourt was released, IPS published a story, "The General Ingrid Hugged," about the national commander of the Colombian Army, General Mario Montoya. Montoya has been linked to a secret commando group from the late 1970s that bombed and massacred political opponents of the right wing. While the initial flurry of photo ops, with Betancourt hugging Montoya and standing with Uribe, has boosted public acclaim for the Uribe administration and the Colombian military, Betancourt is beginning to assert her traditionally oppositional status. She told RFI radio in France,

President Uribe, and not just President Uribe but Colombia as a whole, should change some things ... I think the time has come to change the language of radicalism, extremism and hatred, the very strong words that cause deep hurt to a human being ... There comes a time when one has to agree to talk to the people you hate.

CHEVRON, SHELL,
AND THE TRUE COST OF OIL

The economy is a shambles, unemployment is soaring, the auto industry is collapsing. But profits are higher than ever at oil companies Chevron and Shell. Yet across the globe, from the Ecuadorian jungle, to the Niger Delta in Nigeria, to the courtrooms and streets of New York and San Ramon, California, people are fighting back against the world's oil giants.

Shell and Chevron are in the spotlight this week, with shareholder meetings and a historic trial being held.

On May 13, the Nigerian military launched an assault on villages in that nation's oil-rich Niger Delta. Hundreds of civilians are feared killed in the attack. According to Amnesty International, a celebration in the delta village of Oporoza was attacked. An eyewitness told the organization, "I heard the sound of aircraft; I saw two military helicopters, shooting at the houses, at the palace, shooting at us. We had to run for safety into the forest. In the bush, I heard adults crying, so many mothers could not find their children; everybody ran for their life."

Shell is facing a lawsuit in U.S. federal court, *Wiwa v. Shell*, based on Shell's alleged collaboration with the Nigerian dictatorship in the 1990s in the violent suppression of the grass-roots movement of the Ogoni people of the Niger Delta. Shell exploits the oil riches there, causing displacement, pollution, and deforestation. The suit also alleges that Shell helped suppress the Movement for the Survival of the Ogoni People and its charismatic leader, Ken Saro-Wiwa. Saro-Wiwa had been the writer of the most famous soap opera in Nigeria, but decided to throw his lot in with the Ogoni, whose land near the Niger Delta was crisscrossed with pipelines. The children of Ogoniland did not know a dark night, living beneath the flame—apartment-building-sized gas flares that burned day and night, and that are illegal in the United States.

I interviewed Saro-Wiwa in 1994. He told me, "The oil companies like military dictatorships, because basically they can cheat with these dictatorships. The dictatorships are brutal to people, and they can deny the human rights of individuals and of communities quite easily, without compunction." He added, "I am a marked man." Saro-Wiwa returned to Nigeria and was arrested by the military junta. On November 10, 1995, after a kangaroo show trial, Saro-Wiwa was hanged with eight other Ogoni activists.

In 1998, I traveled to the Niger Delta with journalist Jeremy Scahill. A Chevron executive there told us that Chevron flew troops from Nigeria's notorious mobile police, the "kill 'n' go," in a Chevron company helicopter to an oil barge that had been occupied by nonviolent protesters. Two protesters were killed, and many more were arrested and tortured.

Oronto Douglas, one of Saro-Wiwa's lawyers, told us, "It is very clear that Chevron, just like Shell, uses the military to protect its oil activities. They drill and they kill."

Chevron is the second-largest stakeholder (after French oil company Total) of the Yadana natural gas field and pipeline project, based in Burma. The pipeline provides the single largest source of income to the military junta, amounting to close to $1 billion in 2007. Nobel Peace Prize laureate Aung San Suu Kyi, popularly elected the leader of Burma in 1990, has been under house arrest for 14 of the past 20 years, and is standing trial again this week. (On Tuesday the government said it had ended the house arrest of Suu Kyi, but she remains in detention pending the outcome of the trial.) The U.S. government has barred U.S. companies from investing in Burma since 1997, but Chevron has a waiver, inherited when it acquired the oil company Unocal.

Chevron's litany of similar abuses, from the Philippines to Kazakhstan, Chad-Cameroon, Iraq, Ecuador, and Angola and across the United States and Canada, is detailed in an "alternative annual report" prepared by a consortium of nongovernmental organizations and is being distributed to Chevron shareholders at this week's annual meeting, and to the public at TrueCostofChevron.com.

Chevron is being investigated by New York State Attorney General Andrew Cuomo about whether the company was "accurate and complete" in describing potential legal liabilities. It enjoys, though, a long tradition of hiring politically powerful people. Condoleezza Rice was a longtime director of the company, and the recently hired general counsel is none other than disgraced Pentagon lawyer William J. Haynes, who advocated for "harsh interrogation techniques," including waterboarding. General James L. Jones, President Barack Obama's national security adviser, sat on the Chevron board of directors for most of 2008, until he received his high-level White House appointment.

Saro-Wiwa said before he died, "We are going to demand our rights peacefully, nonviolently, and we shall win." A global grass-roots movement is growing to do just that.

THE FREE MARKET'S MARKED MEN

Ken Saro-Wiwa and Alberto Pizango never met, but they are united by a passion for the preservation of their people and their land, and by the fervor with which they were targeted by their respective governments. Saro-Wiwa was executed by the Nigerian government November 10, 1995. Pizango this week was charged by the Peruvian government with sedition and rebellion, and narrowly eluded capture, taking refuge in the Nicaraguan Embassy in Lima. Nicaragua has just granted him political asylum. Two indigenous leaders—one living, one dead—Pizango and Saro-Wiwa demonstrate that effective grass-roots opposition to corporate power can take a personal toll. Saro-Wiwa's family and others just won a landmark settlement in U.S. federal court, ending a 13-year battle with Shell Oil. Pizango's ordeal is just beginning.

Peru and Nigeria are a world apart on the map, but both host abundant natural resources for which the United States and other industrialized nations hunger.

The Niger Delta is one of the world's most productive oil fields. Shell Oil began extracting oil there in 1958. Before long, the indigenous peoples of the Niger Delta suffered from pollution, destruction of the mangrove forests, and depletion of fish stocks that sustained them. Gas flares constantly lit up the sky, fouling the air and denying generations a glimpse of a dark night. The despoliation of traditional Ogoni land in the Niger Delta inspired Saro-Wiwa to lead an international, nonviolent campaign targeting Shell. For his commitment, Saro-Wiwa was arrested by the Nigerian dictatorship, subjected to a sham trial, and hanged with eight other Ogoni activists. I visited the Niger Delta and Ogoniland in 1998, and met Ken's family. His father, Jim Wiwa, did not mince words: "Shell has a hand in the killing of my own son."

Family members sued Shell Oil, charging it with complicity in the executions. They were granted their day in U.S. court under the Alien Tort Claims Act, which allows people outside the United States to bring charges against an offender in U.S. courts when the charges amount to war crimes, genocide, torture, or, as in the case of the Ogoni Nine, extrajudicial, summary execution. Despite Shell's efforts to have the case (*Wiwa v. Shell*) thrown out, it was set to be tried in a New York federal court two weeks ago. After several delays, Shell settled, agreeing to pay $15.5 million.

Saro-Wiwa's son, Ken Wiwa, said,

> We now have an opportunity to draw a line on the sad past and ... face the future with some hope that what we've done here will have helped to change the way in which businesses regard their operations abroad ... We need to focus on the development needs of the people ... We've created evidence, an example, that with enough commitment to nonviolence and dialogue, you can begin to build some kind of creative justice. And we hope that people will take their signals from that and push for similar examples of creative justice, where communities and all the stakeholders where oil production is are able to mutually benefit from oil production, rather than exploitation and degradation of the environment.

Peruvian indigenous populations have been protesting nonviolently since April, with road blockades a popular tactic. At issue is the so-called U.S./Peru Trade Promotion Agreement, which would override protections of indigenous land, granting access to foreign corporations for resource extraction.

This week, eyewitnesses allege that Peruvian special forces police carried out a massacre at one of the blockades. Pizango, the leader of the national indigenous organization the Peruvian Jungle Interethnic Development Association, accused the government of President Alan Garcia of ordering the attack:

> Our brothers are cornered. I want to put the responsibility on the government. We are going to put the responsibility on Alan Garcia's government for ordering this genocide ... They've said that we indigenous peoples are against the system, but, no, we want development, but from our perspective, development that adheres to legal conventions ... The government has not consulted us. Not only am I being persecuted, but I feel that my life is in danger, because I am defending the rights of the peoples, the legitimate rights that the indigenous people have.

Saro-Wiwa told me in 1994, just before he returned to Nigeria, "I'm a marked man." Pizango has challenged the powerful Peruvian government and the corporate interests it represents. Pizango is now marked, but still alive. Will the international community allow him and the indigenous people he represents to suffer the same fate as Saro-Wiwa and the Ogoni people?

UNDO THE COUP

The first coup d'etat in Central America since the Cold War occurred last Sunday in Honduras. Honduran soldiers roused democratically elected President Manuel Zelaya from his bed and flew him into exile in Costa Rica. The coup, led by Honduran General Romeo Vasquez, has been condemned by the United States, the European Union, the United Nations, the Organization of American States, and all of Honduras' immediate national neighbors. Mass protests have erupted on the streets of Honduras, with reports that elements in the military loyal to Zelaya are rebelling against the coup.

The United States has a long history of domination in the hemisphere. President Barack Obama and Secretary of State Hillary Clinton can chart a new course, away from the dark days of military dictatorship, repression, and murder. Obama indicated such a direction when he spoke in April at the Summit of the Americas: "[A]t times we sought to dictate our terms. But I pledge to you that we seek an equal partnership. There is no senior partner and junior partner in our relations."

Two who know well the history of dictated U.S. terms are Dr. Juan Almendares, a medical doctor and award-winning human rights activist in Honduras, and the American clergyman Father Roy Bourgeois, a priest who for years has fought to close the U.S. Army's School of the Americas (SOA) at Fort Benning, Georgia. Both men link the coup in Honduras to the SOA.

The SOA, renamed in 2000 the Western Hemisphere Institute for Security Cooperation (WHINSEC), is the U.S. military facility that trains Latin American soldiers. The SOA has trained more than 60,000 soldiers, many of whom have returned home and committed human rights abuses, torture, extrajudicial execution, and massacres.

Almendares, targeted by Honduran death squads and the military, has been the victim of that training. He talked to me from Tegucigalpa, the Honduran capital: "Most of this military have been trained by the School of the Americas ... They have been guardians of the multinational business from the United States or from other countries ... The army in Honduras has links with very powerful people, very rich, wealthy people who keep the poverty in the country. We are occupied by your country."

Born in Louisiana, Bourgeois became a Catholic priest in 1972. He worked in Bolivia and was forced out by the (SOA-trained) dictator General Hugo Banzer. The assassination of Archbishop Oscar Romero and the murders of four Catholic churchwomen in El Salvador in 1980 led him to protest where some of the killers were trained: Fort Benning's SOA. After six Jesuit priests, their housekeeper, and her daughter were murdered in El Salvador in 1989, Bourgeois founded SOA Watch and has built an international movement to close the SOA.

Honduran coup leader Vasquez attended the SOA in 1976 and 1984. Air Force General Luis Javier Prince Suazo, who also participated in the coup, was trained at the SOA in 1996.

Bourgeois' SOA Watch office is just yards from the Fort Benning gates. He has been frustrated in recent years by increased secrecy at SOA/WHINSEC. He told me, "They are trying to present the school as one of democracy and transparency, but we are not able to get the names of those trained here—for over five years. However, there was a little sign of hope when the U.S. House approved an amendment to the defense authorization bill last week that would force the school to release names and ranks of people who train here." The amendment still has to make it through the House-Senate conference committee.

Bourgeois speaks with the same urgency that he has for decades. His voice is well known at Fort Benning, where he was first arrested more than 25 years ago when he climbed a tree at night near the barracks of Salvadoran soldiers who were training there at the time.

Bourgeois blasted a recording of the voice of Romero in his last address before he was assassinated. The archbishop was speaking directly to Salvadoran soldiers in his country: "In the name of God, in the name of this suffering people whose cry rises to heaven more loudly each day, I implore you, I beg you, I order you: Stop the repression."

Almost 30 years later, in a country bordering Romero's El Salvador, the United States has a chance to change course and support the democratic institutions of Honduras. Undo the coup.

GRASSROOTS
ACTIVISM

FROM THE BAYOU TO BAGHDAD:
MISSION ACCOMPLISHED?

During the second anniversary of Hurricane Katrina, several dozen public-housing residents and activists marched to the headquarters of the Housing Authority of New Orleans. The marchers occupied the offices for hours. As the military and police surrounded the building, Sharon Sears Jasper, a displaced resident of the St. Bernard housing project, spoke:

> We are not going to stop. We refuse to let you tear our homes down and destroy our lives. The government, the president of the United States, you all have failed us. Our people have been displaced too long. Our people are dying of stress, depression, and broken families. We demand that you open all public housing. Bring our families home now.

In contrast, the day before, I had asked Mayor Ray Nagin if he made any demands of President Bush as they dined together the previous night. Bush had just spoken at a school named for Dr. Martin Luther King Jr., whose issues of race and poverty are starkly laid bare in New Orleans. Unlike those who had lost their homes, the mayor replied, "It wasn't a time for demands."

Tracie Washington is the president of the Louisiana Justice Institute and a lifelong resident of New Orleans. She says only a quarter of the more than 5,000 affordable housing units in New Orleans are filled. "There is a feeling by our government that public housing of old needs to be dismantled, buildings shut. We have litigation going right now to change that, but it's horribly slow, and it's tragic."

She describes the plan by which public housing will be converted to "mixed-income" developments: "Some of these developments that are closed down took in no water. But the decision was made to take advantage of an opportunity. Hurricane Katrina came. 'Look what we can do. We can keep these people away from here, bring in the bulldozers, tear down this housing.'"

It is not just renters. Private housing is being demolished as well. Washington described how the city instituted a stunning policy to allow the legal demolition of homes. Whereas once homeowners would have at least 120 days and several layers of appeals to prevent their homes from being demolished, Nagin instituted an "Imminent Health Threat Demolition" ordinance. He now gives residents only 30 days to stop demolition.

To the tens of thousands of New Orleanians scattered across the country, the city's scant notice—a sticker attached to the property plus mentions on a city website and in the Times-Picayune newspaper—is clearly insufficient. According to the Times-Picayune, in addition to homes being destroyed, liens are placed on properties for the cost of the demolition, setting the stage for the displaced owners to lose their property to the city.

That is why groups like Common Ground Collective, the Louisiana Justice Institute, and People's Hurricane Relief Fund and Oversight Coalition are taking action, on the streets and in the courts.

According to Common Ground's founder, Malik Rahim, of the more than 12,000 people previously in the lower Ninth Ward, only about 400 live there now. Where once there was a dense, vibrant African-American neighborhood, I walked with Rahim through tall marsh grass, vacant lots, and destroyed churches and schools. A few isolated, damaged brick homes remain.

Curtis Muhammad, a longtime resident of New Orleans and a member of the People's Organizing Committee, believes the economic interests driving the failing reconstruction must be investigated. "People see [Donald] Trump down here trying to buy real estate, the big tycoons. The gated communities are growing faster and faster. Look at public housing. They could have knocked that out in a week if they wanted to, cleaned it up. That's a lot of people that they could have just brought home. You can't explain that."

Two years after Katrina, as Bush flew from the bayou to Baghdad, a People's Hurricane tribunal—putting every level of government on trial—was wrapping up in New Orleans. A group was selling a T-shirt there that reads, "Don't believe the hype. Gulf Coast recovery is not 'slow'—it is a privatization scheme that takes away our homes, schools, hospitals and human rights." Mission accomplished?

TIME IS RUNNING OUT
FOR BROTHER AND SISTER

Troy Anthony Davis and his sister, Martina Correia, are fighting for their lives. Troy faces death by lethal injection at the hands of the state of Georgia, and Martina has breast cancer. Their parallel battles against insuperable odds will remain an inspiring story—provided they live. Time is running out.

Troy Davis turned 39 years old behind bars on October 9. He was accused of the shooting death of off-duty police officer Mark Allen McPhail in a Burger King parking lot in Savannah, Georgia, late one August night in 1989. A homeless man was being beaten over a can of beer. Davis intervened, but fled when the assailant threatened him with a gun. McPhail, working that night as a security guard at the Greyhound bus station, intervened next and was killed. Davis has maintained his innocence throughout.

The state of Georgia presented 15 witnesses in its prosecution of Davis, an African American. He was found guilty and sentenced to death. Since his conviction, seven of the nine non-police witnesses have recanted their testimony, alleging police coercion in gaining their testimony. One of those who has not recanted is Sylvester Coles, whom others identified as the shooter. Despite these witness recantations, the courts have refused to re-open the case. Davis faces execution by lethal injection, a method several states have moratoriums against. Last week, the U.S. Supreme Court agreed to hear arguments on the constitutionality of lethal injection.

Throughout Davis' ordeal, his sister, Martina Correia, has fought for his release. She spoke before the Georgia State Board of Pardons and Paroles the day before Davis was to be executed last July. The board granted a stay of execution. Correia described the hearing:

> Troy's clemency hearing was the longest clemency hearing in the history of Georgia. And they came back and decided to give Troy an up-to-90-day stay.
>
> But what took place was, five of the seven witnesses who recanted came forward, including the man who was being attacked that night, and said, "I never saw Troy Davis in the parking lot." One gentleman said he was a police snitch, and the police had paid him several times to lie on people, and that he just went by the headlines, and the police gave him everything else. Another witness stated he couldn't read and write. The police officer was giving them pre-typed statements. So nobody knew what was going on, but they were threatened and intimidated. And they came before the Georgia Parole Board, and they said that under oath.

Congressman John Lewis spoke on behalf of Davis. He told me, "Troy Davis is innocent, and that's why I testified before the parole board. No person, when you have all these questions, should be put to death."

While Martina battles for her brother's life, she is fighting for her own:

> I've been battling metastatic breast cancer for six and a half years. In 2001, I was told that I had six months to live, and I asked God to just give me the strength to see my son grow up and watch my brother Troy walk free. And I've dedicated my life—even though I have not worked in almost seven years due to constant chemotherapy and treatment, I volunteer in my community, and I work and do human rights work to not only help Troy but to help other people who are facing the same situation. So my battle is more than just for Troy. My battle is for everyone to fight injustice.

Davis' case is a textbook example of the racial disparity in the United States, principally the Deep South, in the imposition of the death penalty.

The American Bar Association has singled out Georgia's racial disparities in capital-offense sentencing, saying it has allowed inadequate defense counsel and been "virtually alone in not providing indigent defendants sentenced to death with counsel for state habeas proceedings."

The Georgia Supreme Court has agreed to hear Davis' motion for a new trial, scheduled for November 13. In a new trial, the prosecution could face the bulk of its witnesses recanting their earlier testimonies. This month, on October 13, there will be a major march on Davis' behalf in Savannah, a city familiar with Martina's face: her picture adorns the side of the mammography van that serves indigent women.

Three million women in the United States have breast cancer. African-American women have an overall lower survival rate than white women. The coming months will tell whether Martina and Troy can defy the odds.

APRIL 16, 2008

THE ORANGEBURG MASSACRE

Senator Barack Obama is clearly a bad bowler. The networks rolled the video clip of his gutter ball endlessly across our TV screens. It was an Internet favorite. The media served it and the public ate it up. MSNBC's Chris Matthews, the host of *Hardball*, hammed it up when interviewing Obama on the campus of West Chester University in Pennsylvania:

> Matthews: One of the perks, Senator, of being president of the United States is that you have your own bowling alley. Are you ready to bowl from day one?

> Obama: Obviously, I am not.

But in fact, it was not too long ago when African Americans were not allowed in some bowling alleys. In Orangeburg, South Carolina, three young African-American men were killed for protesting against that town's segregated bowling alley.

It was February 8, 1968, months before the assassinations of Martin Luther King Jr. and Robert F. Kennedy. It was more than two years before the massacre of students at Kent State University in Ohio. Students at

South Carolina State University were protesting for access to the town's only bowling alley. Cleveland Sellers, a student at the time at that historically black college, was also a member of the Student Nonviolent Coordinating Committee and an organizer of the protests. In a recent interview, he said about that night 40 years ago,

> It was a cold night ... this was the fourth day of activities around the effort to desegregate the bowling alley ... The students had built a bonfire to keep themselves warm and build morale. They were trying to work out some strategy. What should they do next? Should they go back to the bowling alley, where they had been arrested on Tuesday night? Should they go to the City Hall? Should they go to the state Capitol? And they thought that they were in an area that was pretty safe and secure, and they never expected the police to open fire.

Sellers is now director of the African-American studies program at the University of South Carolina. His memory is vivid: "The darkness turned to light as the police opened fire, nine highway patrolmen and one local police officer firing rifles and shotguns and pistols. It was a shock to many of the students that there [were] no bullhorns, no whistles, no anything that indicated that this kind of extremely lethal action would be taken on these students."

Survivor Robert Lee Davis recalled the event in an oral history project conducted by Jack Bass, who was a reporter at the time and now is a professor at the College of Charleston:

> It was a barrage of shots ... maybe six or seven seconds. Boom, boom, boom, boom, boom, boom, boom! Students was hollering, yelling and running ... I got up to run, and I took one step, and that's all I could remember. I took that one step. I got hit in the back ... this was when I got paralyzed. Students was trampling over me, because they was afraid.

Sellers put the largely unreported and forgotten Orangeburg Massacre in context:

> It's ironic that here we are 40 years later, and the issue of poverty and the issue of war are still issues that are pertinent all around America again. And I think that it just says that in 1968, with the assassination of Dr. King and

with the decline in the civil rights movement during that period, that a number of issues were left unachieved.

There have been advances in the 40 years since the Orangeburg Massacre. Now, rather than protesting for access to a bowling alley, an African-American man is a leading candidate for the Democratic nomination for president of the United States, his bowling flubs merely the object of ridicule. But the three young African-American men murdered that night in Orangeburg—Samuel Hammond, Delano Middleton, and Henry Smith—are not with us to share in the progress. They are hardly remembered at all.

The media this week recognize the one-year anniversary of the deadly shootings at Virginia Tech, in which a lone, disturbed gunman killed 30 students and faculty members. It is an important date on which to reflect. The Orangeburg Massacre deserves a place in our national consciousness as well. We need media that provide historical context, that offer more than a one-year perspective on our society. Instead, the mainstream media keep throwing gutter balls.

DON'T CAGE DISSENT

The bulwark against tyranny is dissent. Open opposition, the right to challenge those in power, is a mainstay of any healthy democracy. The Democratic and Republican conventions will test the commitment of the two dominant U.S. political parties to the cherished tradition of dissent. Things are not looking good.

Denver's CBS4 News just reported that the city is planning on jailing arrested Democratic convention protesters at a warehouse with barbed-wire-topped cages and signs warning of the threat of stun gun use. Meanwhile, a federal judge has ruled that a designated protest area is legal, despite claims that protesters will be too far from the Democratic delegates to be heard.

The full spectrum of police and military will also be on hand at the Democratic convention in Denver, many of these units coordinated by a "fusion center." These centers are springing up around the country as an outgrowth of the post–9/11 national-security system. Erin Rosa of the online Colorado Independent recently published a report on the Denver fusion center, which will be sharing information with the U.S. Secret

Service, the FBI, and the U.S. Northern Command. The center is set up to gather and distribute "intelligence" about "suspicious activities," which, Rosa points out, "can include taking pictures or taking notes. The definition is very broad."

Civil rights advocates fear the fusion center could enable unwarranted spying on protesters exercising their First Amendment rights at the convention. Documents obtained by I-Witness Video, a group that documents police abuses and demonstrations, revealed that the CIA and the Defense Intelligence Agency were receiving intelligence about the protests at the 2004 Republican National Convention in New York City. The growing problem is that legal, peaceful protesters are ending up on federal databases and watch lists with scant legal oversight.

Former FBI agent Mike German is now a national security policy counsel for the American Civil Liberties Union. He said, "It's unclear who is actually in charge and whose rules apply to the information that's being collected and shared and distributed through these fusion centers." Maryland State Police were recently exposed infiltrating groups like the Baltimore Coalition Against the Death Penalty. German explains how police expand

> beyond normal law-enforcement functions, and start becoming intelligence collectors against protest groups. The reports that we obtained ... make clear that there was no indication of any sort of criminal activity. And yet, that investigation went on for 14 months, and these reports were uploaded into a federal database ... When all these agencies are authorized to go out and start collecting this information and putting it in areas where it's accessible by the intelligence community, it's a very dangerous proposition for our democracy.

After Barack Obama became the presumptive Democratic nominee, the protest coalition in Denver splintered, as many were motivated originally by the anticipated nomination of the more hawkish Hillary Clinton. An anarchist group, Unconventional Denver, actually offered to call off its protests if Denver would redirect the $50 million federal grant it is receiving for security to "reinvest their police budget toward real community security: new elementary schools; health care for the uninsured; providing clean, renewable energy." The plea has not been answered. The city, meanwhile, is stocking up on "less-lethal" pepper-ball rifles and has set aside a space for permitted protesting that some are referring to as the "Freedom Cage."

In the Twin Cities on the evening Obama was giving his Democratic acceptance speech in June, the St. Paul Police Department arrested a 50-year-old man peacefully handing out leaflets promoting a September 1 march on the Republican National Convention. After mass arrests at the RNC in Philadelphia in 2000 and roughly 1,800 arrests in New York City in 2004, ACLU Minnesota predicts hundreds will be arrested in St. Paul, and is organizing and training 75 lawyers to defend them.

For now, the eyes of the world are on the Beijing Olympics. Sportswriter Dave Zirin is reporting on the suppression of protests that are occurring there. He has an interesting perspective, as he is a member of the Baltimore Coalition Against the Death Penalty, the anti-death-penalty group infiltrated in Maryland. He told me, "Our taxpayer dollars went to pay people to infiltrate and take notes on our meetings, and it's absolutely enraging … a lot of this Homeland Security funding is an absolute sham … it's being used to actually crush dissent, not to keep us safer in any real way." The lack of freedom of speech in China is getting a little attention in the news. But what about the crackdown on dissent here at home? Dissent is essential to the functioning of a democratic society. There is no more important time than now.

A TALE OF TWO NOBEL NATIONS

STOCKHOLM, Sweden—The days are short here in Stockholm, which is so far north that winter daylight is limited to about four hours a day. But the city is buzzing with visitors, media, and activities, for the Nobel Prizes are being given this week. While the Nobels recognize lifetime achievements in medicine, chemistry, physics, literature, economics, and peace, and Sweden is a paragon among progressive social democracies, there is another side to Sweden and the Nobels that warrants a closer look.

Alfred Nobel made a fortune as an inventor, principally for his invention of dynamite. He died in 1896, leaving most of his fortune to endow the Nobel Prizes. Nobel lived in a time when European rivalries and wars were the norm. He believed the destructive power of his inventions could promote peace. He wrote to his lifelong friend, peace activist Bertha von Suttner, who would win the Nobel Peace Prize almost a decade after his death, "Perhaps my factories will put an end to war even sooner than your Congresses; on the day when two army corps will be able to annihilate each other in a second, all civilised nations will recoil with horror and disband their troops."

If only. Now countries can destroy each other many times over, but instead of recoiling in horror, they just continue buying ever more destructive weapons, ironically making Sweden one of the world leaders, per capita, in weapons exports. Nobel turned Swedish munitions into a stable, multinational enterprise. In 1894, he acquired the weapons company Bofors, now a subsidiary of the weapons maker BAE Systems. While the world's eyes are on the Nobel Prize winners, several Swedes are facing prison time for taking direct action against Bofors.

Cattis Laska is a member of the antiwar groups Ofog and Avrusta, Swedish for "mischief" and "disarm." She told me about their protests against the Swedish weapons industry:

> We went into two weapon factories the same night. Two went into Saab Bofors Dynamics (while General Motors bought Saab's auto division, Saab in Sweden makes weapons) ... and they disarmed about 20 [grenade launchers] ... to prevent them from being used in wars. They did it by using a hammer. There's very much details in those launchers, so they have to be perfect. So it's enough just to scrape inside to disable them. And then, me and another person went into the BAE Systems Bofors factory, where we disabled some parts for howitzers going to India. We also used hammers.

Like the Plowshares activists in the United States, they follow the biblical prescription from Isaiah 2:4, turning "swords into plowshares."

Annika Spalde also participated in the actions: "We sell weapons to countries at war and to countries who seriously violate human rights, and still these sales just grow bigger and bigger, so we feel that we, as ordinary citizens, have a responsibility to act then and to physically try to stop these weapons from being shipped off." Spalde is awaiting trial. Laska has been sentenced to three months in prison.

Traditional Swedish politics also are in flux. Brian Palmer is an American, a former Harvard lecturer, who has immigrated to Sweden and become a Swedish citizen. Palmer has penned a biography of Sweden's prime minister, Fredrik Reinfeldt. Palmer credits Reinfeldt, 43, with leading the shift away from the progressive social policies for which Sweden has become world-famous. He said Reinfeldt, in 1993, "wrote a book, *The Sleeping People*, where he said that the welfare state should only prevent starvation, nothing beyond that. After being elected ... one of his first major visits abroad was to George Bush in the White House."

Reinfeldt and his Moderate Party hired Karl Rove as a political consultant to help with the election coming in 2010. Palmer went on, "We have a real kind of silent war on the labor movement. We have a rather dramatic change in the tax system, abolishing the inheritance tax and most property taxes, cutbacks in social-welfare institutions." This week, a new coalition of center-left political parties formed to challenge this rightward drift.

The U.S. electorate has thoroughly rebuked the Bush administration, handing Barack Obama and the Democrats a mandate for change on issues of war and health care, among others. One of the world's leading laboratories for innovative social policies, Sweden is now wrestling with its own future. Those seeking change in the United States would be wise to watch Sweden, beyond Nobel week.

BUSH AND THE MONKEY WRENCH GUY

OR: ONE MAN'S BID TO AID THE ENVIRONMENT

Tim DeChristopher is an economics student at the University of Utah in Salt Lake City. He had just finished his last final exam before winter break. One of the exam questions was: If the oil and gas companies are the only ones who bid on public lands, are the true costs of oil and gas exploitation reflected in the prices paid?

DeChristopher was inspired. He finished the exam, threw on his red parka and went off to the controversial Bureau of Land Management (BLM) land auction that the Southern Utah Wilderness Alliance called "the Bush administration's last great gift to the oil and gas industry." Instead of joining the protest outside, he registered as a bidder, then bought 22,000 acres of public land. That is, he successfully bid on the public properties, located near the Arches and Canyonlands National Parks and Dinosaur National Monument, and other pristine areas. The price tag: more than $1.7 million.

He told me: "Once I started buying up every parcel, they understood pretty clearly what was going on ... they stopped the auction, and some federal agents came in and took me out. I guess there was a lot of chaos, and they didn't really know how to proceed at that point."

Patrick Shea, a former BLM director, is representing DeChristopher. Shea told the *Deseret News*, "What Tim did was in the best tradition of civil disobedience, he did this without causing any physical or material harm. His purpose was to draw attention to the illegitimacy and immorality of the process."

There is a long tradition of disrupting land development in Utah. In his memoir, *Desert Solitaire*, Edward Abbey, the writer and activist, wrote, "Wilderness. The word itself is music ... We scarcely know what we mean by the term, though the sound of it draws all whose nerves and emotions have not yet been irreparably stunned, deadened, numbed by the caterwauling of commerce, the sweating scramble for profit and domination."

Abbey's novel *The Monkey Wrench Gang* inspired a generation of environmental activists to take "direct action," disrupting "development." As the *Salt Lake Tribune* reported on DeChristopher,

> He didn't pour sugar into a bulldozer's gas tank. He didn't spike a tree or set a billboard on fire. But wielding only a bidder's paddle, a University of Utah student just as surely monkey-wrenched a federal oil- and gas-lease sale Friday, ensuring that thousands of acres near two southern Utah national parks won't be opened to drilling anytime soon.

Likewise, the late Utah Phillips, folk musician, activist, and longtime Utah resident, often invoked the Industrial Workers of the World adage: "Direct action gets the goods."

More than just scenic beauty will be harmed by these BLM sales. Drilling impacts air and water quality. According to *High Country News*, "The BLM had not analyzed impacts on ozone levels from some 2,300 wells drilled in the area since 2004 ... nor had it predicted air impacts from the estimated 6,300 new wells approved in the plan." ProPublica reports that the Colorado River "powers homes for 3 million people, nourishes 15 percent of the nation's crops and provides drinking water to one in 12 Americans. Now a rush to develop domestic oil, gas and uranium deposits along the river and its tributaries threatens its future."

After being questioned by federal authorities, DeChristopher was released. The U.S. attorney is currently weighing charges against the student. DeChristopher reflects,

This has really been emotional and hopeful for me to see the kind of support over the last couple of days ... for all the problems that people can talk about in this country and for all the apathy and the eight years of oppression and the decades of eroding civil liberties, America is still very much the kind of place that when you stand up for what is right, you never stand alone.

His disruption of the auction has temporarily blocked the Bush-enabled land grab by the oil and gas industries. If DeChristopher can come up with $45,000 by December 29, he can make the first payment on the land, possibly avoiding any claim of fraud. If the BLM opts to re-auction the land, that can't happen until after the Obama administration takes over.

The outcome of the sales, if they happen at all, will probably be different, thanks to the direct action of an activist, raising his voice—and his bidding paddle—in opposition.

SEATTLE'S LESSONS FOR LONDON

Protests dominate the news as world leaders gather in London for the Group of Twenty meeting. War, the economy, corporate globalization, and grass-roots opposition to financial bailouts are at the forefront.

Executives receive golden parachutes while workers and unions are forced to make concessions. President Barack Obama has inherited a slew of deep, interlocked crises, yet elicits broad global hope that he can be an agent of change.

Obama last week held an "Open for Questions" town hall meeting, streamed online, with questions posed by the public and voted on to rank their popularity. Obama answered a question about marijuana:

> Three point five million people voted. I have to say that there was one question that was voted on that ranked fairly high and that was whether legalizing marijuana would improve the economy and job creation. And I don't know what this says about the online audience … this was a fairly popular question; we want to make sure that it was answered. The answer is, no, I don't think that is a good strategy to grow our economy.

That question's popularity might indicate audience concern with U.S. drug policy, and the enormous toll on our society of the so-called war on drugs.

I am traveling around the country this spring, visiting more than 70 cities. In Seattle, I interviewed a strong critic of U.S. drug laws, who said, "I ... support the legalization of all drugs."

These words come from an unlikely advocate: former Seattle Police Chief Norm Stamper. Stamper is an advisory board member of the National Organization for the Reform of Marijuana Laws and a speaker for the organization Law Enforcement Against Prohibition. He explained,

> We have spent a trillion dollars prosecuting that war ... and what do we have to show for it? [D]rugs are more readily available today at lower prices and higher levels of potency than ever before. So it's a colossal failure. And the only way to put these cartels out of business and to restore health and safety to our neighborhoods is to regulate that commerce as opposed to prohibiting it.

As Stamper pushes for reform, his successor as Seattle police chief, Gil Kerlikowske, is, as Stamper blogged, "on his way to the other Washington to assume the mantle of 'drug czar' ... to make his case for a continuation of the nation's drug laws."

Secretary of State Hillary Clinton admitted recently, en route to Mexico, "Our insatiable demand for illegal drugs fuels the drug trade." It also fuels a rising U.S. prison population (some cash-strapped states are simply releasing nonviolent drug offenders to save money), the militarization of the U.S.–Mexico border, and the epidemic of drug-related violence in Mexico. Drug cartels purchase AK-47 assault rifles and other arms in the United States, then smuggle them into Mexico. Paul Helmke, president of the Brady Center to Prevent Gun Violence, told me recently, "The folks in Mexico have figured out what criminals in the U.S. figured out a long time ago: our weak and nearly nonexistent laws in the U.S. are making it very easy for these guns to get to Mexico."

With the increasing state-by-state acceptance of the medical uses of marijuana, with decriminalization of possession of small amounts in various jurisdictions and with the high cost of imprisonment versus treatment, public sentiment seems disposed to favor a change.

It took Stamper years to learn the hard lessons of the failed war on drugs. Hard lessons seem to be his forte.

He was the Seattle police chief during the World Trade Organization protests of 1999: "I made major mistakes leading up to that week and during that week ... Not vetoing a decision to use chemical agents, also known as tear gas, against hundreds of nonviolent demonstrators." He now sounds more like one of the WTO protesters his forces tear-gassed: "We're now reaping what we have sown in the form of unbridled globalization and unfettered free trade ... it's time for all of us in this country, as we attempt to pull ourselves out of this global economic meltdown, to really take a look at what issues of social and economic justice mean within the context of globalization."

The leaders of the G-20 in London, and those at the NATO summit to follow, have an opportunity to learn from Norm Stamper, to instruct their security to put away the Tasers and the tear gas, and to shock the world by seriously considering the voices of the protesters outside.

DISCLOSURE OF "SECRETS" IN THE '70S DIDN'T DESTROY THE NATION

President Barack Obama promised "more transparent ... more creative" government. His release of the torture memos, and the Pentagon's expected release of more photos of detainee abuse, is a step in the right direction. Yet he assured the CIA that he will not prosecute those who followed the instructions to torture from the Bush administration. Congress might not agree with this leniency, with prominent senators calling for investigations.

Senator Carl Levin, D-MI, the chairman of the Senate Armed Services Committee, just released a 262-page report titled "Inquiry Into the Treatment of Detainees in U.S. Custody." Levin said the report "represents a condemnation of both the Bush administration's interrogation policies and of senior administration officials who attempted to shift the blame for abuse ... to low-ranking soldiers. Claims ... that detainee abuses could be chalked up to the unauthorized acts of a 'few bad apples' were simply false." Senators Patrick Leahy, D-VT, and Dianne Feinstein, D-CA, also are proposing investigations.

The Senate interest in investigation has backers in the U.S. House, from Speaker Nancy Pelosi, D-CA, to Chairman of the House Judiciary

Committee John Conyers, D-MI, who told the Huffington Post recently, "We're coming after these guys."

Amrit Singh, staff attorney for the American Civil Liberties Union, said the Pentagon's photos "provide visual proof that prisoner abuse by U.S. personnel was not aberrational but widespread, reaching far beyond the walls of Abu Ghraib. Their disclosure is critical for helping the public understand the scope and scale of prisoner abuse as well as for holding senior officials accountable for authorizing or permitting such abuse." The ACLU also won a ruling to obtain documents relating to the CIA's destruction of 92 videotapes of harsh interrogations. The tapes are gone, supposedly, but notes about the content of the tapes remain, and a federal judge has ordered their release.

In December 2002, when the Bush torture program was well under way, then–Secretary of Defense Donald Rumsfeld signed off on a series of harsh interrogation techniques described in a memo written by William Haynes II (one of the "Bush Six" being investigated by Spanish Judge Baltasar Garzon). At the bottom of the memo, under his signature, Rumsfeld scrawled: "I stand for 8–10 hours a day. Why is standing limited to 4 hours?" Rumsfeld zealously classified information in his years in government.

A similar crisis confronted the U.S. public in the mid-1970s. While the Watergate scandal was unfolding, widespread evidence was mounting of illegal government activity, including domestic spying and the infiltration and disruption of legal political groups, mostly antiwar groups, in a broad-based, secret government crackdown on dissent. In response, the Senate Select Committee to Study Governmental Operations with Respect to Intelligence Activities was formed. It came to be known as the Church Committee, named after its chairman, Idaho Democratic Senator Frank Church. The Church Committee documented and exposed extraordinary activities of the CIA and FBI, such as CIA efforts to assassinate foreign leaders, and the FBI's COINTELPRO (counterintelligence) program, which extensively spied on prominent leaders, like Dr. Martin Luther King Jr.

It is not only the practices that are similar, but the people. Frederick A. O. Schwarz Jr., general counsel to the Church Committee, noted two people who were active in the Ford White House and attempted to block the committee's work: "Rumsfeld and then [Dick] Cheney were people who felt that nothing should be known about these secret operations, and there should be as much disruption as possible."

Church's widow, Bethine Church, now 86, continues to be very politically active in Idaho. She was so active in Washington in the 1970s that she was known as "Idaho's third senator." She said there needs to be a similar investigation today:

> When you think of all the things that the Church Committee tried to straighten out and when you think of the terrific secrecy that Cheney and all of these people dealt with, they were always secretive about everything, and they didn't want anything known. I think people have to know what went on. And that's why I think an independent committee [is needed], outside of the Congress, that just looked at the whole problem and everything that happened.

TWO STANDARDS OF DETENTION

Scott Roeder, the anti-abortion zealot charged with killing Dr. George Tiller, has been busy. He called the Associated Press from the Sedgwick County Jail in Kansas, saying, "I know there are many other similar events planned around the country as long as abortion remains legal." Charged with first-degree murder and aggravated assault, he is expected to be arraigned July 28. The Associated Press recently reported that Roeder has been proclaiming from his jail cell that the killing of abortion providers is justified. According to the report, the Reverend Donald Spitz of the Virginia-based Army of God sent Roeder seven pamphlets defending "defensive action," or killing of abortion clinic workers.

Spitz's militant Army of God website calls Roeder an "American hero," proclaiming, "George Tiller would normally murder between 10 and 30 children ... each day ... when he was stopped by Scott Roeder."

The site, with biblical quotes suggesting killing is justified, hosts writings by Paul Hill, who killed Dr. John Britton and his security escort in Pensacola, Florida, and by Eric Rudolph, who bombed a Birmingham, Alabama, women's health clinic, killing its part-time security guard.

On Spitz's website, Rudolph continues to write about abortion: "I believe that deadly force is indeed justified in an attempt to stop it."

Juxtapose Roeder's advocacy from jail with the conditions of Fahad Hashmi. Hashmi is a U.S. citizen who grew up in Queens, New York, and went to Brooklyn College. He went to graduate school in Britain and was arrested there in 2006 for allegedly allowing an acquaintance to stay with him for two weeks. That acquaintance, Junaid Babar, allegedly kept at Hashmi's apartment a bag containing ponchos and socks, which Babar later delivered to an al-Qaeda operative. Babar was arrested and agreed to cooperate with the authorities in exchange for leniency.

While the evidence against Hashmi is secret, it probably stems from the claims of the informant Babar.

Fahad Hashmi was extradited to New York, where he has been held in pretrial detention for more than two years. His brother Faisal described the conditions:

> He is kept in solitary confinement for two straight years, 23- to 24-hours lockdown ... Within his own cell, he's restricted in the movements he's allowed to do. He's not allowed to talk out loud within his own cell ... He is being videotaped and monitored at all times. He can be punished ... denied family visits, if they say his certain movements are martial arts ... that they deem as incorrect. He has Special Administrative Measures (SAMs) ... against him.

Hashmi cannot contact the media, and even his lawyers have to be extremely cautious when discussing his case, for fear of imprisonment themselves. His attorney Sean Maher told me,

> This issue of the SAMs ... of keeping people in solitary confinement when they're presumed innocent, is before the European Court of Human Rights. They are deciding whether they will prevent any European country from extraditing anyone to the United States if there is a possibility that they will be placed under SAMs ... because they see it as a violation ... to hold someone in solitary confinement with sensory deprivation, months before trial.

Similarly, animal rights and environmental activists, prosecuted as "eco-terrorists," have been shipped to the Federal Bureau of Prisons' new "communication management units" (CMUs). Andrew Stepanian was recently released and described for me the CMU as "a prison within the actual prison ... The unit doesn't have normal telephone communication to your family ... normal visits are denied ... you have to make an appointment to make one phone call a week, and that needs to be done with the oversight of ... a live monitor."

Stepanian observed that up to 70 percent of CMU prisoners are Muslim—hence CMU's nickname, "Little Guantánamo." As with Hashmi, it seems that the U.S. government seeks to strip terrorism suspects of legal due process and access to the media—whether in Guantánamo or in the secretive new CMUs. The American Civil Liberties Union is suing U.S. Attorney General Eric Holder and the Bureau of Prisons over the CMUs.

Nonviolent activists like Stepanian, and Muslims like Hashmi, secretly and dubiously charged, are held in draconian conditions, while Roeder trumpets from jail the extreme anti-abortion movement's decades-long campaign of intimidation, vandalism, arson, and murder.

OBAMA'S MILITARY IS SPYING
ON U.S. PEACE GROUPS

Antiwar activists in Olympia, Washington, have exposed U.S. Army spying and infiltration of their groups, as well as intelligence gathering by the U.S. Air Force, the federal Capitol Police, and the Coast Guard.

The infiltration appears to be in direct violation of the Posse Comitatus Act preventing U.S. military deployment for domestic law enforcement, and may strengthen congressional demands for a full-scale investigation of U.S. intelligence activities, like the Church Committee hearings of the 1970s.

Brendan Maslauskas Dunn asked the City of Olympia for documents or e-mails about communications between the Olympia police and the military relating to anarchists, Students for a Democratic Society (SDS), or the Industrial Workers of the World (Dunn's union). Dunn received hundreds of documents. One e-mail contained reference to a "John J. Towery II," who activists discovered was the same person as their fellow activist "John Jacob."

Dunn told me: "John Jacob was actually a close friend of mine, so this week has been pretty difficult for me. He said he was an anarchist. He was really interested in SDS. He got involved with Port Militarization Resistance

(PMR), with Iraq Vets Against the War. He was a kind person. He was a generous person. So it was really just a shock for me."

"Jacob" told the activists he was a civilian employed at Fort Lewis Army Base, and would share information about base activities, which could help PMR organize rallies and protests against public ports being used for troop and Stryker military vehicle deployment to Iraq and Afghanistan. Since 2006, PMR activists have occasionally engaged in civil disobedience, blocking access to the port.

Larry Hildes, an attorney representing Washington activists, says the U.S. attorney prosecuting the cases against them, Brian Kipnis, specifically instructed the army not to hand over any information about its intelligence-gathering activities, despite a court order to do so.

Which is why Dunn's request to Olympia and the documents he obtained are so important.

The military is supposed to be barred from deploying on U.S. soil, or from spying on citizens. Christopher Pyle, now a professor of politics at Mount Holyoke College, was a military intelligence officer. He recalled: "In the 1960s, army intelligence had 1,500 plainclothes agents watching every demonstration of 20 people or more. They had a giant warehouse in Baltimore full of information on the law-abiding activities of American citizens, mainly protest politics." Pyle later investigated the spying for two congressional committees: "As a result of those investigations, the entire U.S. Army Intelligence Command was abolished, and all of its files were burned. Then the Senate Intelligence Committee wrote the Foreign Intelligence Surveillance Act of 1978 to stop the warrantless surveillance of electronic communications."

Representatives Barbara Lee, D-CA, Rush Holt, D-NJ, and others are pushing for a new, comprehensive investigation of all U.S. intelligence activities, of the scale of the Church Committee hearings, which exposed widespread spying on and disruption of legal domestic groups, attempts at assassination of foreign heads of state, and more.

Demands mount for information and accountability for Vice President Dick Cheney's alleged secret assassination squad, President George W. Bush's warrantless wiretapping program, and the CIA's alleged misleading of Congress. But the spying in Olympia occurred well into the Obama administration (and may continue today). President Barack Obama supports retroactive immunity for telecom companies involved in the wiretapping, and has maintained Bush-era reliance on the state secrets privilege. Lee and Holt should take the information uncovered by Brendan Dunn and the Olympia activists and get the investigations started now.

ELECTIONS

NEW VERMONT SENATOR
NOT STANDARD FARE

Bernard Sanders is the new U.S. senator in Vermont. He ran as an independent, but he is the first self-described socialist to be elected to the Senate.

In a fitting matchup for a socialist, Sanders' opponent was multimillionaire businessman Republican Rich Tarrant. As Sanders said before the election, "We are running against the richest man in Vermont, who will spend more per capita than anyone in the history of the U.S. Senate." And, as he pointed out, "I don't mind really if millionaires vote against me; they probably should."

I caught up with Sanders at a pre-election victory rally in Montpelier, the state capital, on the Saturday before the election. The packed high-school cafeteria was decorated with red balloons declaring the name by which he is known across Vermont: Bernie. One attendee looked at his free dinner of chicken and pasta and said, "This is the same stuff they fed me 20 years ago when I went here."

But Bernie, the candidate the diners had gathered for, is not standard fare. With global attention focused on the control of Congress, and the prognosticating political pundits working at a fever pitch, scant notice has been paid to this Senate socialist.

Vermont, the small New England state known traditionally for its steady, stoic, plain-speaking farmers and pragmatic Republicanism, has also in the past 25 years proven to be an incubator for progressive politics. Vermont's congressional delegation is the only one in the country to vote unanimously against the invasion of Iraq. It's a delegation of three: retiring Senator Jim Jeffords, whose switch from Republican to independent in 2001 briefly restored Senate control to the Democrats, Democratic Senator Patrick Leahy and Sanders. Sanders has been the point person in building Vermont's progressive politics.

Sanders is a native of Brooklyn, New York, with an accent and irascibility to prove it, but has been in the Green Mountain State since the late '60s. He was the first Senate candidate of the upstart Liberty Union Party in the early 1970s, where he secured a solid protest vote of 2 percent. Ten years and a few unsuccessful statewide campaigns later, Sanders won the Burlington mayor's race by ten votes, and ushered in the Progressive Era of Vermont politics. In his political autobiography, *Outsider in the House*, Sanders writes of that first mayoral campaign, "The coalition we had brought together—low-income people, hard-pressed working-class homeowners, environmentalists, renters, trade unionists, college students, professors, and now the police—reinforced each other. I cannot emphasize enough how important it was that we developed a 'coalition politics.'" (Why the police? They were union. The Burlington Patrolmen's Association joined the coalition after Sanders vowed to bargain fairly with them, unlike the incumbent mayor.)

How do his socialist policies play with conservative Republican Vermonters?

Truth of the matter is … conservative Republicans don't have health care, don't have money to send their kids to college; conservative Republicans are being thrown out of their jobs as our good paying jobs move to China. And if you talk about those issues, you know what those people say? "I want someone to stand up to protect my economic well-being." Conservative people are very worried about Bush's attacks on our constitutional rights. So the job is to say, "We're not going to agree on every issue, but don't vote against your own interests."

After eight years as Burlington's mayor, and 16 years in the U.S. House of Representatives, Sanders is heading to the Senate. Senators have longer terms, more procedural power, a more prominent bully pulpit. Sanders has policy ideas that cross the simple partisan divides, that unite people by impacting them where they live. He thumbs his nose at millionaires, yet is joining the Senate, which has more than 40 of them. With a lame-duck president and nearly evenly split Senate, where coalitions matter and every vote counts, Bernie Sanders, the socialist senator from Vermont, is poised to make a difference.

NOT ALL IS DEBATED
IN LOVE AND WAR

One pundit called the Democratic presidential debate in Las Vegas "a lovefest." It may well have been, but only because the corporate sponsor of the debate, General Electric–owned NBC News and its cable news channel MSNBC, rescinded its invitation to candidate Dennis Kucinich. NBC decided earlier that it would invite the top four Democratic candidates to the debate. Then New Mexico Governor Bill Richardson dropped out of the race, which elevated Kucinich to the fourth position.

Jenny Backus of NBC sent an e-mail to the Kucinich campaign, saying Kucinich "met the criteria set by NBC and the debate sponsors." So Kucinich was surprised when, less than two days later, NBC News political director Chuck Todd called the Kucinich campaign to rescind the invitation. Kucinich responded with a lawsuit, filed in Nevada state court, claiming that NBC had broken its contract with him to include him in the debate.

District Judge J. Charles Thompson ruled in Kucinich's favor, enjoining NBC from holding the debate without him. Thompson told the *Las Vegas Review-Journal*, "If the criteria was one set of rules and you changed the rules in the middle of the game so as to exclude somebody after having invited them, I'm offended by that." NBC escalated its efforts to exclude Kucinich, appealing to the Nevada Supreme Court. NBC claimed that "Mr. Kucinich's claim is nothing more than an illegitimate private cause of action designed to impose an equal-access requirement that entirely undermines the wide journalistic freedoms enjoyed by news organizations under the First Amendment."

NBC also argued, "A television station does not have to grant unlimited access to a candidate debate. If anyone's First Amendment rights are being infringed, they are MSNBC's."

As the hour of the debate neared, MSNBC hyped the event. The Nevada Supreme Court was debating whether to sustain Thompson's decision, which would have forced NBC to include Kucinich. Chris Matthews, host of MSNBC's *Hardball*, said, "This promises to be the hottest debate of the political season, because only a few candidates will be up there on the stage." He did not burden his audience with the news that his network was working behind the scenes to exclude a candidate. The host of MSNBC's most popular program, Keith Olbermann, mentioned the successful Kucinich lawsuit and NBC's appeal, and reported when, 50 minutes before the debate, the Nevada Supreme Court sided with NBC, excluding Kucinich.

Late Tuesday night, after the debate, Kucinich learned that the House of Representatives in Washington, D.C., was going to take up a defense appropriations bill on Wednesday. He took a red-eye flight back from Las Vegas.

Unlike the candidates whom General Electric/NBC News allowed into the debate, Kucinich stands alone in opposing war funding: "I'm the only person running for president who not only voted against the war, but voted 100 percent of the time against funding the war.

> They either voted for the war, in the case of Sen. Edwards and Sen. Clinton, or they voted to fund the war, in the case of Sen. Edwards, Sen. Clinton and Sen. Obama, who, by the way, campaigned saying, well, he opposed the war from the start, but then when he was elected to the Senate, his voting record is indistinguishable from Sen. Clinton's with respect to funding the war.

Kucinich wants Congress to fulfill its obligation to use its power of the purse to shut off funding for the war in Iraq. He told me, "I'm going to be there to challenge the bill, to speak on it and call for a vote and, hopefully, keep alive the issue of a contest over defense spending policies."

He went on,

> It goes right to the question of democratic governance, whether a broadcast network can choose who the candidates will be, based on their narrow concerns, because they've contributed—GE, NBC and Raytheon ... have all contributed substantially to Democratic candidates who were in the debate. And the fact of the matter is, with GE building nuclear power plants, they have a vested interest in Yucca Mountain in Nevada being kept open ... So NBC ends up being their propaganda arm to be able to advance their economic interests.

A quick search of Federal Election Commission data showed that employees of those three companies—GE, NBC, and Raytheon—have contributed in total $68,656 to the Democratic presidential candidates. Most of that went to the three GE-approved candidates who were on the stage Tuesday night.

In his farewell address, President Dwight Eisenhower famously said, "In the councils of government, we must guard against the acquisition of unwarranted influence, whether sought or unsought, by the military-industrial complex." Add to that complex the media, with a company like GE, with its vested interests in selling weaponry and nuclear power plants, using its subsidiary, NBC, to exclude candidates like Kucinich, who is for an immediate withdrawal from Iraq, no nuclear energy, no Yucca Mountain radioactive waste dump, and for single-payer health care.

If there was a lovefest at the Las Vegas debate, it was between the corporate-funded Democrats and their sponsor, GE/NBC.

MILLIONS WITHOUT A VOICE

As I raced into our TV studio for our Super Tuesday morning-after show, I was excited. Across the country, initial reports indicated there was unprecedented voter participation, at least in the Democratic primaries, several times higher than in previous elections. For years I have covered countries like Haiti, where people risk death to vote, while the United States has one of the lowest participation rates in the industrialized world. Could it be this year would be different?

Then I bumped into a friend and asked if he had voted. "I can't vote," he said, "because I did time in prison." I asked him if he would have voted. "Sure I would have. Because then I'm not just talking junk, I'm doing something about it."

Felony disenfranchisement is the practice by state governments of barring people convicted of a felony from voting, even after they have served their time. In Virginia and Kentucky, people convicted of any felony can never vote again (this would include "Scooter" Libby, even though he never went to jail, unless he is pardoned). Eight other states have permanent felony disenfranchisement laws, with some conditions that allow people to rejoin the voter rolls: Alabama, Arizona, Delaware, Florida, Mississippi, Nevada, Tennessee, and Wyoming.

Disenfranchisement—people being denied their right to vote—takes many forms, and has a major impact on electoral politics. In Ohio in 2004, stories abounded of inoperative voting machines, too few ballots, or too few voting machines. Then there was Florida in 2000. Many continue to believe that the election was thrown to George W. Bush by Ralph Nader, who got about 97,000 votes in Florida. Ten times that number of Floridians are prevented from voting at all. Why? Currently, more than 1.1 million Floridians have been convicted of a felony and thus aren't allowed to vote. We can't know for sure how they would have voted, but as scholar, lawyer, and activist Angela Davis said recently in a speech honoring Dr. Martin Luther King Jr. in Mobile, Alabama, "If we had not had the felony disenfranchisement that we have, there would be no way that George Bush would be in the White House."

Since felony disenfranchisement disproportionately affects African-American and Latino men in the United States, and since these groups overwhelmingly vote Democratic, the laws bolster the position of the Republican Party. The statistics are shocking. Ryan King, policy analyst with the Sentencing Project in Washington, D.C., summarized the latest:

About 5.3 million U.S. citizens are ineligible to vote due to felony disenfranchisement; two million of them are African American. Of these, 1.4 million are African-American men, which translates into an incredible 13 percent of that population, a rate seven times higher than in the overall population. Forty-eight states have some version of felony disenfranchisement on the books. All bar voting from prison, then go on to bar participation while on parole or probation. Two states, Maine and Vermont, allow prisoners to vote from behind the walls, as does Canada and a number of other countries.

The politicians and pundits are all abuzz with the massive turnouts in the primaries and caucuses. There are increasing percentages of women participating, and initial reports point to more young people. The youth vote is particularly important, as young people have less invested in the status quo and can look with fresh eyes at long-standing injustices that disenfranchise so many. In this context, one of the Sentencing Project's predictions bears repeating here: "Given current rates of incarceration, 3 in 10 of the next generation of black men can expect to be disenfranchised at some point in their lifetime. In states that disenfranchise ex-offenders, as many as 40 percent of black men may permanently lose their right to vote."

The Sentencing Project's King said, "We are constantly pushing for legislative change around the country. But public education is absolutely key. There are so many different laws that people simply don't know when their right to vote has been restored. That includes the personnel who work in state governments giving out the wrong information."

I called my friend to tell him he was misinformed. He hadn't been on probation or parole for years. "You can vote," I told him. "You just have to register." I could hear him smile through the phone.

AS GOES VERMONT

While the Iraq war is off the front pages, and Senators Hillary Clinton and Barack Obama embark on what may well be a scorched-earth primary battle against each other, let's keep our eye on where the real scorched earth lies: who profits and who dies.

Clinton proclaimed in her victory speech in Ohio on March 4, after winning three of the four primary contests that day, "as goes Ohio, so goes the nation." She should take note, however, of how goes Vermont. That state might be a better bellwether, especially concerning the U.S. quagmire in Iraq.

While no one was surprised that Obama beat Clinton in the Vermont primary by a landslide, several details of the Vermont vote bear mention. Vermont's electoral system is based on the town meeting, a storied exercise in direct democracy. In the Vermont town meeting, local issues and ordinances are hashed out in an open forum, with all townspeople who want to speak given time. This is arguably the closest we come in the United States to real democracy. Part of why this is possible is the rural nature of Vermont, which Vermonters prize and protect.

In Brattleboro, the townspeople decided to arrest President George Bush and Vice President Dick Cheney, should they visit. (This may be a moot point, as Vermont is the one state out of 50 that George W. Bush has not visited while president.) The question before the people of Brattleboro read, "Shall the Selectboard instruct the Town Attorney to draft indictments against President Bush and Vice President Cheney for crimes against our Constitution, and publish said indictments for consideration by other authorities, and shall it be the law of the town of Brattleboro that the Brattleboro Police, pursuant to the above-mentioned indictments, arrest and detain George Bush and Richard Cheney in Brattleboro if they are not duly impeached, and prosecute or extradite them to other authorities that may reasonably contend to prosecute them?"

The question passed, after a spirited discussion, by a vote of 2,012 for, 1,795 against. I asked former Governor Madeleine Kunin, the only woman ever elected to that position in Vermont, what she thought of the vote. Kunin (a Democrat) said,

> I support the fact that these communities were able to do that. That's Town Meeting in Vermont. Anything can happen. Would I have voted for it? Probably not. But I do respect their speaking out and taking a stand. I think there are a lot of people in Vermont who are frustrated that there's no impeachment process going on of Bush and Cheney.

Exit polls in Vermont indicated that the Iraq war remains the number one issue concerning people there. And it isn't some knee-jerk liberal position. Vermont, the first state to outlaw slavery, has a long Republican tradition, but one that is fiercely independent, more along the lines of the slogan on the Revolution-era flag: "Don't Tread on Me."

A central reason that the war hits home in Vermont is that the war touches almost everyone there. Vermont has the highest per capita death rate among U.S. servicemembers, more than twice the rate of most other states. People feel the loss, see the suffering, see the businesses fail as family breadwinners are pulled away for years on multiple deployments. And it is in this elemental crucible of democracy, this Norman Rockwell setting, that anger and frustration find voice.

WHO'S PAYING FOR
THE CONVENTIONS?

The election season is heating up, with back-to-back conventions approaching—the Democrats in Denver followed by the Republicans in St. Paul, Minnesota. The conventions have become elaborate, expensive marketing events, where the party's "presumptive" nominee has a coronation with much fanfare, confetti, and wall-to-wall media coverage. What people don't know is the extent to which major corporations fund the conventions, pouring tens of millions of dollars into a little-known loophole in the campaign-finance system.

Stephen Weissman of the nonpartisan Campaign Finance Institute (CFI) explains the unconventional funding:

> It's totally prohibited to give unlimited contributions to political parties. It's totally prohibited for a corporation or a union to just go right into its treasury and give money to political parties. Yet, under an exemption that was created by the Federal Election Commission, which essentially is made up of representatives of the two major parties, all of this money can be given if it's given through a host committee under the pretense that it's merely to promote the convention city.

According to CFI's new report, "Analysis of Convention Donors," since the last presidential election the corporations funding the conventions have spent more than $1.1 billion lobbying the federal government. Add to it the millions they pour into the conventions. Says Weissman,

> In return for this money, the parties, through the host committees, offer access to top politicians, to the president, the future president, vice president, cabinet officials, senators, congressmen. They promise these companies who are giving that they will be able to not only get close to these people by hosting receptions, by access to VIP areas, but they'll actually have meetings with them.

Disclosure of what corporations are giving is not required until 60 days after each convention, which is essentially Election Day, so there is no time to challenge a candidate on particular corporate donors. Weissman reports that most of the corporations that are giving to the convention "host committees" also have serious business before the federal government. Take AT&T, for example. Glenn Greenwald of Salon.com recently pointed out that the Democratic conventioneers and registered media in attendance will receive a tote bag prominently emblazoned with the AT&T logo. It's a perfect metaphor for a much larger gift, the one Democrats and Republicans just gave AT&T and other telecoms: retroactive immunity for spying on U.S. citizens. While Senators Russ Feingold and Chris Dodd fought the bill, Senator Barack Obama, until recently a staunch opponent of telecom immunity, reversed his position and supported it, reneging on a pledge to filibuster. Perfect timing.

The conventions are also training grounds for the next generation of elected officials. Many state legislators attend the conventions as delegates, where they marinate in the ways of big-money politics. From the corporate parties to the hospitality suites, they learn that there is nothing to be gained by challenging the status quo.

Obama has sworn off special-interest and lobbying money for his campaign, and he made historic strides in using the Internet to marshal millions of small donors and amass a campaign war chest with $72 million in cash on hand at the end of June. Yet the Denver convention is looking more and more like business as usual. Weissman writes in his report, "Lavish conventions with million-dollar podiums, fancy skyboxes and Broadway production teams are not necessary to the democratic process."

What is necessary, Weissman says, is stripping soft money out of the convention process:

> Congress should pass a law that says no more soft money for these conventions, no corporate treasury, union treasury, no unlimited individual money. Instead, the parties—let's discard this host-committee fiction—can go out there and ask people to help the convention, but with the same limits where they're asking people to help them normally.

Deep Throat is said to have told Bob Woodward during Watergate to "follow the money." It looks as if this summer you need only go to the Democratic and Republican national conventions. It's time to close this loophole.

"IT'S A GLOBAL ELECTION"

TALLINN, Estonia—When I arrived in Estonia last week—a former Soviet republic that lies just south of Finland—everyone had an opinion on Barack Obama's speech in Berlin. The headline of the British *Daily Telegraph* we picked up in Finland blared "New Walls Must Not Divide Us," with half-page photos of the American presidential candidate silhouetted against a sea of 200,000 people.

One of the first people I met in Tallinn, the capital of Estonia, was Abdul Turay, the editor in chief of the *Baltic Times*, an English-language weekly that covers Estonia, Latvia, and Lithuania, the three Baltic nations. Granted, he's not a typical resident for this country of largely fair-haired, light-skinned people: Turay is a black Briton whose parents come from the West African nations of Liberia and Sierra Leone. And he is Muslim. While Estonia has no mosques, he notes with pride that the Quran has just been translated into Estonian, and to the publisher's surprise, it's been an instant best-seller here.

I asked Turay what Obama's candidacy means to him. "It'll open doors for me personally if he becomes president," he said. "It's a momentous thing to have a black president, given America's history. Some people say it's not a big deal, but it is a very big deal. The U.S. is a model for the world. If people see a black man can be president of the U.S., maybe they will see me differently. If he's special, I'm special."

As for Obama's politics, Turay says he doesn't actually think Obama's foreign policy will be that different from fellow presidential candidate John McCain's. He said he was surprised after reading Obama's first book, *Dreams from My Father*: "He's almost talking about black nationalism. He's very liberal. He's very much a black politician, whereas today he's a politician who happens to be black." I asked him to explain. "I think that's a question for Barack Obama, not me," he said.

Turay marvels at the importance of the U.S. elections here: "There's more interest in the American election than in the Lithuanian election, which is right next door. It's a global election."

Estonia may be a world away from the United States, but it is intimately tied to U.S. foreign policy. When the United States went looking for other countries to join the coalition to attack Iraq and Afghanistan, to give the occupations international legitimacy, Estonia was a charter member— along with numerous other former Soviet bloc countries of Eastern Europe. President Bush went to Estonia in 2006 to thank them. In 2004, none other than Senators McCain and Hillary Clinton visited the Baltic nation together as part of a congressional delegation. The story goes that Clinton challenged McCain to a vodka-drinking contest, an Estonian tradition. McCain accepted. When a Clinton aide was asked about it, he replied, "What happens in Estonia, stays in Estonia."

Many feel the Baltic nations' participation in the occupations was quid pro quo for their membership in NATO. Estonia has paid a price, as its soldiers have lost their lives in both Iraq and Afghanistan—the latter a place where Estonian soldiers have died before, as conscripts of the Soviet army when it invaded Afghanistan in 1979.

A decade later, Estonia was the scene of a nonviolent revolution. Singing has long been a national pastime, and song festivals, in which thousands come together to sing, are a tradition. In April 1988, this gathering turned into a vehicle for mass mobilization. In the Estonian capital, with the country's banned blue, black, and white flag unfurled on the back of a motorbike, hundreds of thousands began singing the forbidden national anthem. The movement gained momentum throughout the three Baltic nations. In August 1989, two million people joined hands in a Baltic chain spanning hundreds of miles, from Tallinn to Riga to Vilnius, the capitals of Estonia, Latvia, and Lithuania, respectively. Estonia and its Baltic neighbors won their independence in 1991, as the Soviet Union collapsed.

Now, Turay observes, "Estonia looks to America." With Berlin's wall now gone, Turay hopes other walls will soon fall, too. "If the president of America is a black person, other countries will realize that we have people who look like the president who are doing something important ... I think it will happen everywhere."

AUGUST 27, 2008

POVERTY IS THE REAL SCANDAL

DENVER—Former Senator John Edwards was supposed to speak in Denver at the Democratic National Convention. His wife, Elizabeth Edwards, was to speak also. Poverty was their focus. But they are not here because John Edwards had an affair. Will the Democrats now forget about poverty?

Chris Chafe is a former senior adviser to the Edwards campaign. He is now the executive director of the Change to Win coalition, the group of unions well known for their early endorsement of Obama. They split from the AFL-CIO in 2005. I asked Chafe about the absence of Edwards and his message at the convention:

> We miss him being here. He is an important voice in our party ... It is certainly a loss ... We have to look within ourselves in a moment of crisis when we have somebody of symbolic and strong value and leadership who takes a fall ... we have to continue moving forward with all of the values, strengths, priorities and leadership that he brought to the race, we have to carry that forward ... far beyond this election season.

Change to Win supports the unionization of workers at Wal-Mart. Last month, the *Wall Street Journal* revealed that Wal-Mart has been

warning managers that a Barack Obama victory would lead to unionization. In recent weeks, thousands of Wal-Mart store managers and department heads have been summoned to mandatory meetings discussing the
downside of unionization and told that a vote for Obama is tantamount
to inviting unions in. Chafe said,

> The company had been holding what we would consider captive-audience
> meetings where they are on company time, they are paid but they are re-
> quired to go to meetings ... This is going beyond the normal routine of in-
> timidation. Now they are trying to deny workers rights at the ballot box,
> and that is something we felt we could not allow to take place and had to let
> the world know this is happening in the country's largest employer ... You
> are not allowed to tell your employees how they are supposed to vote. It is
> the most sacred right in our democracy.

Change to Win and others have filed a complaint with the Federal Election Commission, challenging Wal-Mart's actions.

During the primaries in the blue-collar battleground states, Obama ef-
fectively pointed out that Hillary Clinton served on the Wal-Mart board
for six years, implying an anti-worker, anti-union association. Shortly
after she dropped out of the race, however, the Obama campaign ap-
pointed Jason Furman as a senior economics adviser. Furman has rankled
labor activists, writing that the benefits of Wal-Mart's low prices outweigh
its low wages. On that appointment, Chafe said,

> We've met privately with [Obama] about it, and we've met privately with
> Jason. The senator brought Jason on to manage the day-to-day war-room
> operations of their message to illustrate contrast with [John] McCain ...
> We made it clear, as did the senator, that there were certainly differences of
> viewpoint between he and Jason on a series of issues. We believe that
> Barack Obama has stood firm and clear on our agenda and the [Wal-Mart]
> workers' agenda.

On low prices trumping low wages, Chafe chafed:

> Absolute hogwash ... Wal-Mart gets a pass because they pass along sav-
> ings, they are passing along poverty. Poverty to workers across the world
> who are producing their goods. Poverty to the people that are working in

their stores representing them who are trying to make a living, many of whom probably have multiple jobs to afford to raise their families ... You name it, they find every way to cut corners and cut their workers out of their success.

The U.S. Census Bureau released a poverty report on August 26. More than 37 million people are in poverty in the United States. With Edwards iced out of the discussion, and free-trade economists advising the Obama campaign, the question remains: What of poverty?

Obama's nomination acceptance speech comes on the 45th anniversary of Dr. Martin Luther King Jr.'s "I Have a Dream" address. King related poverty and justice:

> We refuse to believe that there are insufficient funds in the great vaults of opportunity of this nation. So we have come to cash this check—a check that will give us upon demand the riches of freedom and the security of justice. We have also come to this hallowed spot to remind America of the fierce urgency of now ... Now is the time to make real the promises of democracy.

THE PARTY POLICE

The Democratic and Republican national conventions have passed, but controversy surrounds how they were funded and how they were run. Mass arrests of peaceful protesters, excessive police violence, wholesale disregard for the Bill of Rights, and the targeting and arrest of journalists marred what should have been celebrations of democracy. The "host committees," the legal entities that organize and pay for the conventions, act as large party slush funds, outside of campaign-finance restrictions. Scores of major corporations (and a couple of unions), barred from giving unlimited funds to political parties, could give whatever they wanted to the host committees of Denver and St. Paul, Minnesota.

According to a recent article in *National Underwriter* magazine, "Both the Republican National Committee and Democratic National Committee refused to comment on their insurance purchasing decisions, or even reveal who was providing coverage for their respective conventions." Bruce Nestor, president of the Minnesota chapter of the National Lawyers Guild, who organized scores of legal observers around the Twin Cities to protect citizens' legal rights, told me,

St. Paul actually negotiated a special insurance provision with the Republican host committee so that the first $10 million in liability for lawsuits arising from the convention will be covered by the host committee. The city is very proud of this negotiation. It's the first time it's been negotiated between a city and the host committee. But it basically means we [the city] can commit wrongdoing, and we won't have to pay for it.

According to the Minnesota Independent, more than 40 journalists were arrested or detained during the Republican National Convention.

Like what happened to *Democracy Now!* producer Nicole Salazar, videotaping protests in downtown St. Paul. She was violently forced to the ground, her nose bloodied, was held down with a man's knee or boot on her back, with another person pulling on her leg. Fellow producer Sharif Abdel Kouddous was thrown against a wall and kicked in the chest and back. The police might normally intervene and arrest the perpetrators. Except here, it was the police who were the assailants. And they arrested their victims. Arriving on the scene, I tried to have my colleagues freed, as we were all accredited journalists, and the police arrested me. And we were not the only ones.

As the mayors and police of St. Paul and Minneapolis patted each other on the back for a job well done, the nonprofit group FreePress, the head of the local chapter of the Newspaper Guild, and other media advocates and reporters delivered more than 50,000 signatures to the mayor's office demanding that the charges against the journalists be dropped. We were met by St. Paul Deputy Mayor Ann Mulholland. Free Speech TV CEO Denis Moynihan asked about the Republican host committee indemnification of the city, "Isn't that just giving a $10 million ticket to the police to violate civil rights?" Mulholland countered, "We are very proud of that ... the $10 million was critical for our city. We would not have been able to host the convention otherwise."

The two major-party conventions have become protracted, expensive advertising spectacles for the presidential candidates. It makes sense that Democrats and Republicans would want to control the message. But democracy is not an advertisement, nor is it under the sole dominion of the two parties. People were engaged in Denver and St. Paul in a vast array of civic dialogue, public gatherings, marches, protests, concerts, art openings—in fact, there was more democracy happening outside the convention halls than inside them. The convention center names tell the story: it was the Pepsi Center in Denver, the Xcel Energy Center in St. Paul. Xcel, which pushes nuclear power, gave $1 million to each convention. Both top candidates support nuclear power as a viable option.

In Denver, but particularly in St. Paul, dissent was crushed with a massive array of paramilitarized police, operating under the U.S. Secret Service, granted jurisdiction over the "National Special Security Events" that the conventions have been dubbed. Corporations pay millions to the host committees, earning exclusive access to lawmakers and candidates. The host committees, in turn, unleash police on the public, all but guaranteeing injuries, unlawful arrests, and expensive civil litigation for years to come. More than just a campaign-finance loophole that must be closed, this is a national disgrace.

Throughout the convention week, one of the 25 remaining typeset copies of the Declaration of Independence was on display at St. Paul City Hall—not far from where crowds were pepper-sprayed, clubbed, teargassed, and attacked by police with concussion grenades. As the clouds clear, it is instructive to remember the words of one of the Declaration's signers, Benjamin Franklin: "They who can give up essential liberty to obtain a little temporary safety, deserve neither liberty nor safety."

OPEN THE DEBATES

The reviews are in, and the latest U.S. presidential debate, the "town hall" from Nashville, Tennessee, was a snore. One problem is that in a debate it is important for the debaters to actually disagree. Yet Senators Barack Obama and John McCain substantively agree on many issues. That is one major reason that the debates should be open, and that major third-party or independent candidates should be included.

Take the global financial meltdown. Both senators voted for the controversial bailout bill that first failed in the U.S. House of Representatives. It passed resoundingly in the Senate and, larded with financial favors to woo uncooperative House members, finally passed the House. The news each day suggests that the bailout hasn't solved the problem. Rather, the economic contagion is going global, with European and Asian banks teetering on the brink of collapse. Iceland—not just its banks, but the country—faces financial ruin.

Earlier Tuesday, before the debate, the U.S. Federal Reserve announced that it would for the first time ever begin buying up the debt of private companies to help them meet short-term cash needs for things like payroll.

Shortly after the debate ended, major central banks around the world, again for the first time ever, cut their prime lending rates in unison. Yet on the debate floor, there was no sense that the global financial system needed more than a tax cut here, a voucher there. The major thing lacking from the debate was, well, debate.

Bob Barr, the Libertarian Party's presidential candidate, reacted to the debate, writing, "Sen. McCain, Sen. Barack Obama and the other members of Congress who have supported one bailout after another have turned fiscal responsibility into a sucker's game ... There's no meaningful difference between the two major parties." The independent campaign of Ralph Nader put out a debate-watching e-mail, asking supporters to listen for key words and phrases, among them "working class," "Taft-Hartley Act," "labor unions," "military-industrial complex," "single-payer health care," "impeachment," "carbon tax," and "corporate power." None of these was mentioned.

Obama supporters noted that McCain did not mention "middle class" once. Yet neither candidate mentioned poverty. Obama and McCain fought to prove who was more sympathetic to the nuclear-power industry. They each bowed to the coal industry, with its controversial "clean coal" gambit. They split hairs over who would more cagily bomb Pakistan.

At the core of the problem with U.S. presidential debates is that they are run by a private corporation, the Commission on Presidential Debates (CPD), founded in 1987 by the Republican and Democratic parties. The CPD took over the debate process from the League of Women Voters. Just once since then has a third-party candidate made it into the debate—Ross Perot in 1992. After he did well, he was excluded in 1996. The CPD requires contenders to poll at 15 percent before they qualify for any debate.

Nader calls the 15 percent threshold "a Catch-22 level of support that is almost impossible for any third-party candidate to reach without first getting in the debates."

George Farah directs Open Debates, a group that works "to ensure that the presidential debates serve the American people first." He told me that

historically, it has been third parties, not the major parties, that have supported and are responsible for the abolition of slavery, women's suffrage, public schools, public power, unemployment compensation, minimum wage, child labor laws. The list goes on and on. The two parties fail to address a particular issue; a third party rises up, and it's supported by tens of millions of Americans, forcing the Republican and Democratic parties to co-opt that issue, or the third party rises and succeeds, which is why the Republican Party jumped from being a third party to being a major party of the United States of America.

There is a move to organize a third-party debate, in New York City, a day or so after the final McCain-Obama debate on October 15. The CPD could still liven its last debate, and serve the electorate and history, by opening up that debate to all candidates who have at least obtained significant ballot access. Both Ralph Nader and Bob Barr are on the ballot in close to 45 states, Cynthia McKinney of the Green Party is on the ballot in 30 states, and Constitution Party candidate Chuck Baldwin is on in more than 35 states. Let's open the debates and have a vigorous and honest discussion about where this country needs to go. It will not only make for better television, it will make for better democracy.

WHO GETS TO VOTE?

The 2008 presidential election may see the highest participation in U.S. history. Voter-registration organizations and local election boards have been overwhelmed by enthusiastic people eager to vote. But not everyone is happy about this blossoming of democracy.

ACORN, the Association of Community Organizations for Reform Now, has become a lightning rod for the right wing. ACORN's website notes that "the electorate does not reflect the citizenry of the United States of America. It skews whiter, older, more educated and more affluent than the citizenry as a whole." Bertha Lewis, ACORN's lead organizer, told me,

> We organize low- and moderate-income people, usually folks who are minorities—African Americans, Latinos, Asians, and working-class white people. And most of these folks have always been disenfranchised out of the electoral process ... We've registered 1.3 million new voters across the country over an 18-month period of time. We had over 13,000 hard-working voter-registration workers. And we may have had a few bad apples, but I don't know any organization that didn't.

Barack Obama himself was questioned about ACORN's problematic registrations. He said,

> Having run a voter-registration drive, I know how problems arise. This is typically a situation where ACORN probably paid people to get registrations, and these folks, not wanting to actually register people, because that's actually hard work, just went into a phone book or made up names and submitted false registrations to get paid. So there's been fraud perpetrated on probably ACORN, if they paid these individuals and they actually didn't do registrations. But this isn't a situation where there's actually people who are going to try to vote, because these are phony names.

ACORN has seen some clearly fraudulent registrations submitted, with names like "Mickey Mouse" turned in. ACORN says it reviews all the registration forms. However, it does not serve as the ultimate arbiter of which registrations are fraudulent. In fact, ACORN cannot legally throw away any voter-registration cards. It flags suspicious cards and submits them to the appropriate state election authority to make the judgment.

Republicans are increasingly alarmed at the shifting demographics of the United States. Minorities tend to vote Democratic, and the United States is slowly becoming a majority minority country—by 2050, whites will no longer represent a majority in the United States. As right-wing commentator Patrick Buchanan lamented in 2004, "In 1960, when JFK defeated Nixon, America was a nation of 160 million, 90 percent white and 10 percent black, with a few million Hispanics and Asians sprinkled among us. We were one nation, one people. We worshiped the same God, spoke the same English language." Buchanan's xenophobia highlights a political reality: immigration and mobilization of the urban poor are shifting the electorate to the Democrats, especially in key swing states like New Mexico, Colorado, Florida, and Ohio.

The federal Help America Vote Act was passed in 2002 in response to the electoral crisis of 2000. But it requires new voters to present identification at the polling place, which critics allege is a modern-day Jim Crow law. Robert F. Kennedy Jr. (the son of the assassinated 1968 presidential candidate) said recently, "I have an ID, and most Americans have an ID. But one out of every 10 Americans don't have a government-issued ID, because they don't travel abroad, so they don't have passports, and they don't drive a car, so they don't have driver's licenses. The number rises to one in five when you're dealing with the African-American community." The online Michigan Messenger revealed that Michigan Republicans were planning to use a list of people with foreclosed homes to purge voter rolls. And a federal judge in Detroit has just ordered that 1,500 people be restored to the Michigan voter rolls, based on "voter caging"—purging people if mail to them is returned as undeliverable. The scandal around the firing of U.S. attorneys, which ultimately led to the resignation of U.S. Attorney General Alberto Gonzales, was based largely on the refusal of the Republican prosecutors to pursue unfounded voter-fraud cases.

Citizen groups like Election Protection and Video the Vote are organizing to document and report problems at the polls on November 4. It is more likely that they will see honest people denied the right to vote, purged from the voter rolls, than an attempt by Mickey Mouse to vote for Obama.

ELECTION PROTECTION

Election Day approaches, and with it a test of our election system's integrity. Who will be allowed to vote; who will be barred? Who will get paper ballots; who will use electronic voting machines? Will polls be open long enough to accommodate what is expected to be a historic turnout?

Veteran activist Harvey Wasserman has co-written four books on elections and voter rights. He says John Kerry won Ohio in 2004. Why look back? Wasserman is concerned about the attempt by the Ohio Republican Party, with help from the Bush White House, to challenge the registration of new Ohio voters:

> The GOP is trying to disenfranchise these 200,000 people by challenging their right to vote, asking the secretary of state here, Jennifer Brunner, to let the counties investigate and knock off the voter rolls, if they choose to, people who have minor discrepancies in their Social Security numbers or driver's license numbers. And the secretary of state has rightfully showed that many of these mistakes come from typographical errors when the numbers are entered in at the agencies.

The U.S. Supreme Court ruled that only the U.S. Department of Justice can purge these new registrants from the voter rolls. Republican House Minority Leader John Boehner, of Ohio, and President Bush urged U.S. Attorney General Michael Mukasey to take action, potentially purging these 200,000 people. Advocates feared the homeless in Ohio would be disenfranchised because they lack a traditional address or identification. (Wasserman notes that many of them may be veterans.) U.S. District Judge Edmund Sargus ruled that Ohio counties must allow voters who list their addresses as park benches or other non-building locations.

Wasserman's two main concerns about the integrity of the election are mass disenfranchisement through computerized purging and the failures of electronic voting machines, which can skew vote tallies and cause impossibly long lines at polling places (as can the provision of too few voting machines, whether they work well or not). These issues are both coming to a head in Colorado. There, Secretary of State Mike Coffman, a Republican who is also running for Congress, has been sued by Common Cause, Mi Familia Vota, and the Service Employees International Union for purging 30,000 voters within a 90-day window before an election. Six thousand seven hundred new registrants were purged for failing to check a box on the voter-registration form. Colorado has seen enthusiastic participation in early voting (some estimates nationally put the number of early voters at an astounding ten million, with days to go), and also has seen many voters opt for mail-in ballots. However, more than 11,000 voters in Denver did not receive their mail-in ballots because of a mistake made by Sequoia Voting Systems, the company that was supposed to have delivered 21,000 ballots to a Denver mail-processing facility on October 16. Election officials promise the ballots will be delivered.

Brad Friedman of BradBlog.com told me: "Sequoia is one of the big-four voting-machine companies. Of course, they have failed in state after state." Friedman also reports on "vote flipping," a problem with electronic, touch-screen voting machines. "It's West Virginia, it's Tennessee, it's Texas, Missouri, Nevada ... people go in and vote for a Democratic straight-party ticket or for Barack Obama, and the vote flips to a Republican or some other candidate." The companies claim the machines can be calibrated to work properly. Friedman disagrees: "These machines need to be pulled out, because even when they work, the problem is that there is absolutely no way to ever verify that any vote ever cast on a touch-screen machine like this has been recorded as per the voter's intent."

In response to video of Georgia early voters waiting eight hours, Friedman blogged, "Thank you to those voters who were willing to hang in there! Shame on you to those officials who set up this system that can't even accommodate the limited numbers of early voters! God save us all next Tuesday. Stay strong and brave people!"

The National Association for the Advancement of Colored People has sued Virginia's Democratic governor, Tim Kaine, on the grounds that he is unprepared to deal with a massive onslaught of voters there November 4. Virginia is not among the 31 states with early voting.

Thousands of lawyers and citizen-activists will be monitoring the polling places on Election Day. People are posting videos of election problems at videothevote.org. When you go to cast your vote, take a friend or neighbor, take your ID, and take a camera as well. Election protection is everyone's job.

OBAMA

OBAMA STRIKES A CHORD
WITH A DISAFFECTED REPUBLICAN

David Iglesias is an evangelical, Hispanic Republican—yes, that one, the former U.S. attorney for New Mexico—and he has positive things to say about Barack Obama.

I interviewed Iglesias the morning after Obama became the presumptive presidential nominee of the Democratic Party: "Obama represents all the promise of America, that a biracial man from a broken family can rise and have a strong shot of becoming our next president." Asked if he's endorsing Obama, Iglesias replied, "I'm not endorsing anybody. Our country has elected white males from northern European countries going back now 230-or-so years. This finally represents that the top position in American government is really open to everyone, and I think that's sending a powerful message not only to Americans, but throughout the world."

While Iglesias does not dislike John McCain, his own party's nominee, his comments bear directly on strategy for a campaign of Obama versus McCain. As the Puerto Rican primary results suggested, Obama still has to make major inroads into the Latino community. Iglesias' home state, New Mexico, is a "majority minority" state—that is, people of color outnumber whites in the state (others include California, Texas, and Hawaii).

Iglesias represents another population at play in this election: disaffected Republicans. In his new book *In Justice: Inside the Scandal That Rocked the Bush Administration*, Iglesias paints a picture of a highly politicized U.S. Department of Justice, allegedly following Republican Party strategy to prosecute people accused of voter fraud in cases where voter registrations could be seen to help Democratic candidates. Iglesias was not prosecuting these alleged voter-fraud cases, which did not sit well with New Mexico Republicans. Al Gore won New Mexico in 2000 by a mere 366 votes, and George Bush edged out John Kerry there in 2004 by about 6,000 votes. New Mexico is definitely a swing state. Congresswoman Heather Wilson barely held on to her congressional office in 2006. Every vote counts in New Mexico, and the Republicans know it: all three House seats are up for grabs in November, along with the Senate seat being vacated by Pete Domenici. Wilson is giving up her House seat to run for his.

While the voter-fraud cases that riled the Republicans were not solid cases, Iglesias explained to me voter-suppression tactics that concern him, those that benefit Republican candidates. Chief among them is "voter caging," which Iglesias says "is when you send voter information to a group of people that you have reason to believe are no longer there, such as military personnel who are overseas, such as students at historically black colleges. When it comes back as undeliverable, the party uses that information to remove that person from the voter rolls, claiming they are no longer there. It is a reprehensible practice. I had never heard of it until after I left office."

Iglesias predicted that the Republican Party will be reined in as a result of the U.S. attorney firing scandal:

> I hope the media keeps shining the spotlight on groups like the American Center for Voting Rights, which has been engaging in this type of voter-suppression action, especially targeting the elderly people and minorities. If you are an American citizen who is not a felon, you have the right to vote. I would just hope that in swing states like Missouri, Wisconsin, New Mexico

and a handful of other states, that the Democratic Party and the media really keep a lot of pressure on this.

David Iglesias' father is a Kuna Indian from Panama. David grew up in Panama, Oklahoma, and New Mexico. This once rising star of the Republican Party has much to teach all parties in this crucial, volatile political season.

JULY 2, 2008

IT'S NOT THE MAN,
IT'S THE MOVEMENT

I was on a panel at the Aspen Ideas Festival in Colorado this week when *Newsweek*'s Jonathan Alter asked me, "Is Obama a sellout?" The question isn't whether he is a sellout or not—it's about what demands are made by grass-roots social movements of those who would represent them. The question is, who are these candidates responding to, answering to?

Richard Nixon's campaign strategy was to run in the primaries to the right, then move to the center in the general election. Bill Clinton's strategy was called "triangulation," navigating to a political "third way" to please moderates and undecided voters. This past week, Barack Obama has made some signal policy changes that suggest he might be doing something similar. Will it work for him?

Take the Foreign Intelligence Surveillance Act, for example. A December 17, 2007, press release from Obama's Senate office read,

> Senator Obama unequivocally opposes giving retroactive immunity to telecommunications companies and has cosponsored Senator Dodd's efforts to remove that provision from the FISA bill. Granting such immunity

undermines the constitutional protections Americans trust the Congress to protect. Senator Obama supports a filibuster of this bill, and strongly urges others to do the same.

Six months later, he supports immunity for the companies that spied on Americans.

I asked Senator Russ Feingold, D-WI, about Obama's position on the FISA bill. He told me, "Wrong vote. Regrettable. Many Democrats will do this. We should be standing up for the Constitution. When Senator Obama is president, he will, I'm sure, work to fix some of this, but it's going to be a lot easier to prevent it now than to try to fix it later."

Feingold and Senator Christopher Dodd, D-CT, are planning on filibustering the bill. It will take 60 senators to overcome their filibuster. It looks like Obama will not be one of them. Disappointment with Obama's FISA position is not limited to his senatorial colleagues. On Obama's own campaign website, bloggers are voicing strident opposition to his FISA position. At the time of this writing, an online group on Obama's site had more than 10,000 members and was growing fast. The group's profile reads: "Senator Obama—we are a proud group of your supporters who believe in your call for hope and a new kind of politics. Please reject the politics of fear on national security, vote against this bill and lead other Democrats to do the same!"

Then there were the recent U.S. Supreme Court decisions on gun control and the death penalty. Obama supported the court in overturning the 32-year-old ban on handguns in the nation's violence-ridden capital. It's the court's most significant ruling on the Second Amendment in nearly 70 years. And in a blow to death-penalty opponents, Obama disagreed with the high court's prohibiting execution of those who were found guilty of raping children.

In a January 21, 2008, primary debate, Obama called the North American Free Trade Agreement (NAFTA) "a mistake" and "an enormous problem." He recently told *Fortune* magazine, "Sometimes during campaigns the rhetoric gets overheated and amplified ... my core position has never changed ... I've always been a proponent of free trade." This, after the primary-campaign scandal of the alleged meeting between Obama economic adviser Austan Goolsbee and a member of the Canadian consulate. A Canadian memo describing the meeting suggested Obama was generally satisfied with NAFTA. Goolsbee described the accounts as inaccurate. Now people are beginning to question Obama's genuine opposition to NAFTA and "free trade."

Then there is the floating of potential vice presidential candidates. Jonathan Capehart of the *Washington Post* was on the Aspen panel and noted that he has been receiving e-mails from gay men who angrily oppose former Senator Sam Nunn as an Obama running mate. They can't forget Nunn's key role in shaping "Don't Ask, Don't Tell," which prohibited gay men and lesbians from serving openly in the military. The e-mails trickled up, prompting the writing of an influential Capehart column, "Don't Ask Nunn."

It may be the strategy of the Obama campaign to run to the middle, to attract the independents, the undecided. But he should look carefully at the lessons of the 2004 Kerry campaign. John Kerry made similar calculations, not wanting to appear weak on the war in Iraq. Uninspired, people stayed home. There are millions who care about the issues from which Obama is distancing himself, from FISA to gun control to gay rights to free trade to the death penalty. Rather than staying home, they should recall the words of Frederick Douglass: "Power concedes nothing without a demand."

CHANGE BIG DONORS
CAN BELIEVE IN

Change is at hand. Barring a repeat of the protracted Florida recount of 2000, there will be a victor soon in the U.S. presidential election.

With the economic crisis, change is something in your pocket that you want to hold on to.

The campaigns are not dealing in small change, though. Their coffers, particularly the Democrats', are swelling with larger and larger bundles of cash, ensuring that politicians will remain beholden to special interests and wealthy donors. Don't hold your breath waiting for the extended television discussions of this, because it's the broadcasters who profit the most.

Barack Obama broke records with recently announced September fundraising levels that exceeded all predictions, bringing in $150 million. Since Obama opted out of the public financing system, he can spend freely from his war chest right up to the election. John McCain accepted public financing and has limits imposed on his campaign, with $84.1 million in public money to spend in the general election. McCain is now outspent on advertising by the Obama camp by 4 to 1.

The Obama campaign has "flooded the zone" with advertising. It has a full-time "Obama Channel" on Dish Network. Ads have been inserted into video games like "Guitar Hero." The campaign has bought a full 30 minutes of prime-time airtime on NBC, CBS, and Fox, six days before the election. Fox moved the start time of the World Series to accommodate the ad buy.

Obama's campaign is credited with receiving an unprecedented number of small donations from among its historic 3.1 million donors. Campaign manager David Plouffe says the campaign's average donation is under $100. A *Washington Post* analysis of Federal Election Commission data shows, though, that only a quarter of this vast number of donors fall into the "small" category (under $200), which is a smaller percentage than that achieved by George Bush in his 2004 run.

According to the Center for Responsive Politics, a nonprofit group that tracks campaign contributions, the funds raised in presidential campaigns has skyrocketed. The 1976 campaign, the first campaign that included public financing, saw a total of $171 million raised (about $570 million, adjusted for inflation). The current campaign weighs in at close to $1.6 billion, and the group expects the total to reach $2.4 billion. While donations to candidates are supposed to be limited to $2,300 for the general election (an additional $2,300 is allowed for the primary season, per candidate), huge loopholes exist. Most notable are the "joint fundraising committees," in which the presidential candidate partners with his party to form a fundraising organization. McCain and the Republican National Committee's is called McCain Victory 2008 and can receive donations as high as $70,000, which then get distributed to the presidential campaign, the national party, and to key state parties. Obama and the Democratic National Committee created the Obama Victory Fund, to which donors could give $28,500. As the *Washington Post* just reported, the Democrats found that sum too limiting, so they created the Committee for Change, which allows donors to give up to $65,500. That's a helluva lot of change.

Bill Buzenberg, executive director of the Center for Public Integrity, told me, "What is wrong with this is, after this election, the people [who] have bundled and put together big pots of money are going to come back to who[m]ever is elected, and they will be looking for access and influence."

The $2 billion presidential race also guarantees vast profits for the broadcasters, the national networks, and the local television stations. Hundreds of television stations are using the public airwaves, imposing themselves between the candidates and the public.

Access to the public airwaves for political candidates should be free. Says Buzenberg, "Every local television station I have been to, I say, 'How do you do in election years?' They say, 'We buy new cameras, new sets.' It is a huge benefit to them. The commercial broadcasters are cleaning up this year like never before, and you'll never hear them questioning the system that allows so much money to come back to them."

Is public financing of campaigns dead? A year ago, Senator Obama said, "I have been a longtime advocate for public financing of campaigns combined with free television and radio time as a way to reduce the influence of moneyed special interests." Regardless of who the winner is, the next president will enter the White House with a long list of major donors to thank.

ORGANIZER IN CHIEF

You could almost hear the world's collective sigh of relief. This year's U.S. presidential election was a global event in every sense. Barack Hussein Obama, the son of a black Kenyan father and a white Kansan mother, who grew up in Indonesia and Hawaii, represents to so many a living bridge—between continents and cultures. Perhaps the job that qualified him most for the presidency was not senator or lawyer, but the one most vilified by his opponents: community organizer, on the South Side of Chicago. As Alaska Governor Sarah Palin mocked, "This world of threats and dangers is not just a community, and it doesn't just need an organizer."

But perhaps that's just what it needs. Obama achieved his decisive electoral victory through mass community organizing, on the ground and online, and an unheard-of amount of money. It was an indisputably historic victory: the first African American elected to the highest office in the United States. Yet community organizing is inherently at crosscurrents with the massive infusion of campaign cash, despite the number of small donations that the Obama campaign received.

Senator Obama rejected public campaign financing (sealing that policy's fate) and was flooded with cash, much of it from corporate donors. Those powerful, moneyed interests will want a return on their investment.

There are two key camps that feel invested in the Obama presidency: the millions who each gave a little, and the few who gave millions. The big-money interests have means to gain access. They know how to get meetings in the White House, and they know what lobbyists to hire. But the millions who donated, who volunteered, who were inspired to vote for the first time, actually have more power when organized.

A century and a half earlier, another renowned African-American orator, Frederick Douglass, an escaped slave and leading abolitionist, spoke these words that have become an essential precept of community organizing: "If there is no struggle, there is no progress ... Power concedes nothing without a demand. It never did and it never will."

Before heading over to Grant Park in Chicago, Senator Obama sent a note (texted and e-mailed) to millions of supporters. It read, in part, "We just made history. And I don't want you to forget how we did it ... We have a lot of work to do to get our country back on track, and I'll be in touch soon about what comes next." But it isn't enough for people now to sit back and wait for instructions from on high. It was 40 years ago in that very same place, Grant Park, that thousands of antiwar protesters gathered during the 1968 Democratic National Convention, demanding an end to the Vietnam War. Many from that generation now celebrate the election of an African-American president as a victory for the civil rights movement that first inspired them to action decades ago. And they celebrate the man who, early on, opposed the Iraq war, the pivotal position that won him the nomination, that ultimately led to his presidential victory.

The Obama campaign benefited from the participation of millions. They and millions more see that the current direction of the country is not sustainable. From the global economic meltdown to war, we have to find a new way. This is a rare moment when party lines are breaking down. Yet if Obama buckles to the corporate lobbyists, how will his passionate supporters pressure him? They have built a historic campaign operation—but they don't control it. People need strong, independent grass-roots organizations to effect genuine, long-term change. This is how movements are built. As Obama heads to the White House, his campaign organization needs to be returned to the people who built it, to continue the community organizing that made history.

PRESIDENT OBAMA CAN
REDEEM THE WHITE HOUSE

Alice Walker is the first African-American woman to win the Pulitzer Prize for fiction. But Monday, I called her to talk about a true story. The Obamas had just visited the White House. The first African American elected president of the United States had visited his soon-to-be residence, a house built by slaves. Walker told me, "Even when they were building it, you know, in chains or in desperation and in sadness, they were building it for him. Ancestors take a very long view of life, and they see what is coming." The author of *The Color Purple*, who writes about slavery and redemption, went on, "This is a great victory of the spirit and for people who have had to live basically by faith."

Many decades ago, Alice Walker had broken anti-miscegenation laws in Mississippi by marrying a white man. She is a descendant of slaves.

While Barack Obama is not—he is the son of a Kenyan man and a white Kansan woman—his wife, Michelle, is, and so, too, are their daughters, Sasha and Malia. Michelle Obama's ancestors come from South Carolina; her grandfather was part of the great migration north to Chicago.

Melissa Harris-Lacewell, associate professor of politics and African-American studies at Princeton University, reflected on the Obamas' forthcoming move:

> There are two African-American girls, little girl children, who are going to grow up with 1600 Pennsylvania Avenue as their home address. That's an astonishing difference for our country. It does not mean the end of racial inequality. It does not mean that most little black girls growing up with their residence on the South Side of Chicago or in Harlem, or Latino boys and girls growing up at their addresses, that the world is all better for them. But it does mean that there is something possible here.

Construction of the White House started in 1792, with sandstone quarried by slaves in Aquia, Virginia, then transported up the Potomac River and hauled into place by slaves. The White House Historical Association lists several of the slaves on that historic construction crew: "Tom, Peter, Ben, Harry and Daniel, three of whom were slaves owned by White House architect James Hoban." Stonecutters, or sawyers, "on government payrolls, such as 'Jerry,' 'Jess,' 'Charles,' 'Len,' 'Dick', 'Bill' and 'Jim' undoubtedly were slaves leased from their masters." Randall Robinson, in his book *The Debt*, wrote of slave labor in the construction of the U.S. Capitol:

> The worn and pitted stones on which the tourists stood had doubtless been hauled into position by slaves, for whom the most arduous of tasks were reserved. They had fired and stacked the bricks. They had mixed the mortar. They had sawn the long timbers in hellishly dangerous pits with one slave out of the pit and another in, often nearly buried alive in sawdust.

Looking forward, Barack Obama can make history in another way. The executive orders he issues will set the tone of his presidency and could usher in a new era. Human rights groups are calling for the closing of the Guantánamo prison camp and CIA "black sites," where torture has been commonplace.

Which brings us back to slavery. When Frederick Douglass, the renowned abolitionist, was young, he was enslaved on a plantation on Maryland's Eastern Shore, called Mount Misery, owned by Edward Covey, a notorious "slave breaker." There, physical and psychological torture were standard.

That property today is owned by Donald Rumsfeld, the former secretary of defense who was one of the key architects of the U.S. military's program of torture and detention.

With the stroke of a pen on Inauguration Day, President Obama could outlaw torture. It would be a tribute to those slaves who built his new home, the White House, a tribute to those slaves who built the U.S. Capitol Building, a tribute to those who were tortured at Mount Misery.

CHEVRON IN THE WHITE HOUSE

President-elect Barack Obama introduced his principal national-security Cabinet selections to the world Monday and left no doubt that he intends to start his administration on a war footing. Perhaps the least well known among them is retired Marine General James Jones, Obama's pick for national security adviser. The position is crucial—think of the power that Henry Kissinger wielded in Richard Nixon's White House. A look into who James Jones is sheds a little light on the Obama campaign's promise of "Change We Can Believe In."

Jones is the former supreme allied commander of NATO. He is president and chief executive of the U.S. Chamber of Commerce's Institute for 21st Century Energy. The institute has been criticized by environmental groups for, among other things, calling for the immediate expansion of domestic oil and gas production and issuing reports that challenged the use of the Clean Air Act to combat global warming.

Recently retired from the military, Jones has parlayed his 40-year military career into several corporate directorships. Among them is Cross Match Technologies, which makes biometric identification equipment.

More germane to Jones' forthcoming role in Obama's inner circle, though, might be Jones' seat as a director of Boeing, a weapons manufacturer, and as a director of Chevron, an oil giant.

Chevron has already sent one of its directors to the White House: Condoleezza Rice. As a member of that California-based oil giant's board, she actually had a Chevron oil tanker named after her, the *Condoleezza Rice*. The tanker's name was changed, after some embarrassment, when Rice joined the Bush administration as national security adviser. So now Chevron has a new person at the highest level of the executive branch. With Robert Gates also keeping his job as secretary of defense, maybe Obama should change his slogan to "Continuity We Can Believe In."

But what of a Chevron director high up in the West Wing? Obama's attacks on John McCain during the campaign included a daily refrain about the massive profits of ExxonMobil, as if that was the only oil company out there. Chevron, too, has posted mammoth profits. Chevron was also a defendant in a federal court case in San Francisco related to the murder, ten years ago, of two unarmed, peaceful activists in the oil-rich Niger Delta region of Nigeria. On May 28, 1998, three Chevron helicopters ferried Nigerian military and police to the remote section of the Delta known as Ilajelánd, where protesters had occupied a Chevron offshore drilling platform to protest Chevron's role in the destruction of the local environment. The troops opened fired on the protesters. Two were killed, others were injured. (Rice was in charge of the Chevron board's public policy committee when it fought off shareholder resolutions demanding that Chevron improve its human rights and environmental record in Nigeria.)

One of those shot was Larry Bowoto, who, along with the family members of those killed, filed suit in California against Chevron for its role in the attack. Just after Jones was named Obama's national security adviser Monday, a jury acquitted Chevron. Bowoto told me, "I was disappointed in the judgment by the jury. I believe personally the struggle continues. I believe the attorney representing us will not stay put. He will take the initiative in going to the court of appeals." I met Bowoto in 1998, just months after he was shot. He showed me his bullet wounds when I interviewed him in the Niger Delta. I also met Omoyele Sowore, who has since come to the United States and started the news website SaharaReporters.com.

Sowore has followed the case closely. Though disappointed, he said,

We have achieved one major victory: Chevron's underbelly was exposed in this town ... Also there is Nigeria: Protesters won't give up ... This will not discourage anybody who wants to make sure Chevron gives up violence as a way of doing business. American citizens are increasingly protective of their economy ... Chevron played into fears of ... the jurors, saying these are people [the Nigerian protesters] who made oil prices go through the roof. This was a pyrrhic victory for Chevron. If I was in their shoes, I wouldn't be popping champagne.

Nigerians know well the power of the military-industrial complex in their own country. While Obama was swept into office promising change, his choice of Marine General James Jones as national security adviser probably has U.S. corporate titans breathing easy, leaving the poor of the Niger Delta with the acrid air and oil-slicked water that lie behind Chevron's profits.

A LONG TRAIN RIDE

It started with a train ride. Barack Obama rode to Washington, D.C., for his presidential inauguration on a whistle-stop tour. "To the children who hear the whistle of the train and dream of a better life—that's who we're fighting for," Obama said along the tour, which was compared to the train ride taken by Abraham Lincoln from Springfield, Illinois, to Washington, D.C., in February 1861, en route to his first inauguration. The comparisons between Obama and Lincoln abound, describing the arc between the abolition of slavery in the United States and the election of the first African-American president.

The train holds a deeper symbolism, though, that undergirds Obama's historic ascension to the White House, harking back to the civil rights struggle, reflecting the unprecedented grass-roots activism that formed the core of the Obama campaign and laying out where the nation under the Obama administration might go.

A. Philip Randolph was a legendary labor organizer and civil rights leader. He organized the Brotherhood of Sleeping Car Porters, the men who tended to the overnight guests on the sleeper cars that Pullman built.

While the porter positions were better-paying than many jobs available to African Americans at the time, there were still injustices and indignities. The common practice, for example, was to call the porters "George," regardless of their real name, after the owner of the company, George Pullman. Thousands of porters sought improvements through collective bargaining. (Ironically, after Pullman's death in 1897, the Pullman Co. was run by Abe Lincoln's only surviving son, Robert Todd Lincoln, until the mid-1920s.) Randolph's organizing struggle took 12 years, starting in 1925 and going through the economic collapse of 1929 and into the Franklin Delano Roosevelt administration.

Harry Belafonte recalled in an interview with Tavis Smiley recently a story he was told by Eleanor Roosevelt. She related a public event when her husband, FDR, introduced A. Philip Randolph and asked him, Belafonte recalled, "what he thought of the nation, what he thought of the plight of the Negro people and what did he think … where the nation was headed." Continuing the story, Belafonte recounted what FDR replied upon hearing Randolph's remarks:

> You know, Mr. Randolph, I've heard everything you've said tonight, and I couldn't agree with you more. I agree with everything that you've said, including my capacity to be able to right many of these wrongs and to use my power and the bully pulpit … But I would ask one thing of you, Mr. Randolph, and that is go out and make me do it.

This story was retold by Barack Obama at a campaign fundraiser in Montclair, New Jersey, more than a year ago. It was in response to a person asking Obama about finding a just solution to the Israel/Palestine conflict. After recounting the Randolph story, Obama said he was just one person, that he couldn't do it alone. Obama's final answer: "Make me do it."

That's the challenge.

After settling the Pullman labor struggle, Randolph continued on. He challenged FDR, by beginning to organize a march on Washington set for 1941, to desegregate the military and to ensure that the economic activity around the war effort was equally available to African Americans. FDR issued an executive order, and later, President Harry S. Truman desegregated the military. Randolph, Bayard Rustin, and Martin Luther King Jr.

organized the 1963 March on Washington, which itself has served as a strong symbolic backdrop to Obama's victory. This historic weekend also coincides with Dr. King's birthday. If King had survived, he would have just turned 80 years old.

As Obama begins his first week as president, some might caution that it's only fair to wait and see what he might do. But the peace group Code Pink is not waiting. Along the inaugural parade route, they were handing out thousands of pink ribbons, encouraging people to join them in holding President Obama to his campaign peace promises: end the war in Iraq; shut down Guantánamo; reject the Military Commissions Act; stop torture; work to eliminate nuclear weapons; hold direct, unconditional talks with Iran; and abide by Senate-approved international treaties.

Just follow Obama's own advice: make him do it.

U.S. MUSLIMS STILL UNDER SIEGE

As President Barack Obama made his public appearance with Turkish President Abdullah Gul on Monday as part of his first trip to a Muslim country, U.S. federal agents were preparing to arrest Youssef Megahed in Tampa, Florida. Just three days earlier, on Friday, a jury in a U.S. federal district court had acquitted him of charges of illegally transporting explosives and possession of an explosive device.

Obama promised, when meeting with Gul, to "shape a set of strategies that can bridge the divide between the Muslim world and the West that can make us more prosperous and more secure."

Megahed, acquitted by a jury of his peers, thought he was secure, back with his family. He was enrolled in his final course needed to earn a degree at the University of South Florida. Then the nightmare he had just escaped returned. His father told me,

> Yesterday around noon, I took my son to buy something from Wal-Mart ... when we received a call from our lawyer that we must meet him immediately ... When we got to the parking lot, we found ourselves surrounded by

more than seven people. They dress in normal clothes without any badges, without any IDs, surrounded us and give me a paper.

And they told me, "Sign this." "Sign this for what?" I ask him. They told me, "We are going to take your son ... to deport him."

Megahed is being held by U.S. Immigration and Customs Enforcement for a deportation proceeding. The charges are the same ones on which he was completely acquitted. In August 2007, Megahed and a fellow USF student took a road trip to see the Carolinas. When pulled over for speeding, police found something in the trunk that they described as explosives. Megahed's co-defendant, Ahmed Mohamed, said they were homemade fireworks.

Prosecutors pointed to an online video by Mohamed, said to show how to convert a toy into an explosives detonator. Facing 30 years behind bars, Mohamed took a plea agreement and is now serving 15 years. Megahed pleaded not guilty, and the federal jury in his trial agreed with his defense: He was an unwitting passenger and completely innocent of any wrongdoing.

That's where ICE (Immigration and Customs Enforcement) comes in. Despite being cleared of the charges in the federal criminal case, it turns out that people can still be arrested and deported based on the same charges. The U.S. Constitution protects people from "double jeopardy," being charged twice with the same offense. But in the murky world of immigrant detention, it turns out that double jeopardy is perfectly legal.

Ahmed Bedier, the president of the Tampa Human Rights Council and co-host of *True Talk*, a global-affairs show on Tampa community radio station WMNF focusing on Muslims and Muslim Americans, criticizes the pervasive and persistent attacks on the U.S. Muslim community by the federal government, singling out the Joint Terrorism Task Forces, or JTTFs. The JTTFs, Bedier says, "include not only federal FBI agents, but also postal inspectors, IRS agents, deputized local police officers and sheriff's deputies, any type of law enforcement," and when one agency fails to take down an individual, another agency steps in. "It's like an octopus," he says.

When the not-guilty verdict was read in court last Friday, Megahed's father, Samir, walked over to the prosecutors. Bedier recalled, "It startled many people. He walked over to the prosecution, the people that have been after his son for a couple of years now, and shook their hands, extended his hand, and he shook hands with the prosecution team and the FBI themselves and then also shook hands with the judge. The judge shook hands with Youssef and wished him 'good luck in your future' ... the case was over."

Obama said in Turkey, "[W]e do not consider ourselves a Christian nation or a Jewish nation or a Muslim nation; we consider ourselves a nation of citizens who are bound by ideals and a set of values."

Until Monday, Samir Megahed praised the justice system of the United States. He told me, "I feel happiness, and I'm very proud, because the system works." At a press conference after his son's ICE arrest, he said, "America is the country of freedom. I think there is no freedom here. For Muslims there is no freedom."

FREE SPEECH VS. SURVEILLANCE
IN THE DIGITAL AGE

Tools of mass communication that were once the province of governments and corporations now fit in your pocket. Cell phones can capture video and send it wirelessly to the Internet. People can send eyewitness accounts, photos, and videos, with a few keystrokes, to thousands or even millions via social networking sites. As these technologies have developed, so too has the ability to monitor, filter, censor, and block them.

A *Wall Street Journal* report this week claimed that the "Iranian regime has developed, with the assistance of European telecommunications companies, one of the world's most sophisticated mechanisms for controlling and censoring the Internet, allowing it to examine the content of individual online communications on a massive scale." The article named Nokia Siemens Networks as the provider of equipment capable of "deep packet inspection." DPI, according to the Electronic Privacy Information Center, "enables Internet Service Providers to intercept virtually all of their customers' Internet activity, including web surfing data, e-mail and peer-to-peer downloads."

Nokia Siemens has refuted the allegation, saying in a press release that the company "has provided Lawful Intercept capability solely for the monitoring of local voice calls in Iran." It is this issue, of what is legal, that must be addressed. "Lawful intercept" means that people can be monitored, located, and censored. Global standards need to be adopted that protect the freedom to communicate, to dissent.

China has very sophisticated Internet monitoring and censoring capabilities, referred to as "the Great Firewall of China," which attracted increased attention prior to the 2008 Summer Olympic Games. A document leaked before a U.S. Senate human rights hearing implicated Cisco, a California-based maker of Internet routers, in marketing to the Chinese government to accommodate monitoring and censorship goals. The Chinese government now requires any computer sold there after July 1, 2009, to include software called "Green Dam," which critics say will further empower the government to monitor Internet use.

Josh Silver, executive director of Free Press, a media policy group, says the actions of Iran and China should alert us to domestic surveillance issues in the United States. He told me, "This technology that monitors everything that goes through the Internet is something that works, it's readily available, and there's no legislation in the United States that prevents the U.S. government from employing it ... It's widely known that the major carriers, particularly AT&T and Verizon, were being asked by the NSA [National Security Agency], by the Bush administration ... to deploy off-the-shelf technology made by some of these companies like Cisco." The equipment formed the backbone of the "warrantless wiretapping" program.

Thomas Tamm was the Justice Department lawyer who blew the whistle on that program. In 2004, he called the *New York Times* from a subway pay phone and told reporter Eric Lichtblau about the existence of a secret domestic surveillance program. In 2007, the FBI raided his home and seized three computers and personal files. He still faces possible prosecution.

Tamm told me, "I think I put my country first ... our government is still violating the law. I'm convinced ... that a lot more Americans have been illegally wiretapped than we know."

The warrantless wiretapping program was widely considered illegal. After abruptly switching his position in midcampaign, then-Senator Barack Obama voted along with most in Congress to grant telecom companies like

AT&T and Verizon retroactive immunity from prosecution. The *New York Times* recently reported that the NSA maintains a database called Pinwale, with millions of intercepted e-mails, including some from former President Bill Clinton.

U.S. Attorney General Eric Holder was recently asked by Senator Russ Feingold if he felt that the original warrantless wiretap program was illegal:

> Feingold: "[I]s there any doubt in your mind that the warrantless wire-tapping program was illegal?"
>
> Holder: "Well, I think that the warrantless wiretapping program, as it existed at that point, was certainly unwise, in that it was put together without the approval of Congress."
>
> Feingold: "But I asked you, Mr. Attorney General, not whether it was unwise, but whether you consider it to have been illegal."
>
> Holder: "The policy was an unwise one."

Dissenters in Iran and China persist despite repression that is enabled in part by equipment from U.S. and European companies. In the United States, the Obama administration is following a dangerous path with Bush-era spy programs that should be suspended and prosecuted, not extended and defended.

LUMINARIES

KING'S MESSAGE:
STOP THE WAR, HELP THE POOR

The blood still stains the concrete balcony outside room 306 of the Lorraine Motel in Memphis, Tennessee, where the Reverend Martin Luther King Jr. was assassinated on April 4, 1968. King was in Memphis supporting black sanitation workers striking for a union contract.

This past weekend, I came to Memphis for the National Conference on Media Reform but went directly from the airport to this sacred ground.

King is typically remembered for his pioneering civil-rights work and his commitment to nonviolent social change, immortalized in his "I Have a Dream" speech at the 1963 March on Washington, D.C. Even as he stood with President Johnson as he signed the Civil Rights Act of 1964 and the Voting Rights Act in 1965, King was moving on.

The central issues that drove King in his final years were war and the poor.

On April 4, 1967, exactly one year before he was gunned down, King gave his watershed "Beyond Vietnam" address at the Riverside Church in New York: "A few years ago there was a shining moment. It seemed as if there was a real promise of hope for the poor, both black and white, through the poverty program. Then came the buildup in Vietnam, and I watched this

315

program broken and eviscerated. So I was increasingly compelled to see the war as an enemy of the poor." He went on, "I am convinced that if we are to get on the right side of the world revolution, we as a nation must undergo a radical revolution of values."

The speech charted the course for King's final year. He broadened the scope of his work, opposing the war and promoting a new, broad-based Poor People's Campaign at home.

He also broadened his roster of enemies. FBI wiretaps continued. J. Edgar Hoover described the Nobel Peace Prize winner as "an instrument in the hands of subversive forces." He was investigated by the Internal Revenue Service. Within the movement, he battled a rising, younger generation of militants who did not subscribe to his philosophy of nonviolence. Mainstream newspapers editorialized against him.

At Ebenezer Baptist Church in Atlanta on April 30, 1967, King included the press in his critique:

> I knew that I could never again raise my voice against the violence of the oppressed in the ghettos without having first spoken clearly to the greatest purveyor of violence in the world today—my own government. There is something strangely inconsistent about a nation and a press that would praise you when you say, "Be non-violent toward (Sheriff) Jim Clark," but will curse and damn you when you say, "Be non-violent toward little brown Vietnamese children!" There is something wrong with that press.

Actor and activist Danny Glover was in Memphis this past weekend as well, advocating media reform. In November 2001, after Glover criticized the Bush administration's use of military tribunals, the city of Modesto, California, almost uninvited him from its commemoration of Martin Luther King Jr. Day 2002. Glover wondered then: If King had lived, would he have been welcome at his own birthday celebration?

Memphis is still poor. It has one of the highest infant mortality rates in the United States. We are a nation in a protracted war that is increasingly and aptly compared with Vietnam. To best honor King, consider the words of Judge D'Army Bailey, the founder of the National Civil Rights Museum, which is built around the Lorraine Motel: "This is not a day for ceremony. It ought to be a day for action."

As we move from our celebration of King's birthday to Black History Month, we should collectively remember the fundamental struggles King waged against racism, poverty, and militarism. That's what he lived for, that's what he died for. Instead of the eight-second "I have a dream" sound bite, we should make that dream a reality.

BANG POTS AND PANS
FOR MOLLY IVINS

Molly, I hardly knew ye.

The untimely death of Molly Ivins last week, after a long battle with breast cancer, has provoked a surge of impassioned eulogies—yes, that would be the appropriate use of the term "surge."

Ivins was first and foremost a journalist, in the highest and best sense of the word. She spent the time, did the digging. She had a remarkable gift for words, a command of English coupled with her flamboyant Texas wit. She directed her reportorial skill at the powerful, holding to account the elected and the self-appointed. She first questioned authority, then skewered it.

I had the good fortune to meet Molly, but on too few occasions. I went to Austin, Texas, for the fiftieth anniversary celebration of the *Texas Observer*, the plucky, progressive news magazine that was Molly's journalistic home for so long. Texas' former governor, Ann Richards, was there. Richards, a Democrat, was not immune to Molly's practiced barbs. The governor said of the writer,

I know it's been a shock to all of us, but over the last ten or 15 years our girl Molly Ivins has learned to dress, run a comb through her hair now and then and give a fairly decent speech. A truly remarkable woman who goes around America making speeches and telling lies about me. And I welcome her attentions any time. May God bless this woman who has more survivor blood in her veins than anyone I have ever known.

Richards preceded Molly in death by cancer by just a few months.

Molly's legacy rings out, clarion calls to action from the beyond. After she was diagnosed with cancer in 1999, she implored her readers, "Get. The. Damn. Mammogram. Now." The American Cancer Society predicts that there will be more than 40,000 breast cancer deaths in the United States in 2007. Death rates are declining, although detection and survival rates are lower for women of color. Improvements can be attributed in part to women following Molly's advice: "Get. The. Damn. Mammogram. Now."

In her final column, titled "Stand Up Against the Surge," Molly wrote, "We are the deciders. And every single day, every single one of us needs to step outside and take some action to help stop this war. Raise hell ... We need people in the streets, banging pots and pans and demanding, 'Stop it, now!'"

Her hallmark was to call it as she saw it, and on Iraq she was clear: "It is not a matter of whether we will lose or we are losing. We have lost." She took Senator John McCain to task for supporting the "surge." The coordinated acts of civil disobedience at his Senate offices in Washington, D.C., and in Arizona on February 5 were a fitting tribute to Molly. Meanwhile, houston.indymedia.org announced the formation of the Molly Ivins Brigade, to protest the war with pots and pans.

I asked Molly about the *Texas Observer*. "As we watch the concentration of ownership of mass media," she said, "it's more and more important to keep these little independent voices alive. I think that's where the hope of journalism lies."

Fighting cancer. Fighting to stop the war. Fighting fiercely to protect independent media institutions such as the *Texas Observer*. Molly, while I hardly knew ye, we know you by your good works. Molly has died, but the fight goes on. She asked that donations be made to the nonprofit *Texas Observer* (texasobserver.org). In this time of the Clear Channeling of America, it is pennies well spent.

The final performer at the *Texas Observer* anniversary event was the venerable Willie Nelson, whose sonorous voice and trenchant lyrics have become synonymous with Texas. He sang,

> Fly on, fly on past the speed of sound ...
> Leave me if you need to
> I will still remember
> Angel flying too close to the ground.

Molly has made her sound in the world. Now it's up to us to bang those pots and pans.

HARRY BELAFONTE:
THE LION AT EIGHTY

Harry Belafonte just turned 80. The "King of Calypso" was the first person to have a million-selling album and the first African American to win an Emmy, and is perhaps the most recognizable entertainer in the world. On Saturday, March 3, I attended his birthday party at a restaurant adjoining the New York Public Library.

The setting seemed very appropriate, as Belafonte himself is a living library of not only the civil rights movement but of liberation struggles around the world. In 1944, just before shipping out as a U.S. Navy sailor in World War II, he was banned from the Copacabana nightclub in New York. Ten years later, he headlined there. He knew Rosa Parks, Paul Robeson, and Eleanor Roosevelt. He corresponded with the imprisoned Nelson Mandela when the U.S. government considered the South African leader a terrorist.

Belafonte was a close confidant of the Reverend Martin Luther King Jr. He spoke daily with King. The FBI was listening. Taylor Branch, the award-winning author of a trilogy of books on King, was at Harry's party. Belafonte described how Branch's final book in the trilogy, *At Canaan's Edge*, uncovered extensive FBI wiretaps of their conversations.

For fighting for the right to vote and to end segregation, Belafonte said, "We were looked upon as unpatriotic; we were looked upon as people who were insurgents, that we were doing things to betray our nation and the tranquility of our citizens. That engaged the FBI. Everything we talked about was tapped." The FBI even went to his house when he was away and frightened his wife and children. He told me, "The essential difference between then and now is that no previous regime tried to subvert the Constitution. They may have done illegal acts. They may have gone outside the law to do these, but they did them clandestinely. No one stepped to the table as arrogantly as George W. Bush and his friends have done and said, 'We legally want to suspend the rights of citizens, the right to surveil, the right to read your mail, the right to arrest you without charge.'" His criticism is not limited to President Bush (whom he called, while visiting President Hugo Chavez in Venezuela, "the greatest terrorist in the world").

President Bill Clinton crashed Belafonte's birthday party, which was taking place as the Democratic presidential contenders battled for the African-American vote. Senators Hillary Clinton and Barack Obama were in Selma, Alabama, for the 42nd anniversary of the famous voting-rights march from Selma to Montgomery. (Bill Clinton went to Selma to join his wife for the commemoration.)

In his remarks, Clinton toasted Harry: "I was inspired by your politics more than you can ever know. Every time I ever saw you after I became president, I thought that my conscience was being graded, and I was getting less than an A. And every president should feel that way about somebody as good as you."

I asked Harry how he felt about Clinton showing up: "I'm very flattered, OK, but I'm mindful of all the things that need to be done." In his succinct reply, a lifetime of struggle remembered, a keen-edged skepticism. "He knows what I think. He said I didn't give him an A." I then asked him about both the Clintons and Obama going to Selma.

"We are hearing platitudes, not platforms. What do they plan to do for people of color, Mexicans, for people who are imprisoned, black youth? What are their plans for the Katrinas of America?"

In 1965, Belafonte was on the original Selma march with Dr. King. Just before they reached Montgomery, St. Jude's Catholic Church offered its grounds to the thousands of marchers. Belafonte called in artists from around the country. Tony Bennett came, as did Pete Seeger (both were at Harry's birthday party), Sammy Davis Jr., Mike Nichols, the conductor Leonard Bernstein, Odetta, and Joan Baez. In the rain, they built their stage in the mud with donated caskets from local mortuaries.

The stakes were incredibly high. People were shot and killed; people were beaten. Viola Liuzzo, a white Detroit homemaker, was fatally shot by Klansmen while driving marchers back to Selma. Weeks before, police shot a man named Jimmie Lee Jackson, who later died. Despite all that, Belafonte says that the stakes are higher today.

Like the two stone lions that guard the New York Public Library, Harry Belafonte—fierce, fearless, and focused—protects the soul of struggle. Even as he enters his ninth decade, this lion does not sleep tonight.

HOWARD ZINN:
DISSENT CAN SOMETIMES BE
THE BEST FORM OF PATRIOTISM

Historian Howard Zinn ascended the stage at renowned Faneuil Hall in Boston on Patriot's Day, the Massachusetts holiday commemorating the start of the American Revolution. The "shot heard 'round the world," considered the first shot of that revolution, was fired April 19, 1775, in Concord, Massachusetts.

He spoke about patriotism: "What is patriotism, and what is not? Who is patriotic, and who is not?"

"Patriotism," Zinn began, "is about dissent. It's about criticism and civil disobedience."

Not far from Faneuil Hall, Henry David Thoreau, born in Concord, built a little hut on Walden Pond. Thoreau wrote *Civil Disobedience*, which profoundly influenced Mohandas Gandhi and Martin Luther King Jr.

"He [Thoreau] was arrested for not paying his tax because he was protesting the Mexican-American War in the way there are tax resisters today for protesting the war in Iraq," Zinn continued.

Thoreau went to jail. While he was there, his mentor, the writer Ralph Waldo Emerson, is said to have asked Thoreau, "Henry, what are you doing in there?" Thoreau replied, "What are you doing out there?"

Zinn's *A People's History of the United States*, with well more than 1.5 million copies sold, is essential reading for anyone hoping to truly understand the United States in its current role as sole superpower. He tells the story of America, from the bottom up. Zinn, 84, with a grandfatherly smile and self-deprecating wit, defiantly smashes the icons of American history, exposing the myths that are so often invoked in defense of bad policy.

Zinn continued his homage to patriots like Helen Keller. Everyone is taught that she was deaf and blind, yet went on to great success nevertheless. What the textbooks don't tell children, Zinn says, is about Keller's deep-seated political beliefs.

"Helen Keller was a patriot. She was a radical, an educator, an agitator, a socialist," Zinn said. "She spoke at Carnegie Hall against war, supported the labor unions of her day. She refused to cross a picket line at a theater that was showing a play about her."

Zinn praised Mark Twain's patriotism. Twain spoke out after President Theodore Roosevelt congratulated a general involved in a 1906 massacre in the Philippines. The late Kurt Vonnegut read these words of Twain at an event celebrating the work of Zinn, a fellow World War II veteran: "It should, it seems to me, be our pleasure and duty to make these people free and let them deal with their own domestic questions in their own way; and so I am an anti-imperialist. I am opposed to having the eagle put its talons on any other land."

As Zinn spoke Monday night, they were counting the dead in Blacksburg, Virginia, after the horrific shooting spree at Virginia Tech. The latest figure was 32 dead, plus the shooter himself, also a student at the university. I thought back three months ago, to a similar horror. This one in Baghdad, at Mustansiriya University. On January 16, a double car and suicide bombing there killed 70 students. Those killed were mainly young female students leaving classes.

As our country mourns the dead at Virginia Tech, we have also become inured to the daily slaughter in Iraq. Imagine attacks of this scale happening to Iraqi young people day after day.

Zinn has seen war, has seen its effects. He has seen violent civil strife in the United States. He says the answer is to bring out those voices who say no to the violence:

To omit or to minimize these voices of resistance is to create the idea that power only rests with those who have the guns ... I want to point out that people who seem to have no power, whether working people, people of color or women—once they organize and protest and create movements— have a voice no government can suppress.

Fighting to stop the war in Iraq, fighting to stop gun violence at home: nothing could be more patriotic.

CLARENCE KAILIN:
VOICES FROM THE SPANISH CIVIL WAR

Clarence Kailin is 92 years old. He recently traveled to New York City to attend the annual reunion of the Veterans of the Abraham Lincoln Brigade. The brigade was originally made up of roughly 3,000 U.S. citizens who volunteered to fight in the Spanish Civil War, which raged from 1936 to 1939.

Seventy years later, Kailin recalled his reasons for leaving the comfort of Madison, Wisconsin, to volunteer to fight in defense of Spain's democratically elected government against a military coup led by General Francisco Franco, backed by Adolf Hitler and Italian dictator Benito Mussolini: "It was fighting against Italian fascism and German Nazism. And we felt that if we lost the war, that World War II was pretty much inevitable, which is what happened. It happened because Britain and France and the United States refused to give us any help at all. And so, we fought barehanded at times."

Moe Fishman, a spry 91-year-old Lincoln Brigade veteran, seconds Kailin's point about the United States: "If they had turned to fighting fascism, Hitler would not have attempted a two-front war. There would not have been World War II, where fascism almost won, and 60 million dead, with destruction beyond compare. And, no, there would have been no Holocaust if Hitler had been stopped in Spain in 1936–39."

The Spanish Civil War is little taught in the United States. You might know of it from Pablo Picasso's famous antiwar painting, *Guernica*. Hundreds from around the world gathered in that Basque city on April 26, 2007, for the seventieth anniversary of the German bombing there, one of the first aerial bombardments of civilians. The painting has resonance today. A tapestry of the painting that hangs in the UN was shrouded in 2003, just before then–Secretary of State Colin Powell gave his famous push for war, so that the antiwar image would not form the backdrop to U.S. press statements.

Or you might learn of the Spanish Civil War by reading George Orwell's *Homage to Catalonia* or Ernest Hemingway's *For Whom the Bell Tolls*. In our official history, World War II began for the United States with the bombing of Pearl Harbor, on December 7, 1941. But Kailin and other veterans of the Spanish Civil War are living messengers of a different, authentic history, of the earlier fight against fascism and how World War II might have been prevented.

When the veterans returned home, the U.S. government considered them communist sympathizers. Some were prevented from serving in World War II. The FBI actually labeled them "premature antifascists" (I am not making this up).

Among the 3,000 volunteers were 80 American women. Most of them served in the medical corps. The documentary *Into the Fire: American Women in the Spanish Civil War* features the nurses and brave women writers, like Dorothy Parker of the *New Yorker*, *New York Times* writer Virginia Cowles, and author Martha Gellhorn. Gellhorn was a close friend of Eleanor Roosevelt, who opposed the U.S. arms embargo against Spain but failed to convince her husband, President Franklin Roosevelt, to end it. Gellhorn said, "I was in Germany in 1936, and could not avoid seeing these headlines about the Red Swine Dogs in Spain. I'd been in Spain, but I knew nothing about what had happened … but all I needed was to read in a German paper that it was the Red Swine Dogs to know whose side I was on—theirs."

The Spanish people endured fascism until Franco's death in 1975. They know war. So it is perhaps no surprise that Spain saw some of the largest antiwar protests before the invasion of Iraq, nor is it surprising that when their prime minister allied with Bush/Cheney, they voted him out of office. His replacement, Prime Minister José Zapatero, immediately withdrew Spanish troops from Iraq.

In the United States, the surviving Spanish Civil War veterans are still working to pass on what they learned. They gathered at the Museum of the City of New York to celebrate its exhibit "Facing Fascism." Like Clarence Kailin and Moe Fishman, Brigade veteran Matti Mattson, also in his nineties, preferred to look forward rather than look back. "We have to restore our democratic rights," he said. "We have to get rid of this illegal war." Let us learn from our elders.

JIMMY CARTER:
TEAR DOWN THAT WALL

I sat down with former President Jimmy Carter last week at the Carter Center in Atlanta. The center was hosting a conference of human rights defenders, people at the front lines confronting repressive regimes around the globe. After a quarter-century of humanitarian work through the Carter Center, monitoring elections, working to eradicate neglected tropical diseases, and focusing on the poor, Jimmy Carter now finds himself at the center of the storm in the Israel-Palestine conflict.

After more than three decades of work on the Middle East, Carter released a book titled *Palestine: Peace Not Apartheid*. The book's title alone has created a furor. But Carter is undeterred:

> The word "apartheid" is exactly accurate. This is an area that's occupied by two powers. They are now completely separated. Palestinians can't even ride on the same roads that the Israelis have created or built in Palestinian territory. The Israelis never see a Palestinian, except the Israeli soldiers. The Palestinians never see an Israeli, except at a distance, except the Israeli soldiers. So within Palestinian territory, they are absolutely and totally separated, much worse than they were in South Africa, by the way.

And the other thing is, the other definition of "apartheid" is, one side dominates the other. And the Israelis completely dominate the life of the Palestinian people.

Carter lays much of the blame for the lack of momentum toward a solution on the absence of debate in the United States:

> It's a terrible human rights persecution that far transcends what any outsider would imagine. And there are powerful political forces in America that prevent any objective analysis of the problem in the Holy Land. I think it's accurate to say that not a single member of Congress with whom I'm familiar would possibly speak out and call for Israel to withdraw to their legal boundaries or to publicize the plight of the Palestinians or even to call publicly and repeatedly for good-faith peace talks.

As president, Carter brokered the 1978 Camp David Peace Accords, creating a lasting peace between Israel and Egypt. President Clinton, who officiated over the failed 2000 Camp David Summit between Israel and the Palestinians, has been highly critical of Carter's perspective. Clinton blames the Palestinian leadership for rejecting Israel's "generous offer." Interestingly, Israel's chief negotiator, former Foreign Minister Shlomo Ben-Ami, told me in 2006, "If I were a Palestinian, I would have rejected Camp David as well."

While we were in Atlanta, DePaul University in Chicago reached a settlement with professor Norman Finkelstein. Despite hailing him as a "prolific scholar and an outstanding teacher," DePaul denied him tenure, many believe because of his outspoken criticism of Israeli policy toward Palestinians. The son of Holocaust survivors himself, Finkelstein has been praised by leading scholars.

Just months before he died, Raul Hilberg, revered founder of the field of Holocaust studies, praised Finkelstein's work: "That takes a great amount of courage. His place in the whole history of writing history is assured and that those who in the end are proven right triumph, and he will be among those who will have triumphed, albeit, it so seems, at great cost."

Open debate on Israel-Palestine should not come at such a high cost. It is essential to Middle East peace. The Iraq Study Group, in its bipartisan

Baker-Hamilton Report, stated, "The United States will not be able to achieve its goals in the Middle East unless the United States deals directly with the Arab-Israeli conflict."

Carter's book cover has a picture of the "Separation Barrier." Israel originally designed the wall to run along the internationally recognized 1967 border. Carter noted that Israel decided to "move the wall from the Israeli border to intrude deeply within Palestine to carve out some of that precious land for the Israeli settlers to occupy." The International Court of Justice has ruled it illegal. It is more than half completed, with plans to snake more than 400 miles, mainly through the West Bank. In places the wall is more than 25 feet high and made of concrete.

Carter describes it as "much worse" than the Berlin Wall. Elder Israeli peace activist Uri Avnery writes, "When my friends fall prey to despair, I show them a piece of painted concrete, which I bought in Berlin. It is one of the remnants of the Berlin Wall, which are on sale in the city. I tell them that I intend, when the time comes, to apply for a franchise to sell pieces of the Separation Wall."

That barrier stands in the United States as well—metaphorically—around any kind of rational debate for a fair and just solution in the Middle East. My suggestion: tear down that wall.

JOHN LENNON:
IMAGINE PEACE—A RAY OF LIGHT
IN DARK TIMES

John Lennon would have turned 67 years old last week had he not been murdered in 1980, at the age of 40, by a mentally disturbed fan. On his birthday, October 9, his widow, peace activist and artist Yoko Ono, realized a dream they shared. In Iceland, she inaugurated the Imagine Peace Tower, a pillar of light emerging from a wishing well, surrounded on the ground by the phrase "Imagine Peace" in 24 languages.

The legacy of Lennon is relevant now more than ever. The Nixon administration spied on him and tried to deport him, all because he opposed the war in Vietnam. Parallel details of the Bush administration's warrantless wiretap program and the Pentagon's participation in domestic spying, with mass roundups of immigrants, are chilling, and the lessons vital.

Ono conceived the peace tower 40 years ago, at the outset of her relationship with Lennon. She grew up in Japan, surviving the firebombing of Tokyo. She told me, "Because of that memory of what I went through in the Second World War, it is embedded in me how terrible it is to go through war."

She continued,

> I thought of building a light tower, and John loved that idea, this light tower that just emerges once in a while. And so, he actually invited me in 1967, the first time that he invited me to his house. I thought it was a party or something, but, no, it was a very quiet day. And he said, "Well, actually, I invited you because I wanted to know if you can build the lighthouse in my garden," and I said: "Oh, dear, no, no. It's just a conceptual idea. I don't know how to build anything," and I was just laughing. But that's when he wanted this light tower, and that was 40 years ago.

Forty years ago, the young couple became increasingly active in the anti–Vietnam War movement. The FBI, under the direction of J. Edgar Hoover, spent tremendous resources targeting critics, most engaged in perfectly lawful dissent. This was later exposed as COINTELPRO, the FBI's counterintelligence program, which for decades spied on, infiltrated, and disrupted domestic groups.

Lennon was a pacifist in the tradition of Mahatma Gandhi and Martin Luther King Jr. As the antiwar movement was growing in militancy, Lennon and Ono got married, and used their honeymoon as a public appeal for peace. They decided to spend a week in bed, as a "Bed In." Knowing their action would attract the global news media, the newlyweds ensured that their call for peace was heard and that all photos included the word "Peace." They launched a poster and billboard campaign, using the phrase "The War Is Over—If you want it." The actions were creative and lighthearted—but clearly threatening to the Nixon administration.

They developed a closer connection to the U.S. antiwar movement and, by 1971, were planning a massive get-out-the-vote concert tour to help defeat Nixon. Nixon and Hoover stepped up their campaign to neutralize Lennon.

The FBI increased surveillance and harassment of Lennon, followed by an attempt to deport him. Lennon's activities were also tracked by the CIA, as revealed in recently declassified documents. Arch-conservative Senator Strom Thurmond wrote a secret memo pushing deportation to then–U.S. Attorney General John Mitchell, and the effort moved into full gear. Lennon beat the deportation attempt and, by 1980, with the release of the *Double Fantasy* album, was back demonstrating his creative brilliance, only weeks later to be slain.

Today, revelations about current government wiretaps and surveillance continue. Verizon has just revealed to Congress that it supplied customer records to the government more than 94,000 times since 2005. The American Civil Liberties Union has uncovered collusion between the Pentagon and the FBI in circumventing the law to obtain financial and credit information on people in the United States. I asked Yoko Ono to compare the Nixon and Bush administrations: "I'm not that concerned about professional politicians. I always believe that we can change the world by grassroots movements. It is a very important thing to do. It is the first time that I realized that I respect America so much because there are so many Americans trying to shift the axis of the world to peace."

With major antiwar demonstrations set for cities around the country on Saturday, October 27 (see oct27.org), John Lennon's legacy lives on, from the illuminated sky above Iceland to the heavily surveilled streets here at home.

STUDS TERKEL:
CURIOSITY DIDN'T KILL THIS CAT

"I have, after a fashion, been celebrated for having celebrated the lives of the uncelebrated among us; for lending voice to the face in the crowd." That is the opening line of Studs Terkel's long-awaited memoir, *Touch and Go*. I made a pilgrimage to Chicago to see Terkel, one of the twentieth century's greatest journalists, interviewers, and storytellers.

After writing a dozen books, winning the Pulitzer Prize, having a play produced on Broadway, winning the National Book Foundation Medal for Distinguished Contribution to American Letters, the George Polk Career Award, and the presidential National Humanities Medal, and hosting a daily radio show on WFMT in Chicago for close to half a century, he has, at 95 years old, written his memoir. "I tape, therefore I am," he writes. "I tape, therefore they are. Who are they, these etceteras of history, hardly worth a footnote? Who are they of whom the bards have seldom sung?"

Though he won his Pulitzer for his oral history *The Good War*, about World War II, he says there is a greater generation: "It was in the '60s, there was the civil rights movement, it flourished, at least for a time, and the rise, resurgence, of feminism; the gays and lesbians coming out as free people. So that's the generation, I think the greatest."

While he is a man of the twentieth century, he continues to write about the twenty-first century. In fact, he has just sued AT&T for collaborating with the government in eavesdropping.

Terkel says this is not new. He was wiretapped in the 1950s, during the McCarthy era. Of the government spies and their telecom allies, then and now, Terkel says, "They are un-American. Thomas Paine, the most eloquent visionary of the American Revolution, speaks of this country in which a commoner can look at a king and say, 'Bugger off!' I've known this before, because my phone was tapped in the days when the keyword was 'Commie.'"

Terkel was blacklisted for his views, and lost his show, *Studs' Place*. Then legendary African-American gospel singer Mahalia Jackson insisted that he be hired as the host of her show. CBS demanded Terkel sign a loyalty oath. When he refused, they threatened to fire him. She told them, "Look, if you fire Studs, find another Mahalia Jackson." CBS backed off. Studs recalled, "Do you know what happened? Nothing. You have to face them down."

Terkel is a fierce critic of the Bush administration, but also of the lack of historical context in American society, which has allowed this government to persist, to attack Iraq, to plan on attacking Iran:

> How could it be, at the end of World War II, we were the most honored, powerful nation in the world? "Honored" is the key word. Today we are the most despised. How come? The American public itself has no memory of the past. Gore Vidal uses the phrase "United States of Amnesia." I say, United States of Alzheimer's. What do we know about it—why are we there in Iraq? They say, when you attack our policy, you are attacking the boys. On the contrary, they're defending those boys. Welcoming them back home with their families. The war is built upon an obscene lie. We know that now.

One of the great listeners of the past century, Studs Terkel is now losing his ability to hear. He told me, "When Robert Browning wrote, 'Come and grow old with me, the best is yet to be,' he was lying through his teeth. But the one thing you can retain is the memory." His almost photographic memory is matched only by his continued intense interest in people's lives and the movements that make those lives better. He jokes, "My epitaph has already been formed: Curiosity did not kill this cat."

FEBRUARY 20, 2008

YURI KOCHIYAMA:
LESSONS OF INTERNMENT

Nearing 87 years old, Yuri Kochiyama lives in a small room in an Oakland, California, senior living facility. Her walls are adorned with photos, posters, postcards, and mementos detailing a living history of the revolutionary struggles of the twentieth century. She is quiet, humble, and small, and has trouble at times retrieving the right word. Yet, with a sparkle in her eyes, she has no trouble recalling that incredible history—not from books, not from documentaries, but from living it, on the front lines.

February marks a coincidence of anniversaries in Kochiyama's incredible life: 60 years ago, on February 19, 1942, President Franklin Delano Roosevelt issued Executive Order 9066, authorizing the mass internment of Japanese Americans. Then there is February 21, 1965, the day Malcolm X was assassinated at the Audubon Ballroom in New York City.

Kochiyama was a young woman living with her parents in San Pedro, California, when Pearl Harbor was attacked. Within hours, her father was arrested by the FBI. She recalled,

> [The FBI agents] said, "Is there a Seichi Nakahara living here?" I said, "He just came home from ulcer surgery." And they went in and got him—it was

done so quickly, it didn't even take a half of a minute, I don't think. And I didn't dare ask a question. They were going out the door immediately. And then, I just called my mother, who was right down the street to say, "Come home quick. The FBI just came and took Pop."

He was taken to the San Pedro Hospital, where U.S. sailors and Marines who had been injured in the Japanese attacks were also being treated. Kochiyama's father was the only person of Japanese descent in the hospital. They put him in a bed behind a sheet marked "Prisoner of War." Kochiyama recalled what her mother said:

When she saw the reaction of all the American [patients] who were just brought in from Wake Island, she didn't think he was going to last. And so, she asked the head of that hospital, could he be given a room by himself, and then when he was feeling better, could they take him … to the prison, because that hospital, she said, was probably worse than prison, because here were all these Americans who had been injured.

He was released six weeks later, returned home in a state of extreme illness. Kochiyama recalls, "He came home, it was around dinnertime, 5:30. And they had a nurse come with him. And by the next morning, she woke us up and said, 'He's gone.'" Her father had died.

Yuri and the rest of her family were rounded up and sent to Rohwer Camp in Arkansas as part of the internment of more than 120,000 Japanese Americans. Nearly 70,000 of them were U.S. citizens. She spent more than two years imprisoned there. She married after her release, and she and her family eventually moved to Harlem, New York.

Yuri was a changed woman. Her experience made her aware of the lack of justice suffered not only by Asian Americans, but by African Americans and Latinos as well. She met Malcolm X in 1963. They became friends and allies. He sent her postcards from his transformative trip to Africa. She was in the audience at the Audubon Ballroom in Harlem when he was shot.

She ran up onto the stage: "Malcolm had fallen straight back, and he was on his back. And so I just went there and picked up his head and just put it on my lap. People ask, 'What did he say?' He didn't say anything. He was just having a difficult time breathing. I said, 'Please, Malcolm, please, Malcolm, stay alive.' But he was hit so many times."

Malcolm X's assassination propelled Kochiyama further into a life committed to the struggle for social justice, human rights, racial equality, and prisoner rights. She is a staunch supporter of Mumia Abu-Jamal, who has lived on death row in Pennsylvania for a quarter of a century.

As the Bush administration asserts its authority to detain "enemy combatants" without charge, and zealots in Congress hatch plans to round up 12 million people accused of being "illegal aliens" (100 times the number of Japanese Americans interned), we all have timely lessons to learn from Yuri Kochiyama.

MARTIN LUTHER KING JR.: WHERE DO WE GO FROM HERE?

It has been 40 years since Dr. Martin Luther King Jr. was assassinated in Memphis, Tennessee, while standing on the balcony outside his room at the Lorraine Motel. King was there to support striking sanitation workers, African-American men who endured horrible working conditions for poverty wages. While King's staff was opposed to his going, as they were scrambling to organize King's new initiative, the Poor People's Campaign, King himself knew that the sanitation workers were at the front lines of fighting poverty.

I went to Memphis on Dr. King's birthday. There I interviewed Taylor Rogers, one of the striking sanitation workers who marched with King. He told me, "Back in 1968, 1,300 sanitation workers—we were tired of being mistreated, overworked and underpaid. We decided that we were just going to stand up and be men and do something about our condition. And that's what we did. We stood up, and we told [Mayor] Henry Loeb in the city of Memphis that 'I am a man.'"

While he was organizing against poverty, King also came out forcefully against the Vietnam War, alienating his erstwhile ally, President Lyndon

Johnson. Exactly one year before his assassination, on April 4, 1967, King gave his "Beyond Vietnam" speech at Riverside Church in New York City. He said,

> A few years ago, there was a shining moment in that struggle. It seemed as if there was a real promise of hope for the poor, both black and white, through the poverty program. There were experiments, hopes, new beginnings. Then came the buildup in Vietnam, and I watched this program broken and eviscerated as if it were some idle political plaything of a society gone mad on war. And I knew that America would never invest the necessary funds or energies in rehabilitation of its poor so long as adventures like Vietnam continued to draw men and skills and money like some demonic, destructive suction tube. So I was increasingly compelled to see the war as an enemy of the poor and to attack it as such.

He went on, "I could never again raise my voice against the violence of the oppressed in the ghettos without having first spoken clearly to the greatest purveyor of violence in the world today—my own government."

Time magazine called the speech "demagogic slander that sounded like a script for Radio Hanoi." The *Washington Post* declared that King had "diminished his usefulness to his cause, his country, his people."

King made an essential link between poverty at home and war-making abroad. The connection, sadly, is as relevant today as it was the last year of King's life. A new report from the Institute for Policy Studies, "40 Years Later: The Unrealized American Dream," lays out key elements of the inequality that African Americans experience in the United States around education, employment, and wealth accumulation.

On education, the IPS report states that African-American college graduation rates will not be on par with white graduation rates for another 80 years. The income gap between blacks and whites will not disappear for more than 500 years at current rates. More than one-third of African Americans earn less than $20,000 annually, before taxes.

African Americans are also far behind in the accumulation of wealth. Add to all this higher incarceration, less access to health insurance, and shorter life expectancy. King's Poor People's Campaign went beyond race, as he reached out to poor whites in places like Appalachia. Today, one in five residents of West Virginia is on food stamps, as is one in ten Ohioans, and, according to Jim Weill, president of the Food Research and Action Center, one in three children in Oklahoma has been on food stamps at some point in the past year. It is clear that Dr. King's goal of bringing people "to the promised land" is still far off.

UTAH PHILLIPS HAS
LEFT THE STAGE

"Utah" Phillips died this week at the age of 73. He was a musician, labor organizer, peace activist, and cofounder of his local homeless shelter. He also was an archivist, a historian, and a traveler, playing guitar and singing almost forgotten songs of the dispossessed and the downtrodden, and keeping alive the memory of labor heroes like Emma Goldman, Joe Hill, and the Industrial Workers of the World, "the Wobblies," in a society that too soon forgets.

Born Bruce Duncan Phillips on May 15, 1935, in Cleveland, by his mid-teens he was riding the rails. He told me of those days in an interview in 2004. By then, he was slowed down by congestive heart failure. His long, white beard flowed over his bow tie, plaid shirt, and vest. We sat in a cramped attic of a pirate radio station that was frequently raided by federal authorities. In the early days, he met old-timers, "old, old alcoholics who could only shovel gravel. But they knew songs."

In 1956, he joined the army and got sent to postwar Korea. What he saw there changed him forever: "Life amid the ruins. Children crying— that's the memory of Korea. Devastation. I saw an elegant and ancient culture in a small Asian country devastated by the impact of cultural and economic imperialism. Well, that's when I cracked. I said: 'I can't do this anymore. You know, this is all wrong. It all has to change. And the change has to begin with me.'"

After three years in the army, he went back to the state that earned him his nickname, Utah. There he met Ammon Hennacy, a radical pacifist, who had started the Joe Hill House in Salt Lake City, inspired by the Catholic Worker movement. Hennacy guided Utah Phillips toward pacifism. Utah recalled,

> Ammon came to me one day and said, "You've got to be a pacifist." And I said, "How's that?" He said, "Well, you act out a lot. You use a lot of violent behavior." And I was. You know, I was very angry. "You're not just going to lay down guns and fists and knives and hard angry words. You're going to have to lay down the weapons of privilege and go into the world completely disarmed." If there's one struggle that animates my life, it's probably that one.

Utah's pacifism drove him to run for the U.S. Senate in 1968 on the Peace and Freedom ticket, taking a leave of absence from his civil-service job: "I was a state archivist—and ran a full campaign, 27 counties. We took 6,000 votes in Utah. But when it was over, my job would vanish, and I couldn't get work anymore in Utah."

Thus began his 40 years in "the trade," a traveling, working musician: "The trade is a fine, elegant, beautiful, very fruitful trade. In that trade, I can make a living and not a killing." He eschewed the commercial music industry, once telling Johnny Cash, who wanted to record a number of Utah's songs, "I don't want to contribute anything to that industry. I can't fault you for what you're doing. I admire what you do. But I can't feed that dragon … think about dollars as bullets." He eventually partnered with one of the most successful independent musicians in the United States, Ani DiFranco, who created her own label, Righteous Babe Records. Their collaborative work was nominated for a Grammy Award.

Utah Phillips was a living bridge, keeping the rich history of labor struggles alive. He told me, "The long memory is the most radical idea in America. That long memory has been taken away from us. You haven't gotten it in your schools. You're not getting it on your television. You're being leapfrogged from one crisis to the next. Mass media contributed to that by taking the great movements that we've been through and trivializing important events. No, our people's history is like one long river. It flows down from way over there. And everything that those people did and everything they lived flows down to me, and I can reach down and take out what I need, if I have the courage to go out and ask questions." On his radio show *Loafer's Glory*, he once said, "My work on this planet has been to remember."

A week before he died, Utah Phillips wrote in a public letter to his family and friends, "The future? I don't know. Through all of it, up and down, it's the song. It's always been the song."

EVO MORALES:
A VIEW FROM THE SOUTH

Evo Morales knows about "change you can believe in." He also knows what happens when a powerful elite is forced to make changes it doesn't want.

Morales is the first indigenous president of Bolivia, the poorest country in South America. He was inaugurated in January 2006. Against tremendous internal opposition, he nationalized Bolivia's natural-gas fields, transforming the country's economic stability and, interestingly, enriching the very elite that originally criticized the move.

Yet last September, the backlash came to a peak. In an interview in New York this week, Morales told me, "The opposition, the right-wing parties ... decided to do a violent coup ... They couldn't do it."

In response, presidents from South American nations met in Chile for an emergency summit, led by the two women presidents, Michelle Bachelet of Chile and Cristina Kirchner of Argentina. The group issued a statement condemning the violence and supporting Morales.

Morales continued in our interview, "The reason why I'm here in the U.S.: I want to express my respect to the international community, because everybody condemned the coup against democracy to the rule of law— everybody but the U.S., but the ambassador of the U.S. It's incredible."

After the attempted coup, Morales ejected U.S. Ambassador Philip Goldberg, declaring, "He is conspiring against democracy and seeking the division of Bolivia." Morales went on,

> "He used to call me the Andean bin Laden. And the coca growers, he used to call them Taliban ... Permanently, from the State Department of the U.S., I have been accused of being a drug trafficker and a terrorist. And even now that I'm president, that continues on the part of the embassy. I know it does not come from the American people."

Morales has now given the U.S. Drug Enforcement Administration (DEA) three months to leave the country, and announced at the United Nations Monday that the DEA will not be allowed back. Morales was a *cocalero*, a coca grower. Coca is central to Bolivian indigenous culture and the local economy. As Roger Burbach, director of the Center for the Study of the Americas, writes, "Morales advocated 'Coca Yes, Cocaine No,' and called for an end to violent U.S.-sponsored coca eradication raids, and for the right of Bolivian peasants to grow coca for domestic consumption, medicinal uses and even for export as an herb in tea and other products."

Morales aims to preserve the Bolivian heritage of coca growing, while eliminating the scourge of drug trafficking. He says the United States uses the war on drugs as a cover to destabilize his country: "If they really fought against drug trafficking, it would be very different." He said the South American leaders are finally organizing among themselves: "We are actually setting up a national intelligence in collaboration with our neighbors Argentina, Chile, Brazil. And that way, the fight against drug trafficking is going to be more effective, but it's going to be something that has a political element in it. If we don't permit the DEA to come back, that doesn't mean we'll break relationships with the United States."

The resurgent democracies in Latin America are hoping for better relations with an Obama administration. On the election of the first African-American U.S. president, the first indigenous president of Bolivia told me, "Maybe we can complement each other to look for equality among people, people who are here on Mother Earth." After we spoke, Morales headed off to Washington to visit the Lincoln Memorial and to honor Dr. Martin

Luther King Jr.: "I want to honor my brothers, the movement, the Afro-American movement. I have the obligation to honor the people who preceded us, the ones who fought for the respect of human rights and rights in general."

Thousands are gathering outside Fort Benning, Georgia, this weekend for the annual mass protest and civil disobedience against the U.S. School of the Americas (now called WHINSEC), a military training facility that is alleged to have trained hundreds of Latin American soldiers who have gone home to commit human rights violations. The wounds of U.S. intervention in Latin America are still raw. President-elect Obama has an opportunity to reach out and grab the extended olive branch being offered by President Morales.

TUTU, OBAMA,
AND THE MIDDLE EAST

As President-elect Barack Obama focuses on the meltdown of the U.S. economy, another fire is burning: the Israeli-Palestinian conflict.

You may not have heard much lately about the disaster in the Gaza Strip. That silence is intentional: the Israeli government has barred international journalists from entering the occupied territory.

Last week, executives from the Associated Press, *New York Times*, Reuters, CNN, BBC, and other news organizations sent a letter of protest to Israeli Prime Minister Ehud Olmert criticizing his government's decision to bar journalists from entering Gaza. Israel has virtually sealed off the Gaza Strip and cut off aid and fuel shipments. A spokesman for Israel's Defense Ministry said Israel was displeased with international media coverage, which he said inflated Palestinian suffering and did not make clear that Israel's measures were in response to Palestinian violence.

A cease-fire between Israel and Hamas, the group that won Palestinian elections nearly three years ago and controls Gaza, broke down after an Israeli raid killed six Hamas militants two weeks ago. More Israeli raids have followed, killing approximately 17 Hamas members, and

Palestinian militants have fired dozens of rockets into southern Israel, injuring several people.

UN Secretary-General Ban Ki-moon has criticized Israel over its blockade of the overcrowded Gaza, home to close to 1.5 million Palestinians. The United Nations Relief and Works Agency is warning that Gaza faces a humanitarian "catastrophe" if Israel continues to blockade aid from reaching the territory.

The sharply divided landscape of Israel and the occupied territories is familiar ground for South African Archbishop Desmond Tutu. He won the Nobel Peace Prize for his opposition to apartheid in South Africa. Tutu was in New York last week to receive the Global Citizens Circle Award. I sat down with him at the residence of the South African vice consul. Tutu reflected on the Israeli occupation: "Coming from South Africa ... and looking at the checkpoints ... when you humiliate a people to the extent that they are being—and, yes, one remembers the kind of experience we had when we were being humiliated—when you do that, you're not contributing to your own security."

Tutu said the embargo must be lifted. "The suffering is unacceptable. It doesn't promote the security of Israel or any other part of that very volatile region," he said. "There are very, very many in Israel who are opposed to what is happening."

Tutu points to the outgoing Israeli prime minister. In September, Olmert made a stunning declaration to *Yedioth Ahronoth*, the largest Israeli newspaper. He said that Israel should withdraw from nearly all territory captured in the 1967 Middle East war in return for peace with the Palestinians and Syria: "I am saying what no previous Israeli leader has ever said: We should withdraw from almost all of the territories, including in East Jerusalem and in the Golan Heights."

Olmert said that traditional Israeli defense strategists had learned nothing from past experiences and that they seemed stuck in the considerations of the 1948 War of Independence. He said, "With them, it is all about tanks and land and controlling territories and controlled territories and this hilltop and that hilltop. All these things are worthless."

Olmert appears to have come closer to his daughter's point of view. In 2006, Dana Olmert was among 200 people who gathered outside the home of the Israeli army chief of staff and chanted "murderer" as they protested Israeli killings of Palestinians (Archbishop Tutu was blocked from entering Gaza in his UN-backed attempts to investigate those killings). Ehud Olmert recently resigned over corruption allegations, but remains prime minister until a new government is approved by parliament.

Palestinian Foreign Minister Riyad al-Maliki criticized Olmert for waiting until now to call for an end to the settlements: "We wish we heard this personal opinion when Olmert was prime minister, not after he resigned. I think it is a very important commitment, but it came too late. We hope this commitment will be fulfilled by the new Israeli government."

Israel is a top recipient of U.S. military aid. Archbishop Tutu says of the Israeli-Palestinian conflict, "When that is resolved, what we will find [is] that the tensions between the West and ... a large part of the Muslim world ... evaporates." He said of Obama, "I pray that this new president will have the capacity to see we've got to do something here ... for the sake of our children."

PETE SEEGER CARRIES US ON

It was some garden party. Eighteen thousand people packed into Madison Square Garden Sunday night to celebrate the first 90 years of Pete Seeger's life.

The legendary folk singer is a living history of the twentieth century's grass-roots struggles for worker rights, civil rights, the environment, and peace. Powerful, passionate performances and tributes rang out from the stage, highlighting Seeger's enduring imprint on our society.

Bruce Springsteen opened his set with a tribute to Pete, saying, "As Pete and I traveled to Washington for President Obama's inaugural celebration, he told me the entire story of 'We Shall Overcome,' how it moved from a labor-movement song and, with Pete's inspiration, had been adopted by the civil rights movement. And that day, as we sang 'This Land Is Your Land,' I looked at Pete. The first black president of the United States was seated to his right. I thought of the incredible journey that Pete had taken ... He was so happy that day. It was like, Pete, you outlasted the bastards, man."

Springsteen recalled Pete's only request for the inaugural: "'Well, I know I want to sing all the verses [of 'This Land Is Your Land']. You know,

I want to sing all the ones that Woody [Guthrie] wrote, especially the two that get left out ... about private property and the relief office.' ... That's what Pete's done his whole life: He sings all the verses all the time, especially the ones that we'd like to leave out of our history as a people."

The oft-censored verses, for the record:

In the squares of the city, under shadow of the steeple,
at the relief office, I saw my people.
As they stood there hungry, I stood there whistling,
this land was made for you and me.
A great high wall there tried to stop me.
A great big sign there said private property,
but on the other side it didn't say nothing.
That side was made for you and me.

Seeger's unflinching commitment to social justice landed him before the House Un-American Activities Committee in 1955. He told HUAC, "I resent very much and very deeply the implication of being called before this committee that in some way because my opinions may be different from yours, that I am any less of an American than anyone else." Seeger was blacklisted and didn't appear on television for close to 15 years until he sang on *The Smothers Brothers Comedy Hour*.

Seeger told me,

The Smothers Brothers were a big, big success on CBS television. And ... in the spring of '67, CBS says, "What can we do to make you happier?" And they said, "Let us have Seeger on." And CBS said, "Well, we'll think about it." Finally, in October they said, "OK, you can have him on." And I sang this song "Waist deep in the Big Muddy, the big fool says to push on." ... In New York, they scissored the song out. The Smothers Brothers took to the print media and said, "CBS ... censored Seeger's best song." ... Finally, in late January of '68, CBS said, "OK, OK, he can sing the song."

The song tells of an army captain who drowned while ordering his troops deeper and deeper into a river—an obvious metaphor for U.S. involvement in Vietnam.

In 1949, Pete Seeger and the great "whitelisted" black opera singer and actor Paul Robeson held a concert in Peekskill, New York, an upstate village with an active Ku Klux Klan. A vigilante mob stoned the crowd. Hundreds were injured. Pete took rocks from that assault and incorporated them into his fireplace—so that the stones meant to maim now just protect the flame.

Dear to Pete for his life has been the Hudson River, said to be one of the most polluted bodies of water in the world. In 1966, Pete cofounded the environmental organization Hudson River Sloop Clearwater, which uses a beautiful wooden boat and an annual celebration to engage and educate people on the need to clean the Hudson and protect the environment. There is a movement to nominate Pete Seeger for the Nobel Peace Prize.

At Madison Square Garden, Pete was center stage, playing his banjo. His singing voice is faint now, after 70 years of singing truth to power. He mouthed the words to the songs, but what came out were the voices of the 18,000 people in the audience, singing out. That's Pete's legacy. That's what will carry on.

DR. GEORGE TILLER
DIDN'T HAVE TO DIE

George Tiller did not have to die. He was assassinated while in church in Wichita, Kansas, on Sunday, targeted for legally performing abortions. His death might have been prevented simply through enforcement of existing laws. His alleged killer was seen vandalizing a Kansas City clinic, Aid for Women, both the week before and the day before the murder, putting glue into its door locks. The manager of that clinic, who calls himself "Jeff Pederson" to protect his identity, told me he called the FBI and local police both times, but the vandal, the alleged killer Scott Roeder, was not arrested. Pederson had Roeder's first name and his license-plate number. He had images of him on the security video. He recognized him from previous protests.

Pederson said, "The clinic was closed on Memorial Day weekend. A worker tried to get in on Memorial Day but couldn't. The locks were super-glued. I went to the videotape and I saw the same guy on the videotape who had done it in 2000." Pederson called his contact at the FBI, agent Mark Colburn. "He [Colburn] said the videotape wouldn't be clear enough, and since I had touched the locks, I had ruined it with my DNA. So I bought new color video cameras."

On Saturday, May 30, the clinic manager said "Scott" struck again: "My head nurse calls me, 5:40 Saturday morning. She had come to prep for the patients. When she was coming back from the store she noticed the Taurus [Roeder's car]. She made her way to the back door. She saw him. He saw her and bolted. She followed him to his car and started talking to him.

"He tried to stand in front of the license plate, but she got it, 225 BAB. As she ran back to the clinic, he shouted 'Baby killer!' at her."

Pederson called Colburn, reporting the second vandalism and letting him know he had better video. Pederson said Colburn told him, "The Johnson County prosecutor won't do anything until the grand jury convenes." The next day, Tiller was murdered, allegedly by Roeder.

I called the Kansas City FBI and reached Colburn. He immediately referred me to FBI spokesperson Bridget Patton. I asked her about the incidents at the clinic and why the suspect hadn't been arrested either time. She said, "I am not sure of the timeline, but whenever an act of vandalism occurs at an abortion clinic, we are notified of that vandalism and respond appropriately."

Tiller's medical practice, which included performing late-term abortions, drew rage, protests, and attacks during the decades of his career. His clinic was bombed in the mid-1980s. He survived an assassination attempt in 1993, when he suffered gunshot wounds to each of his arms. Bill O'Reilly on Fox News Channel demonized him as "Tiller the Baby Killer." He was the target of a political prosecution by a former Kansas attorney general, Phill Kline, and was acquitted just months ago on misdemeanor charges that he violated state rules on providing abortions.

Roeder was picked up shortly after the shooting Sunday in his Ford Taurus. On Tuesday, he was charged with first-degree murder.

I asked Pederson if he thought Tiller's murder could have been prevented if the authorities had simply arrested Roeder after he vandalized the Kansas City clinic. Pederson paused. "I don't know," he said.

But Dr. Susan Robinson was adamant. She flies to Wichita every month to perform abortions in Tiller's clinic. She said, "It is generally regarded amongst those who do clinic security, if local authorities are not responsive, if they don't show up or they don't vigilantly enforce the law, that it encourages the anti-abortion people to push it further and further."

She said,

> In Wichita, Dr. Tiller was constantly dealing with the same lack of enforcement. Wichita prohibits placing signs on city property. But they allow the anti-abortion protesters to set up dozens of crosses and leave them all day. Dr. Tiller went to the city attorney over the crosses, and complained that people block the clinic driveway. He told me that the city attorney said, "I would rather be sued by George Tiller than the anti-abortion folks."

The 1994 federal Freedom of Access to Clinic Entrances Act (FACE) makes it a crime to block or damage a reproductive health service facility. Enforcing FACE saves lives. George Tiller will be buried on Saturday.

HENRY LOUIS GATES JR.:
THE 21ST-CENTURY COLOR LINE

W. E. B. Du Bois' classic 1903 work *The Souls of Black Folk* opens with "The problem of the Twentieth Century is the problem of the color line." Du Bois helped form the NAACP, the National Association for the Advancement of Colored People, which just celebrated its 100th anniversary.

Henry Louis Gates Jr., who directs Harvard University's W. E. B. Du Bois Institute for African and African American Research, knows much about the color line—not only from his life's work, but from life experience, including last week, when he was arrested in his own home.

Gates' lawyer, Harvard Law professor Charles Ogletree, said in a statement that the arrest occurred as Gates returned from the airport:

"Professor Gates attempted to enter his front door, but the door was damaged. Professor Gates then entered his rear door with his key, turned off his alarm, and again attempted to open the front door. With the help of his driver they were able to force the front door open, and then the driver carried Professor Gates' luggage into his home." Both Gates and his driver are African American. According to the Cambridge (Massachusetts) Police report, a white woman saw the two black men attempting to enter the home and called the police.

Ogletree continued, "The officer ... asked Professor Gates whether he could prove that he lived there and taught at Harvard. Professor Gates said that he could, and ... handed both his Harvard University identification and his valid Massachusetts driver's license to the officer. Both include Professor Gates' photograph, and the license includes his address." Police officer James Crowley reported that Gates responded to his request for identification, "Why? Because I'm a black man in America?" Despite his positive identification, Gates was then arrested for disorderly conduct.

Meanwhile, in Philadelphia, more than 60 mostly African American and Latino children attending the Creative Steps camp were disinvited from a suburban Valley Swim Club, which their camp had paid for pool access.

Suspicions of racism were exacerbated when Valley Swim Club President John Duesler said, "There was concern that a lot of kids would change the complexion ... and the atmosphere of the club." The U.S. Department of Justice has opened an investigation.

The Senate Judiciary hearings on Supreme Court nominee Sonia Sotomayor were permeated by the race question, especially with white, male senators questioning her comments on how a "wise Latina" might rule in court. If confirmed, one of the first cases she will hear will be that of Georgia death-row prisoner Troy Anthony Davis, an African American.

As it moves into its second century, the NAACP is, unfortunately, as relevant as ever. It is confronting the death penalty head-on, demanding Davis' claims of innocence be heard and asking Attorney General Eric Holder to investigate the case of Pennsylvania death-row prisoner Mumia Abu-Jamal. Another new NAACP initiative asks people to record instances of bias, discrimination, and police brutality with their cell-phone cameras, and upload them to naacp.org.

At the group's centennial, longtime board chair Julian Bond said, paraphrasing Jay Leno, "When I started, my hair was black and my president was white. Now my hair's white, and my president is black. I hold the NAACP responsible for both." While the Cambridge Police Department has dropped the charges against Gates, his charges of racial discrimination remain. W. E. B. Du Bois' color line has shifted—but it hasn't been erased.

KIEFER SUTHERLAND'S GRANDFATHER, TOMMY DOUGLAS: HEALTH CARE REFORM NEEDS AN ACTION HERO

Imagine the scene. America 2009. Eighteen thousand people have died in one year, an average of almost 50 a day. Who's taking them out? What's killing them?

To investigate, President Barack Obama might be tempted to call on Jack Bauer, the fictional rogue intelligence agent from the hit TV series *24*, who invariably employs torture and a host of other illegal tactics to help the president fight terrorism. But terrorism is not the culprit here:

It's lack of adequate health care. So maybe the president's solution isn't Jack Bauer, but rather the actor who plays him.

The star of *24* is played by Kiefer Sutherland, whose family has very deep connections to health care reform—in Canada. Sutherland is the grandson of the late Tommy Douglas, the pioneering Canadian politician who is credited with creating the modern Canadian health care system. As a youth, Tommy Douglas almost lost his ailing leg. His family could not afford treatment, but a doctor treated him for free, provided his medical students could observe. As an adult, Douglas saw the impact of widespread poverty caused by the Great Depression. Trained as a minister, he had a popular oratorical style.

He moved into politics, joining the Co-operative Commonwealth Federation party. After several years in parliament, he led the CCF's decisive victory in the province of Saskatchewan, ushering in the first social democratic government in North America.

Douglas became premier of Saskatchewan, and pioneered a number of progressive policies there, including the expansion of public utilities, unionization and public auto insurance. But Douglas' biggest battle, for which he is best remembered, is the creation of universal health insurance, called Medicare. It passed in Saskatchewan in 1962, guaranteeing hospital care for all residents. Doctors there staged a 23-day strike, supported by the U.S.-based American Medical Association. Despite industry opposition, the Saskatchewan Medicare program was so successful and popular that it was adopted throughout Canada. While Tommy Douglas was fighting for health insurance in Canada, a similar battle was raging in the U.S., resulting in the passage of Medicare and Medicaid, giving guaranteed, single-payer health care to senior citizens and the poor.

Rush Limbaugh, Fox News Channel's Glenn Beck and insurance-industry-funded groups are encouraging people to disrupt town hall meetings with members of Congress. A number of the confrontations have become violent, or at least threatening. Outside President Obama's Portsmouth, N.H., event, a protester with a pistol strapped to his thigh drew further attention with a sign that read, "It is time to water the tree of Liberty." Thomas Jefferson's complete quote, not included on the sign, continues, "... with the blood of tyrants and patriots."

Rush Limbaugh says 24 is one of his favorite shows. He has even visited the set. He should learn from the real-life actor who plays his hero, Jack. Limbaugh and his cohorts may find truth not as satisfying as fiction.

In 2004, a Canadian Broadcasting Corporation poll named Tommy Douglas "The Greatest Canadian." At a protest in 2000 against efforts to roll back the Medicare system in the province of Alberta, Kiefer Sutherland defended Canada's public, single-payer system:

"Private health care does not work. America is trying to change their system. It's too expensive to get comprehensive medical care in the U.S. Why on earth are we going to follow their system here? I consider it a humanitarian issue. This is an issue about what is right and wrong, what is decent and what is not."

Maybe Jack Bauer can save the day.

ACKNOWLEDGMENTS

My deepest thanks go to Denis Moynihan, without whom this book would never have been written, for his commitment to ensuring that the voices of the unheard, undocumented, unrecorded, unquoted get published in newspapers and websites around the world.

I am ever inspired by the braintrust that breaks the sound barrier every day by producing *Democracy Now!*, our daily grass-roots, global news hour: my colleagues Sharif Abdel Kouddous, Mike Burke, Juan Gonzalez, Anjali Kamat, Steve Martinez, Hany Massoud, Aaron Maté, Nicole Salazar, and Robbie Karran.

My undying gratitude to *Democracy Now!* powerhouses Karen Ranucci, who orchestrated the building of our new, green LEED-certified broadcast tv/radio/internet studio, perhaps the first in the country, while we were consumed with our daily investigations, and Julie Crosby, who calmly and wisely guides and manages *Democracy Now!*

Thanks also to the staff, interns and volunteers at *Democracy Now!*, who daily stand up to the madness, including Samantha Chamblee, Nick Gilla, Michael Hoerger, Peter Kurys, Andrés Thomas Conteris, Clara

Ibarra, Angie Karran, Michael Kimber, Nicole Martin, Brenda Murad, Jaisal Noor, Edith Penty, Isis Phillips, Chuck Scurich, Neil Shibata, Becca Staley, Tasia VanderVegt, Hugh Gran, Angie Kiefer, John Randolph, Rah Campenni, Laura Chipley, Travis Collins, Kieran Krug-Meadows, Michael DiFilippo, Joy Hornung, Maria Eva Blotta, Marcela Schenck, Mercedes Camps, Rick Rowley, Jacquie Soohen, Rabia Alghani, Katherine Martinez, Jim Carlson, Jon Gerberg, Linda Greco, Jimmy Tobias, Dolna Smithback, Elizabeth Press, Miguel Nogueira, and Vesta Goodarz.

I also want to thank Glenn Mott at King Features, who believed the weekly column could happen, and Chris Richcreek for bearing with me each deadline until the columns are put to bed.

At Haymarket Books, thanks to the innovative and talented Anthony Arnove, as well as Eric Ruder, Dao X. Tran, Caroline Luft, Chris Dodge, Rachel Cohen, Julie Fain, Brian Jones, and Sarah Macaraeg.

Thanks also to Patrick Lannan, Andy Tuch, Laurie Betlach, Randall Wallace, Brenda Coughlin, Diana Cohn, Sarah Jones, Israel and Edith Taub, Irma Weiss, Mark Friedburg, Kim Jennings, Anastasia White, Dennis Darcy, Joe Dunson, Kevin Allen, Jon Alpert, and Keiko Tsuno. And thanks to Elisabeth Benjamin, Dan Coughlin, Michael Ratner, Jeremy Scahill, Julie Cohen, Maria Carrion, and the little and not so little ones, Rory and Cecilia, Sesa, Gabriela and Estrella, Jake and Ana, Sara and Aliza. To my dear friend Caren Spruch, I share the loss, and celebrate the life, of her mother Norma.

Thanks as always to my family, my brothers David, who worked with me on a number of these stories, Dan and Steve, their wives (and my sisters) Sue, Yujin, and Ruth, my remarkable mother Dorrie and my late dad George Goodman who would have been so proud of his beautiful growing grandchildren Ariel and Jasper, Anna, Sarah, and Eli. And to my grandparents who modeled it all.

INDEX

ABOUT THE AUTHOR

AMY GOODMAN is an internationally acclaimed journalist, and host and executive producer of *Democracy Now!*, a daily grass-roots global news hour that broadcasts on nearly 800 radio and television stations and on democracynow.org. She is a syndicated columnist with King Features. Amy has received numerous awards for her work, including the Robert F. Kennedy Prize for International Reporting, the George Polk Award, the Alfred I. duPont-Columbia University Awards for excellence in broadcast journalism, and the Radio/Television News Directors Award, as well as awards from the Associated Press and United Press International. She is the first journalist to receive the Right Livelihood Award, also referred to as "The Alternative Nobel Prize," presented in the Swedish parliament. Amy was co-winner of the first annual Izzy Award from the Park Center for Independent Media at Ithaca College, named after legendary journalist I. F. Stone. She is co-author with her brother, David Goodman, of three *New York Times* best-sellers: *The Exception to the Rulers, Static,* and *Standing Up to the Madness.* She lives in New York City.

DEMOCRACYNOW.ORG

Democracy Now! is a national, daily, independent, award-winning news program hosted by journalists Amy Goodman and Juan Gonzalez. Pioneering the largest public media collaboration in the United States, *Democracy Now!* is broadcast on nearly 800 stations, including Pacifica, NPR, college, community, and low-power FM radio stations; on public access TV and PBS stations, as well as satellite TV (DISH network: Free Speech TV channel 9415 and Link TV channel 9410; DIRECTV: Link TV channel 375); and on the Internet at democracynow.org. *Democracy Now!*'s video and audio podcasts are among the most popular on the web. *Democracy Now!* is listener, viewer and reader supported non-profit media.

Other books by Amy Goodman, coauthored with her brother David Goodman:

–*The Exception to the Rulers: Exposing Oily Politicians, War Profiteers and the Media That Love Them*

–*Static: Government Liars, Media Cheerleaders, and the People Who Fight Back*

–*Standing Up to the Madness: Ordinary Heroes in Extraordinary Times*

Get signed books, as well as audiobooks, DVDs, and other gifts, from democracynow.org.

ABOUT HAYMARKET BOOKS

Haymarket Books is a nonprofit, progressive book distributor and publisher, a project of the Center for Economic Research and Social Change. We believe that activists need to take ideas, history, and politics into the many struggles for social justice today. Learning the lessons of past victories, as well as defeats, can arm a new generation of fighters for a better world. As Karl Marx said, "The philosophers have merely interpreted the world; the point however is to change it."

We take inspiration and courage from our namesakes, the Haymarket Martyrs, who gave their lives fighting for a better world. Their 1886 struggle for the eight-hour day reminds workers around the world that ordinary people can organize and struggle for their own liberation.

For more information and to shop our complete catalog of titles, visit us online at www.haymarketbooks.org.

ALSO FROM HAYMARKET BOOKS

Between the Lines: Readings on Israel, the Palestinians, and the U.S. "War on Terror" • Tivka Honig-Parnass and Toufic Haddad

Diary of Bergen-Belsen • Hanna Lévy-Hass, foreword by Amira Hass

The Democrats: A Critical History • Lance Selfa

Essays • Wallace Shawn

Field Notes on Democracy • Arundhati Roy

Hopes and Prospects • Noam Chomsky

In Praise of Barbarians: Essays Against Empire • Mike Davis

The Pen and the Sword: Conversations with Edward Said
David Barsamian

War Without End: The Iraq War in Context • Michael Schwartz

Winter Soldier: Iraq and Afghanistan: Eyewitness Accounts of the Occupations • Iraq Veterans Against the War and Aaron Glantz